A NEW HISTORY
OF ENGLAND

A New History of England

of England

JEREMY BLACK

THE HISTORY PRESS

First published in the United Kingdom in 2000 by
Sutton Publishing Limited

This revised second edition published in 2008 by
The History Press
Cirencester Road · Chalford · Stroud
Gloucestershire GL6 8PE

Reprinted in 2001

A catalogue record for this book is available from the British
Library

ISBN 978-0-7509-4784-8

Typeset in Photina MT.
Typesetting and origination by
The History Press.
Printed and bound in England by Ashford Colour Press Ltd.

CONTENTS

JEREMY BLACK MBE is Professor of History at Exeter University. Among his many publications are the best-selling *History of the British Isles* (Macmillan), *Culloden and the '45* (Sutton), *Pitt the Elder: The Great Commoner* (Sutton) and *A New History of Wales* (Sutton).

For Ron Blumer and Muffie Meyer

PREFACE

This is a new history of England for two linked reasons. The first, mundane, one is that I published a heavily-illustrated history of England in 1993, but the second reason is more important. The situation now appears different, in some important respects very different, to when I was writing in 1992. First and foremost, the future and identity of Britain or, to give the current full title of the state, the United Kingdom of Great Britain and Northern Ireland, have become unclear. This owes most to the process of devolution in Scotland and Wales, but also reflects growing interest in regional government. Second, the possibility that the process of 'Euro-convergence' will dramatically alter the character of both England and Britain has become more pressing.

Thus, there is renewed interest in considering the identity of England and it is appropriate to offer an historical dimension to this question. Yet, that does not make clear how best to provide such a dimension, especially for the last three centuries. In particular, the relationship between the history of England and that of Britain, on which I have deliberately written separately, is unclear. Is the history of England that of Britain with the 'other bits' left out? If not, how is a history of England to be written? The following is one scholar's suggestion. Obviously it is not definitive. No work is. Even more so, the contracted length encourages a reflective approach. Many of the readers will be English. I hope that both they and others will consider how they would have written the book, because our different senses of the past, our past and that of others, register history and give it shape. The past provides the framework and vocabulary for experience, just as the future does for hope. By the standards of both, the present is generally found wanting, but past and future also exist in a counterpoint with each other. Those who fear the future tend to praise the past, while those who chart hopeful destinies for the future are often critical of the past. The curse of the past is particularly present for those who seek to empower themselves through past grievances, whether real or imagined; but to abandon history leads to the broken continuity with the past in which identities are lost and values atomised.

I would like to thank Christopher Feeney, a most sympathetic and helpful publisher, Helen Gray, Sarah Flight and Mary Critchley for their valuable editorial work at Sutton Publishing, and Bill Gibson and Robert Peberdy for their helpful comments on an earlier draft. I benefited from the advice of Nigel Aston, John Blair, Sue Bruley, Grayson Ditchfield, Joyce Ellis, Stephen Evans, John Gardiner, David Griffiths, Ann Hughes, Helen Jewell, Diarmaid MacCulloch, Don MacRaild, John Martin, Nigel Saul, Henry Summerson, David Taylor, Alex Walsham, Carl Watkins, Ann Williams, and Jenny Wormald on particular points and sections, and from the opportunity to develop ideas provided by invitations to give lectures in Cambridge, Oxford and on the *Queen Mary II*. This book is dedicated to two friends whose filmmaking combines clarity and accuracy to an exemplary decree. They are also fun people and wonderful hosts.

INTRODUCTION

It is tempting in 2008 to offer a new history of England that focuses on how the past (and present) would have been different had England not been linked to other parts of the British Isles. Such an approach, that of the what if, for which the technical term is counterfactualism, can be attempted, in some cases with apparent precision. For example, it is possible to take electoral results and subtract those from non-English seats. These certainly suggest a very different national history. Conservatives and their allies would have won nearly every election in the last two centuries (although, of course, the shape of politics might have been very different had only England been at stake).

It is also possible, although far more difficult, to consider how English history would have been different without, for example, the (Welsh) Tudors and the (Scottish) Stuarts. More recently, over the last century, it is noteworthy how many politicians have come from outside England, and it is worth assessing how far politics would have been different without say Lloyd George. The modern Labour party has a particularly powerful Scottish tendency.

Envisaging different courses of political development relates to a wider question of national identity. In the twentieth century, English identity was frequently 'constructed', in other words formulated, in terms of images and values that were apparently redolent of a Southern identity. This could be seen, for example, in posters produced both during the major wars and in the inter-war period, with their reassuring, almost domestic, images of Southern Downland. The implicit, and, at times, explicit contrast was with the world of what was termed the Celt. In short, Scotland, Wales and Ireland were assumed to represent a very different culture.

This approach was misleading in a number of ways. Most seriously, it offered essentially unitary accounts both of England and of the Celtic world, and presented these as clearly contrasting. Such unitary accounts were inaccurate, as was the clear contrast. Furthermore, the combination led to the implication that elements that seemed similar to the other were, in some fashion, aberrations, even disloyal or traitorous. This could be seen in the depiction of the industrial regions of northern England as closer to the Celtic world than to English identity and interests: Tyneside, for example, having more in common with Clydeside than with Dorset.

Such an account receives some support from a unitary approach to history. If, for example, the identity of England in the nineteenth and twentieth centuries is to be electorally constructed around images of Southern Downland and/or successive Conservative victories, then Liberal and Labour heartlands indeed appear different because they overlapped considerably with the Celtic world. Yet, this is misleading, because national identity and interests are not uniform, in two senses: geographically uniform and consistent over time; nor are they uncontentious.

The attempt to imply that there is uniformity instead tells us more about images of 'Englishness', important and influential as they are, than it does about the far more complex reality of overlapping and often very different, if not contentious and clashing, senses of identity. Alongside nationhood, people can also identify through social structures, religion, gender, ethnicity and other factors, although there is a risk of putting excessive weight on modern ideas of self-identification through gender, ethnicity and other factors.

It is unclear that such categories were as potent in the past as they are today. While, for example, ethnicity was an issue for the early Norman elite or for Jews in the eleventh and twelfth centuries, village, locality and social group seem more potent markers for the majority of the population. Place, however, is a complex issue. Dominant senses of place may relate not to the country or state, but to the locality or region, or to a wider space defined by identities and issues such as religion.

These points should be understood in the following account, as it is not always possible throughout the text to add, let alone dwell on, the caveats just mentioned. A working definition is also adopted from the outset. It is that the English are those who live in England. This approach has its limitations, but it avoids having to deal with the history of where the English went, and in large numbers; and also does justice to the ethnic mix that composed and recomposed the population of England, which is understood throughout the text as what is currently England.

Separately, it is worth noting that the idea of Britain, especially of the Anglicized bits of Scotland, Wales and Ireland, is, in many (but by no means all) respects, essentially a 'bigger England' view: an English identity was stamped on some of the 'Celtic Fringe' and, in turn, opposition to real or alleged English interests and values helped drive local identities and political activism. This was different historically to the situation within England where a patchwork of sometimes very different regional identities interacted, and cemented, bolstered and changed this England, without the notion of an imposed identity. Alongside the strength of the core of England – Westminster, London, the monarchy, the system – there has been a dynamic interaction of the English regions with the national system, not least thanks to the operation of the social system and of nationally defined political groupings.

Lastly, this book seeks to provide more than just a brief narrative, useful as that is for those who want a shape for the history of the country. Such a shape is indeed best offered by a chronological approach. Yet there is also a need at the outset for a discussion of England itself, a brief mention of its geography, separate consideration of what is in many ways the most important narrative, the human impact on the environment, and also reference to the role of this environment in England's history.

ONE

A Transformed Environment

Popular and artistic images of England relate largely to the countryside. The Downland of South-East England has played a particularly important role, but is far from alone in providing or encapsulating senses of place, not only of England but also of parts of the country. Yet this is very much a changed country, a transformed environment. This transformation is true both of the physical environment and of the plants and animals that also live in England.

The pace of change is obvious today. To travel in England is to see the impact of human activity, not only the ever-spreading roads and towns, the asphalt, brick and concrete, but also a countryside that has been transformed. Prior to the arrival of humans, much of England was woodland, but the virgin woodland had been cleared by the end of the Middle Ages in the fifteenth century, and in lowland England in large part by the beginning of the Iron Age (*c.* 700 BC) and, even more so, before the start of the Middle Ages. Much of England was swamp or marsh, but that has been drained from the Roman period and, more intensively, especially in the case of the East Anglian Fens, from the seventeenth century. Human impact on the environment is apparent even in areas that are not cultivated. Some have been deforested or, like the Suffolk and Norfolk Breckland, subsequently, afforested. In Hampshire, the Waltham and Bere Forests have been destroyed and the Forestry Commission's Micheldever Forest created to the north. Mining, quarrying, gravel extraction, and animal rearing have affected most of the terrain of England that has not been cultivated. The fall of the water table due to extraction by drilling and pumping, has been a particularly marked feature of the last century. It has led to considerable changes in surface conditions, including the intermittent flow of formerly constant streams. More generally, human light and noise have come to dominate the environment: two developments which rapid technological change has accentuated.

Aside from land-use, the terrain has also been organized by human beings. Territory has been delimited, controlled by fences or stone walls, surveyed, named, and mapped, all processes that mark human control. These processes have been largely directed against possible rival human claimants, and, where the enclosure of common land was concerned, elicited violent human reactions. Yet, for much of history, animals had also to be kept out. Thus, dwellings and farms were organized to keep away animals, such as wolves and foxes. Much of this activity was designed to protect not so much humans as the animals they reared and the plants they grew. Human control of the environment was in a way a partnership: oxen, horses, cattle, sheep, pigs and chicken were important, but it was a partnership controlled by humans. The dominance of the environment was an aspect of this control. The bulk of this book will concentrate on history 'between' humans, but it is worth remembering that at every stage there is another history, that of the relationship with the environment.

In this relationship, other animals have been wiped out, controlled or domesticated. This process is a continuing one. It has affected well-known and more obscure species. Some, such as the bear and the wolf, were wiped out, the former by the end of the Roman period, the latter, it is alleged, by Peter Corbet in 1281 on the orders of Edward I. Other species, for example the corncrake, became far less common. The corncrake was traditionally a bird of flower-rich meadows and damp grasslands. It declined from the time of the First World War (1914–18) when cooperative hand-cutting by neighbouring farmers who cut their fields in rotation declined. Mechanization led to earlier cutting, which destroyed nests and broods of young. The decline was exacerbated after the Second World War (1939–45) by early cut silage which reduced the success of nesting. Other causes included the drainage and reseeding of damp pastures, and increased staking which led to the loss of essential tall vegetation at the start of the breeding season.

As conservationism gathered pace in the twentieth century, there were efforts to reintroduce animals. Thus, from 1989 red kites were introduced. These birds of prey had, like the golden eagle, been nearly wiped out by gamekeepers. The last kite in Middlesex disappeared about 1777, and in northern England about 1850. By 1989, they were restricted to Wales, although they have since been reintroduced to parts of England, for example Yorkshire. Signs of recovery are also now evident in the case of the bittern, one of England's rarest and shyest birds. Numbers fell from about seventy booming males in the 1960s to fifteen or sixteen by 1994: population levels are calculated by counting the number of males calling or booming. Large-scale restoration work of the reed beds where they live is now taking place.

It would be misleading to neglect the extent to which the natural environment also played a role in the human story. The geography of the country is important. First, and most importantly, England is the major, most fertile and most populous portion of an island. The natural resources and economic and military power which a unified England possessed enabled her to extend her control to Wales and Ireland, and to become the undisputed predominant partner in the resulting United Kingdom. It was not easy, however, to conquer the entire island and indeed only once, under the Interregnum 'Commonwealth' government of 1650–2, was Scotland conquered, in large part thanks to the victories of Oliver Cromwell over Scottish armies. Yet, although inroads were at times made into northern England, states based in Scotland were not able to conquer England which, therefore, enjoyed security in its home base. Despite this security, control of Ireland was often justified in terms of the strategic threat which an independent Ireland would pose.

On its island, England was also difficult to conquer. There were successful invasions, notably in 1066 and 1688, but it was much harder to invade a country by sea than by land. As a result, throughout the eighteenth and nineteenth centuries and part of the twentieth, Britain prided itself upon its possession of the most powerful navy in the world.

As a result of its military geography, England tended not to have a permanent land military establishment comparable to that of other European states, who relied upon conscript armies to greater or lesser degrees. This had an impact on the government, society and politics of the country, although it is necessary to avoid the assumption of an automatic correlation. Indeed, the determination of numerous rulers to campaign outside the country and England's frequent membership in larger states with external commitments lessened the importance of this factor.

Britain's island existence engendered an insularity which made for suspicious minds when it comes to relationships with Continental Europe, not that these suspicions were necessarily inappropriate. The nineteenth-century tradition of 'splendid isolation' in foreign policy could be regarded as the precursor of Britain's present status as the 'awkward partner' within the European Union.

England's position on an island also helped ensure that fishing and foreign trade played a major role in its history. The expansion of England was in no small part due to the economic power which the importing and exporting of goods made possible. Indeed, England's dependence upon the importation of foreign foodstuffs for the sustenance of her people has made the country vulnerable during wartime. Like Japan, but unlike say Australia, England was not only an island, but also one in which the bulk of the country was readily accessible from the coast. This access was improved through the construction of canals in the eighteenth century, and railways in the nineteenth. In addition, like Japan, but unlike Madagascar or Ceylon (Sri Lanka), the centre of government was not in the interior. The role of the sea was fostered by the nature of the offshore waters and the role of oceanic currents. Both ensured a rich fish life.

The most important of the offshore currents was/is the Gulf Stream. This brought warm waters from the Caribbean to British shores and helped ensure that the climate was far more temperate than other areas at the same latitude, such as Sakhalin, Kamchatka, and Labrador, a position that would be gravely threatened by any movement of the Gulf Stream. The relatively mild climate contributed to a longer growing season that permitted the cultivation of a range of cereal crops.

Furthermore, farm animals were able to live out of doors. Rainfall was such that England avoided drought and did not require expensive and burdensome irrigation systems. The agricultural base is important, as food imports did not become significant until the late eighteenth century, and only came to meet a large portion of English food needs in the late nineteenth. Until then, population figures were, in part, related to the quantity of food that could be produced in England.

Alongside these general characteristics there was/is remarkable geological diversity that ensured a great variety in terrains and soil types within relatively small areas. The geological inheritance was mineral rich, and mineral resources, ranging from plentiful coal and iron-ore to limited gold deposits, were exploited from early on. England was the first country in the world that developed large-scale production of coal, and that was to be important both in its industrialization from the late eighteenth century and to the development of a north–south divide, as the most important coal deposits were found in the North and in the north Midlands, rather than in the South, although there was coal mining in Kent and Somerset.

The diversity of the geological inheritance and related variety in landforms was linked by some commentators to the country's history. Indeed, the notion of environmentalism as a key to history was developed in the nineteenth century and proved very influential in the early twentieth. This idea was extensively applied to English history. In his *Historical Maps of England during the First Thirteen Centuries* (1869), Charles Pearson stated, 'Our geography is in the fact the history of the land'. In *A New Student's Atlas of English History* (1903),

Emil Reich claimed that 'History is largely the make of geography'. Environmental influences appeared the best way to explain why nations and states developed with particular characteristics and interests. Environmentalism could make the process seem natural and necessary. It played a crucial role in the organic theory of the state, and in the treatment of culture as defined by the integration of nature and society. Pearson presented geography as playing a direct role in English history. He argued for example that the extensive woodlands near the south coast 'explain why England was settled from east and west', and suggested that, although 'man triumphs over the elements', this triumph was essentially a matter only of the previous half-century. Certainly the railway construction of the mid-nineteenth century, with the use of explosives to assist tunnelling and the construction of mighty bridges and viaducts, was a major development in the ability of humans to determine lines of communication. The telegraph lines built along railways were also crucial to the new victory over distance.

Pearson also saw geography at work in the great political divisions of the country's history. He termed the mountains 'the conservative element . . . in our history'; and observed that the Roman presence was limited in the upland regions – the south-west and Lancashire – and that 'it was precisely these parts where the nationality was unbroken, that afterwards sustained the struggle against the Saxon'. In the civil war of Stephen's reign (1135–54), Pearson noted 'the Empress Matilda, who represented the not infrequent combination of a legitimate title and an oppressive government', drew her support from the upland west, whereas Stephen was backed by London 'and the commercial towns of the east'. In the 1260s, 'London and the south and east were with the great constitutional leader De Montfort; the north and west sided with the King [Henry III]. In the Wars of the Roses the Yorkist party, which on the whole was that of good government, received partisans from the same district as De Montfort'. Similar comments were made about the Civil War (1642–6), and then, for Charles Edward Stuart and the Jacobite uprising in 1745 'nowhere but in the north-western counties, still only partially civilized, did he find recruits. Our country is so small, that in Cumberland and Westmorland at least, the hills are losing their old influence.'

This interpretation neatly linked a conventional nineteenth-century view of progress through a limitation of royal authority with a sense that upland areas were socially conservative and politically reactionary. Modern scholarship is more sceptical about De Montfort and the Yorkists, although the geographical basis of support for the two sides in the Civil War receives considerable attention and is often related to socio-economic criteria. Pearson's observation about the hills could be a throwback to the pre-nineteenth-century view that mountains were hideous and oppressive. As a result, when, as is commonly the case, you have 'history written by the victors', the defeated were associated with upland areas possibly at least in part as much from inherited prejudice as from acute observation.

Pearson's environmentalism and, in particular, his theme of the difference between upland and lowland was taken up in the *Philips' New School Atlas of Universal History* (1928), with the map 'The Two Halves of England', which showed land over 600 ft, navigable rivers, cathedral cities, universities, chief ports, centres of the wool trade and iron smelting, and was designed to display 'the distinction between the hilly north-western and the level south-eastern halves of England, which has profoundly influenced its history'. As if to indicate the timeless nature of this distinction, the map bore no date.

In the same period, O.G.S. Crawford stressed the geographical approach to history and prehistory in his *Man and his Past* (1921). He was responsible for a series of inter-war historical maps produced by the Ordnance Survey that mapped locations and distributions against the background of physical geography.

Cyril Fox, an archaeologist who greatly influenced inter-war British historical geography, produced, in his lengthy *Archaeology of the Cambridge Region* (1923), a scholarly account of a physically based cultural zone and its historical characteristics. Fox used distribution maps that were coloured to show the physiography of the region: rivers and meres, fen and marsh, and areas probably densely forested. Fox explained 'the cultural differentiation of the eastern plain' in a way that emphasized physical factors but left room for others:

> At the commencement of this analysis the tendency to unity of cultural character in the Cambridge Region in any given age was held to be the natural consequence of the geographical unity which a river basin possesses. The peculiar configuration of the district – a narrow belt of open country bordered by fen and forest and forming a highway into Norfolk and North Suffolk – has, however, permitted this tendency at times to be modified by military or political action.

Fox went on to publish *The Personality of Britain. Its Influence on Inhabitant and Invader in Prehistoric and Early Historic Times* (1943). This emphasized the distinction between lowland and highland zones, but not in any deterministic fashion. Such a relationship is common in subsequent work, certainly on the crucial and long settlement period(s) of English history prior to 1200. It is indeed clear that there was causal interaction with the environment. For example, the lack of natural obstacles and the relatively small area of England encouraged Roman, Anglo-Saxon, Viking and Norman advances, but they also all benefited from the extent of the removal of woodland during the Bronze and Iron Ages.

The role of geography in England's history is not one that has been pushed to the fore, certainly for the history of the last millennium. Whereas the role of geographical factors in affecting settlement patterns in the centuries after the departure of the Romans is well known, this is far less the case for subsequent periods. Yet, geography is in many respects the factor that *helps* to explain the regional variations that are so important in England's history. These variations subvert any emphasis on uniformity, although, in turn, local circumstances also highlight the impact of national developments, for, given the great variety of geographical background, it is striking to note how much there is in the way of similarities. Reference to geographical influence does not, however, make clear how best to explain or assess this influence. It is all too easy to adopt a determinism akin to much of the discussion of socio-economic factors. This is inappropriate. It is more reasonable to stress influence without assuming any automatic response, a theory known as 'possibilism'. This allows for the vitality and variety of human responses, both of which emerge clearly in England's history.

TWO

BEFORE THE ROMANS

England had a long history prior to the Roman conquest in the first century AD. Much of it is obscure, although excellent work has been carried out by archaeologists. Within Europe, early man lived first in the warmer areas of the South but, when the climate permitted, spread from there into Northern Europe. Human remains of early hominids and finds of tool assemblages have been found in many sites in Southern England, including Stoke Newington, Clacton and Swanscombe. Neanderthal hunters also left sites in Southern England, but these were far fewer than in France and Germany, especially South-West France. The Neanderthals were replaced by anatomically modern humans during the Upper Palaeolithic period (c. 35,000 to c. 12,000 years ago). This lengthy age saw a development of social structures and stone blade technology. People retained useful objects for future use, had craftsmen with ideas of symmetry, and performed tasks entailing a division of labour. Cave or rock shelters from the period in England include Gough's Cave, Soldier's Hole and Kents Cavern in the South-West, Boxgrove in Sussex, and Mother Grundy's Parlour, Robin Hood's Cave and Pin Hole in the North Midlands.

The Upper Palaeolithic was followed by a period of climatic improvement, as the last Ice Age came to an end in around 10,000 BC. This led to a northward spread of forest and wildlife in Europe. The trees of a cold climate – birch, pine and hazel – were followed by oak, elm, ash and lime, all of which came to cover England between 7,500 and 5,000 BC.

11

These deciduous forests were rich in plant and animal life. Animal life also changed in its composition and became plentiful, with red and roe deer, and wild pig arriving. This encouraged an expansion in the number of hunter-gatherers in the Mesolithic period (*c.* 8,300 BC to *c.* 6,000 BC). They were equipped with microlithic flints. Mounted in wood or bone hafts, these provided effective tools for use, for example, as knives or as arrowheads. Settlements became more fixed and trade developed. As the ice melted, the sea level rose, and in about 6,500 BC the land-bridge that joined England to the Continent across the southern North Sea was cut.

This did not prevent a spread of agricultural developments from the Continent. Domestic crops and agriculture originated in the Near East and spread into England in the fifth millennium BC, although hunting, fishing and gathering continued. The move towards a more settled human imprint centred on farming, permitted a larger production of food, and that, in turn, led to a greater material culture, not least of pots, for storage and cooking. In addition, trade increased. All of these ensured that the archaeological trace improved, but, nevertheless, there is still much that is obscure. The plough was in use in southern England in about 3,500 BC. This helped increase crop yields, and encouraged the clearing of forest. Analysis of layers of pollen and the dating of the shift from tree pollen to open-country and field species suggest that land clearance occurred in Blea Tarn in Cumbria in about 4,525 BC and Hockham Mere in Norfolk in about 4,045 BC. The spread of domestic animals – sheep, goats, pigs, cattle and, later, horses – was followed by wheeled vehicles. With domestic animals came milk, wool and an ability to pull ploughs.

As the population rose, evidence of settlements increases. The evidence takes the form of 'causewayed camps', ritual monuments, and burial chambers, such as the West Kennet Long Barrow. Such works required much labour, suggesting a rising level of social organization, although it is difficult to assess its nature.

The monuments of the period were far from constant in type. Barrow tombs were followed between 3,200 and 1,500 BC by stone circles and circular ditched enclosures or henges. In England these were concentrated in the West Country, although they were more widely distributed. As they were also found in North-West France, there is evidence of a cultural region linked by sea. Indeed trade along the coasts and also across seas was a crucial development in English history.

The most famous legacy of the period is Stonehenge, a ritual centre that developed in phases. It took possibly 2 million man-hours to complete (by *c.* 1,550 BC), and the blue stones came from as far as the Prescelly Mountains in Wales. The nature of the rituals that took place there are unclear, but the effort and organization necessary for the construction of Stonehenge are obvious. Furthermore, Stonehenge was not alone.

Aside from major constructions, there was also an improvement in the range of craftsmanship, as the use of copper increased with developments in smelting and casting. Metalworking had spread into southern England by the third millennium BC. This increase in the material culture was followed by the dissemination of a new burial pattern, known as 'Beaker', from the distinctive pottery found in the graves. Unlike the communal graves of earlier Megalithic tombs, these were individual burials with rich grave-goods, suggesting a more stratified society.

The Copper Age was followed from 2,300 BC by that of bronze, a harder alloy of copper that was more effective in tools and weapons. Bronze replaced not only copper but also hard stone and flint. The social stratification already in evidence appears to have become more pronounced. Large burial mounds have been linked to areas likely to have benefited from trade, suggesting the existence of an elite. Aside from trade, agriculture increased in response to a rising population, and there is evidence for massive Bronze Age land division: laying-out of fields. More marginal areas were cleared of trees and cultivated. It has also been suggested that Bronze Age England was more bellicose. There is increased evidence of fortifications and weapons, and it has been argued that society was dominated by warriors.

They were to be challenged by the arrival of a new metal, iron. The smelting and forging of iron spread from West Asia and arrived in England by 700 BC. Iron was the most common metal, and its availability ensured that iron goods ceased to be rare and, instead, became widely used. By 500 BC iron tools were being used to clear trees. Iron hoes and nails brought new flexibility to agriculture and construction. Iron also made better weapons, particularly when carbon was added to make steel.

Subsequently, England was exposed to pressure from the Celts, a culture that appeared in South Germany in about 800 BC and then spread over much of Europe, including France. The extent of Celtic influence in England is controversial, although features of Celtic settlement, culture and civilization have been found in southern England. However, it is unclear how much was due to a widespread population movement, to more limited immigration, or to trade. If the first two, it is unclear how much should be attributed to invasion. The likelihood is that there was a mixture of all these influences, unsurprisingly so as the period in question was lengthy. The impact of 'Belgic' peoples from northern France (a Celtic group) has been traced in the development of what can be termed states, such as that of the Trinovantes (later Essex), the use of coins, and the development of towns, such as Wheathampstead, Seaford, Hengistbury, and Colchester, the capital of the Trinovantes.

Iron Age society in England was different to that of its nemesis, imperial Rome. There were proto-towns, known to the Romans as *oppida*, but not a developed urban civilization, and states but not a sophisticated governmental system with differentiated administrative functions. Language was divisive and there was no written culture. Yet there had also been much development. Much of the woodland had been cleared, particularly in areas with light soil, and agriculture was both varied and extensive. It supported a growing population, a settled society and an aristocratic elite. The announcement in 2006 of the discovery of an ancient bronze off Salcombe provides evidence of trade with the central Mediterranean, although this trade may not have been direct.

Although there were 'states', there was not only nothing to match Rome, but also no sign of an identity, political or otherwise, that might be termed England. There was no one state, nor federation of states, that was co-terminous with England. Nor was there any 'proto-England', any state that might, had Rome not intervened, have taken over England, rather as Rome had done in Italy. Nor was there any uniformity of conditions over England; indeed the term had no meaning in this period and is used simply to indicate the area that was later to be termed England. Statehood and urban development were most pronounced in southern England, while the use of coins was restricted to southern England and the Midlands. The term the English also has no meaning for this period.

Counterfactuals are always tricky, and it is unclear what would have happened but for the conquest. The areas of Germany and Scotland that were not conquered by Rome were essentially to develop into a number of small kingdoms that focused on farming but also took part in trade, as did Ireland. Through trade and war, they interacted with their neighbours, including Rome. Yet this interaction was far less than England was to experience as part of the Roman empire.

THREE

THE ROMAN PERIOD

Britain was the only island attacked by Rome outside the better-known and more placid, or, at least, certainly less tidal, waters of the Mediterranean. Julius Caesar's invasions in 55 and 54 BC were bold steps. He claimed that they were necessary to end the support of tribes in southern England for the Celts who were resisting his conquest of Gaul (France). However, it was largely personal prestige and the dictates of politics in Rome that led to his expeditions, as they also did for the following expedition, that of the Emperor Claudius in AD 43. Caesar needed to show that the invasions were necessary for him to remain in control of the army in Gaul, the basis of his power. He also wished to win glory.

In 55 BC, Caesar did not move from his beachhead in Kent. The Romans were victorious in hard fighting, but the damage done to their ships by equinoctial gales and the scale of the resistance led Caesar to come to terms with the local tribes. In 54 BC a larger force made an unopposed landing, again in Kent. Caesar won a victory near Canterbury, defeating the tribal leader, Cassivellaunus, and crossed the River Thames. Cassivellaunus' capital, possibly Wheathampstead, was seized, an attack on the Kent beachhead was beaten off, and Caesar reached a settlement with Cassivellaunus. Hostages and tribute were promised by the local rulers and a client ruler installed for the Trinovantes.

England was no pushover, but the Romans benefited from their opponents' inability to contest the passage of the

Channel, and from their fighting advantage once landed. The disciplined Roman infantry, with its body-armour, javelins and short swords, was more effective than that of the English who had little body armour and lacked effective missile power. English chariots were vulnerable to Roman archers and their hillforts to siegecraft. Furthermore, English farmer-soldiers could not afford to be soldiers all the time, and their farming also made them vulnerable to Roman devastation.

Caesar's expeditions were not followed up for nearly a century. Rebellion in Gaul, and then civil war in the empire took precedence and, once order was restored by Augustus, the German frontier was a higher priority. Caligula planned an invasion, but did not mount one. Had the invasions of 55 and 54 BC been followed up more rapidly it is probable that England would have been conquered earlier, although there is little reason to believe that the Romans would have been able or willing to press on to conquer Ireland and Highland Scotland, and thus unite the Brtitish Isles.

In search of a military reputation, Claudius launched an invasion with about 40,000 men in 43 AD. After an unopposed landing, probably in Kent, the Romans defeated a confederation of forces in three battles, two of which were caused by contested crossings of the Medway and the Thames. The Emperor then arrived, with the first elephants seen in England, and received the surrender of Colchester.

This was not to be a raid or a short-term occupation akin to the Roman advance to the Elbe under Augustus. After Claudius decided to make Britannia a Roman province, the Romans rapidly overran most of the south. The Iceni of East Anglia and the Atrebates of Surrey, Sussex and Hampshire were given client status, while the hillforts of the West

Country were captured. Vespasian, then commander of the II Augusta legion, and later Emperor, destroyed more than twenty hillforts, including Maiden Castle, when he conquered the Durotriges of Dorset and Somerset. Caratacus, the leader of the Catuvellauni, continued resistance from Wales, but was defeated in 50–1 AD. Fleeing north, he was handed over to the Romans by Cartimandua, Queen of the Brigantes of Yorkshire, who became a client ruler.

The most effective response occurred in 60 AD. The Governor, Suetonius Paulinus, was campaigning in North Wales when the Iceni under Boudica (Boadicea is a later corruption of the name) rebelled. The Iceni were enraged by vicious and corrupt mismanagement and expropriation and by the abuse of her family by the Romans, including the flogging of Boudica and the rape of her daughters. The Iceni were supported by the Trinovantes, much of whose land had been confiscated to support the colony of Roman veterans at Colchester (Camulodunum). The major Roman settlements – Colchester, London (Londinium) and St Albans (Verulamium) – were stormed and their inhabitants slaughtered with great cruelty. However, as with the Indian Mutiny against English rule in 1857, there was no united response, in large part because there was no basis for political unity. Cogidubnus, the client ruler of the Atrebates, for example, remained loyal. Furthermore, the regular Roman forces moved rapidly. At a battle somewhere in the Midlands, Paulinus crushed Boudica, who died, probably by suicide. The Iceni and their allies were then 'pacified' with typical Roman brutality.

The Romans pressed on to conquer the whole of England, but this was not automatic. The civil war that began with the Emperor Nero's suicide in 68 was the first of a series of conflicts within the Roman elite that periodically weakened the Roman military effort and presence in England until the eventual fall of the empire. The pace of advance resumed in 71 with the subjugation of the Brigantes (71–73/4) and of Wales (73/4–6). Highland Scotland and Ireland, however, were to escape the Roman grasp, with long-term consequences for their separate development that are difficult to evaluate. Inchtuthil in Perthshire is the northernmost major Roman fort. From about 122, the Emperor Hadrian constructed the most impressive legacy of Roman rule in England, a stone wall 70 miles long at the narrowest part of the island, the Tyne–Solway line. Designed to mark a frontier, this was not the end of Roman attempts to move north. None, however, proved more than short-term.

Roman England displayed the characteristics of other imperial provinces, although its frontier position ensured that there was an extensive military presence. The settlement of people from elsewhere in the empire, many of them former soldiers, was matched by the Romanization of the native elite. Towns had a far greater role than in pre-Roman England. They developed as centres of administration, trade and integration, many of them on the sites of modern cities. The administrative hierarchy and military system were not unchanging, but, by the mid-second century, London, the major port of Roman England, and thus its crucial link with the rest of the empire, was the provincial capital. The city had developed on the lowest bridging point on the Thames. York, Chester and Caerleon in South-East Wales were the long-standing bases of three legions, while Colchester, Lincoln and Gloucester were *coloniae*, towns founded for veterans. Provincial capitals included Canterbury, Chichester, Cirencester,

Dorchester, Exeter, Leicester, St Albans and Winchester. Rectilinear grid street-plans, centred on forums and basilicas, developed in these towns, although some smaller towns were less planned.

The towns were linked by roads, some of which are still used today: Watling Street from London to Chester became, in part, the A5. Roads were built to a high standard, with stone foundations and gravel surfaces, and were frequently straight. No equivalent road-building programme followed in England until the turnpikes of the eighteenth century. The planned network of the roads helped both communications and military control. They were a testimony to the impact of a powerful governmental structure that also organized a large-scale drainage scheme in East Anglia, built the Foss Dyke, a canal to link Lincoln to the River Trent, brought economic changes designed to supply the army, and introduced effective taxation.

As goods and money were moved in a regular fashion across greater distances, and also to and from the Continent, inter-regional contact increased, and new fashions and designs were disseminated, as in the pottery industry. The population rose and the area under cultivation increased, an aspect of the Roman control which extended to the environment.

Agriculture improved. In the late third and fourth centuries, larger ploughs were introduced and coulters were added. This led to the cutting of deeper furrows, which permitted the working of heavier soils. The introduction of two-handed scythes enabled hay to be cut faster and thus larger quantities to be stored for winter forage. Corn-drying kilns were constructed, and crop rotations were introduced.

The greater quantity of archaeological material surviving from the Roman period suggests a society producing and trading far more goods than its Iron Age predecessors.

The prosperity of the rural economy underwrote the cost of building numerous villas: large noble houses in the country constructed in a Roman style and heated from under the floor by a hypocaust system. They were very different to the native tradition of housing. Villas, such as Chedworth, the remains of which can be visited near Cheltenham, were supported by nearby farmsteads. Villas had a major effect on the organization of the landscape and the ability to produce an agricultural surplus. From this surplus stemmed non-agricultural production and trade supported by coinage. However, this needed a superstructure of Roman administration to survive: hence the collapse in the fifth century.

There were also religious and cultural changes. Roman cults spread, although assimilation with native Celtic beliefs was important. When Christianity became the state religion, this brought more systematic cultural links between England and the Continent. The pre-Roman druids, whom the Romans stamped out, and the cults of the Olympian gods which they introduced, had both lacked diocesan structure and doctrinal regulation. The Olympian cults, however, linked England to the Continent. So also did the cult of Mithras which was of Persian origin and closely connected with the Roman army. Mithras was seen as an agent of good or light endlessly fighting evil or darkness. Mithraic congregations normally met in underground or partly underground buildings. Women were excluded, as from much else of Roman life.

In addition, pre-Roman pagan practices still continued. This was an aspect of the limited impact of Roman culture.

Outside the towns, which were the centres of consumption, authority and Roman culture, England was not as thoroughly Romanized as other provinces of the empire, such as Gaul. It was further from the centres of the Roman empire.

Roman England was weakened by the inability of the Roman empire to devise a consistently accepted system of imperial succession, and the willingness of military units to support their commanders in bids for power, although such bids were not continual. After the decades in which Roman rule was established, in Britain there was no civil revolt. Instead, the unreliable sector was the army. In addition, the impact of defending Roman England from outside attacks, including Picts from Scotland, Scots from Ireland, and Saxons from northern Germany and southern Scandinavia, was considerable. Their attacks became serious in the 350s, ending a period of prosperity that had begun in the 270s, and a successful invasion in 367 led to a widespread devastation. Order was restored by Theodosius between 368 and 369. By 370 a chain of ten forts stretched from Brancaster, Norfolk to Portchester, Dorset. This 'Saxon Shore' was designed to protect harbours and estuaries along the vulnerable east and south coasts. The construction of town defences from the third century indicated an attitude of growing defensiveness.

Civil war in the empire and 'barbarian' invasions led to renewed problems in the 400s. In 406 Gaul was invaded, and England, threatened with being cut off from the rest of the empire, created its own emperor, Constantine III. As an English-based self-styled 'Roman Emperor', he was an interesting early instance of a short-term de facto English autonomy but one that was not designed to lead to independence. Indeed Constantine III took a significant part of the island's military forces to Gaul to counter the 'barbarian' threat. These troops did not return. The Romano-Britons, disillusioned with the rebel Constantine's activities, expelled his administrators and appealed to the true emperor, Honorius, for the restoration of legitimate rule. He, hard pressed in Italy by Alaric, the Visigothic leader, who captured Rome in 410, could do no more than tell them to look to their own defence. This was the end of the Roman empire in England.

FOUR
ANGLO-SAXON ENGLAND

The period after the end of the Roman empire is the most obscure in England's history over the past two millennia. The early Germanic invaders were illiterate, and Bede and other later written sources provide a different account from the archaeological evidence. The latter anyway has to be used with care because of the difficulty of interpreting evidence and its uneven spread, reflecting, in part, the varied pattern of excavation and fieldwork activity. Nevertheless, such evidence suggests that there was already a substantial Germanic presence in eastern England before the 450s. Then, according to the *Anglo-Saxon Chronicle* (Saxon annals written considerably later, probably first in Alfred's reign in the ninth century), Jutes, under the probably mythical Hengist and Horsa, founded the kingdom of Kent; although, in fact, there were originally probably two Kentish kingdoms.

The process of 'barbarian' arrival is also unclear. As elsewhere in Western Europe, 'barbarian' mercenaries were hired and probably came to demand power for themselves, although it is unclear how far there were large-scale migrations into England and how much there was therefore a replacement of the earlier population. Some scholars emphasize a considerable measure of continuity in the population.

Jutes established themselves in Kent, the Isle of Wight and parts of Hampshire, the Saxons elsewhere in South-East England (Sussex: South Saxons; Essex: East Saxons), and the Angles further north. Wessex, the kingdom of the West

Saxons, centred on Hampshire, eventually became the most important Saxon kingdom, although the process by which particular ethnic groups came to be associated with specific territories is open to doubt.

The new states, however, were bitterly resisted. Late- and post-Roman society was increasingly militarized and able to mount long-lasting resistance, although the economy of Roman Britain declined after the formal end of imperial government in 409. In addition, the post- (or sub-) Roman British were themselves divided into warring kingdoms and, unlike in the fourth century, could not call for assistance from the Continent. Most of lowland England had been conquered by 600.

The length of time that the Anglo-Saxon conquest took limited its ability to lead to an abrupt change. Furthermore, it means that it is difficult to distinguish between the impact of the invaders and that stemming from the consequences of the end of imperial Roman rule. The break with Roman rule ensured a transitional stage in which governmental power ceased to be wielded by those appointed by Rome.

Anglo-Saxon conquest brought more sweeping change, both because of Germanization, not least linguistically, and because, under the pagan invaders, Christianity, introduced under the Romans, became a tenuous presence. It is likely that the population of England fell dramatically, not least because of plague. In the areas conquered by the Anglo-Saxons, the Romano-Britons largely fled or survived as slaves and peasants, although the latter could lead to a significant level of both survival and continuity with Anglo-Saxon settlement. Furthermore, the conventional view is contested by scholars who argue that there were few Anglo-Saxon settlers, and that the great majority of the population remained British, but acculturated to a militarily dominant invading elite.

Archaeological evidence suggests that the new settlers continued the Romano-British pattern of generally neglecting clay lands, in favour of lighter soils on gravel, sand and chalk. As a consequence, the Anglo-Saxons occupied an already managed landscape, although the common place-name 'ley' (from Old English *lēah*), meaning woodland clearing or clearing where there is a settlement, suggests a process of expansion into woodland. At least initially, Anglo-Saxon agriculture was largely subsistence. Trade declined, although in 600 much of Britain was not yet in Anglo-Saxon hands, and the rest remained in trading contact with the Mediterranean. Within the conquered regions, there was a major transformation unique in the former Roman empire: in contrast Gaul, Italy, Spain and North Africa, all of which were also conquered by 'barbarians', did not lose towns, Latin or Christianity. The impact of what was probably bubonic plague in the seventh century appears to have hit population numbers in Britain hard.

Yet, it would be misleading to see these centuries simply as the Dark Ages, solely as centuries of plague and violence. There is potential in a long-term approach for understanding the 'Dark Ages' in pre-Roman terms, viewing Romanization as something which overlay deeper 'rhythms' of continuity in, for example, settlement, land use and trade. In addition, cemeteries have yielded much early Anglo-Saxon pottery and metalwork. The rich and ornate goods, many from the Continent and Byzantium (the Eastern Roman Empire), found in the ship burials at Sutton Hoo and, to a lesser extent, at

Snape and in Kentish cemeteries, testified to the wealth of the
East Anglian and Kentish dynasties, and the importance of
links with the Continent. The Sutton Hoo burial (*c.* 630) near
Woodbridge, Suffolk, probably contained the tomb of King
Raedwald of East Anglia. The exceptional quality of the
ornamental work found with the burial is evidence of the
wealth and splendour of some elements of seventh-century
society, and prompts speculation about the riches of Anglo-
Saxon civilization that have been lost. In part, this was a case
of new developments as the Sutton Hoo burial would
probably have been inconceivable a century earlier. It
reflected a new political complexity and strengthened contacts
with the Continent.

Much of the resources of Anglo-Saxon civilization was spent
on aggressive warfare. The ethic of the warband seems to
have been very important in Anglo-Saxon culture. After three
hundred years in which conflict within England had been very
limited, the period that began in 400 saw far more frequent
conflict, although it is unclear how destructive it was.
Whereas the Roman conquest of England had taken three
decades, the Anglo-Saxons took over four centuries, although
it was a different type of conquest, in large part a cultural
process. For example, the Saxon occupation of Dorset was
delayed until the late sixth or seventh centuries, Cornwall was
only conquered by Wessex in 838, and the kingdoms in Wales
were never conquered. The remaking of the linguistic map
helped create and define differences within the British Isles.

As a consequence of this lengthy process, conquest and war
remained central to the ethos and structure of Anglo-Saxon
England. Conquest did not prevent a measure of assimilation
and, at times, co-operation, but the persistent trend was of

the pushing back of sub-Romano-British power. Gloucestershire was conquered in the 570s, and the British kingdoms of Elmet, centred on Leeds, and Rheged, around the Solway estuary, were absorbed by the Anglian kingdom of Northumbria in the late sixth and seventh centuries.

This expansion also helped to tip the balance between the Anglo-Saxon kingdoms. Initially, Kent and East Anglia were important, and in the 590s Aethelbert of Kent was what the *Anglo-Saxon Chronicle* was to call a Bretwalda ('wide ruler' or 'over king'). However, these kingdoms, like Lindsey, were not able to benefit from the subsequent advance of the Anglo-Saxon frontier. Instead, the crucial beneficiaries were to be kingdoms further west and on the frontier of settlement: the Saxon kingdom of Wessex and the Anglian kingdoms in the Midlands (Mercia), Yorkshire (Deira), and north of the Tees (Bernicia). Deira, to the north of the Humber, was probably established in the late fifth century; Bernicia at or near Bamburgh in the mid-sixth century. Under Aethelfrith (593–616), Bernicia expanded as far as Lothian and south-west Scotland, while Deira gained the vales of York and Pickering.

Such expansion interacted with the coalescence of the numerous small Anglo-Saxon kingdoms. This lengthy process was an aspect of what could be described as state-building, although it is important not to exaggerate the sophistication of the resulting product. Penda of Mercia (*c*. 632–54) was said to have had an army which included forces contributed by thirty subordinate leaders, many of whom would once have been the independent rulers of small territories. With time, and particularly after 700, ruling houses were increasingly differentiated from landowners, and royal justice was to be differentiated from that of kin, feud and surety.

For much of the seventh century, Northumbria, the kingdom created from Bernicia and Deira, was the most powerful state. Oswald (634–42), Oswy (642–70), and Egfrith (670–85) ruled the lands between the Humber and the Forth, and the Mersey and the Ayr, and were at times treated as overlords by the rulers of Mercia, Wessex, Strathclyde, and the Pict and Scottish territories.

This period was important in the establishment of Christianity. The sources for this were twofold: Rome and the Irish Church. A mission from Pope Gregory the Great, under Augustine, came in 597 to Canterbury, the capital of Kent, whence much of South-East England was converted. The remainder was converted by the Irish Church, via its Scottish base at Iona, from where a mission, under Aidan, founded Lindisfarne in Northumbria in 635. From there, Mercia was converted after the death of the pagan Penda. Oswald of Northumbria was important in the foundation of Lindisfarne, and Oswy played a major role in ensuring that at the Synod (church meeting) of Whitby in 664, Roman, rather than Celtic, customs prevailed. The canons of the Synod of Hertford in 672 were issued for and applied to the whole English Church. Theodore of Tarsus, whom the pope appointed Archbishop of Canterbury, organized the English Church.

The monolithic orthodoxy which established Christianity pursued, as well as its centralized character, marginalized and sought to destroy alternative religions and different cults. Christianity thus helped ensure cultural unification. Paganism lacked the physical or intellectual infrastructure to compete with the strengths of Christianity. The latter included an evolving structure of dioceses, a system of 'minsters' equipped with proselytizing clergy, and a codified body of doctrine.

Ecclesiastical developments were not matched in secular politics. The ability of rulers of Northumbria to act as overlord of most of England was not sustained. Defeat by Mercia (678) and the Picts (685) ended Northumbria's hegemony. In its place, Mercia became the most powerful kingdom. It had already absorbed the West Midland kingdoms of the Hwicce and the Magonsaetan and, from 654, when King Anna was killed, dominated East Anglia. Penda's heir, Peada, was baptized in 653.

Mercia became most powerful under Offa (757–96). He controlled such formerly independent kingdoms as Essex, Kent and Sussex, while Wessex recognized Mercian protection in 786. Offa is most often linked with the earth dyke built to prevent Welsh raiding. Its construction was an impressive display of resources and organization, and extended the earlier Wat's Dyke of *c.* 700.

Mercia, however, was unable to provide any lasting unity. Wessex rejected Mercian protection in 802. Mercia was weakened in the 820s by conflict in Wales and dynastic feuds. In 825, after defeating the Mercians at Wroughton, Egbert of Wessex conquered Essex, Kent, Surrey and Sussex. In 829, Mercia followed, and Northumbria also acknowledged Egbert's overlordship, but effective control over England was beyond Wessex's capability, and Mercia was soon independent. A divided England was to be vulnerable to Viking attack.

People mostly lived in farmsteads and small hamlets, in a society in which kinship bonds played a major role, albeit one tempered by the rise of lordship and kingship. The nucleated villages of high-medieval England still lay in the future. Anglo-Saxon place-names, such as *-ham*, *-tun* and *-worth*, were thereafter to be the most important in rural England, matching the *chesters* and *cesters* that denote Roman towns. However, a small number of major ports, such as Ipswich, London, Southampton and York, developed in the eighth century. Coinage developed in the late seventh and eighth centuries.

Agriculture was handicapped by a serious shortage of fertilizer. Spring marling was a festival of fertilizing land in Saxon England. Fields had to be left fallow (uncultivated) to restore their fertility. Livestock were smaller than their Roman predecessors and far smaller than their modern descendants; and meat and milk yields were much lower. Most agriculture was subsistence. Communications were relatively primitive, both for goods and for people. Long-distance bulk transport was only economic by water, but rivers were affected by freezing and drought, while sea travel was at the mercy of wind, waves and tides.

Yet the agrarian economy underwrote what was, by the standards of the period, a relatively prosperous society and a rich civilization. This was especially true of the Church. The evidence of ports, coinage and monastic endowment all suggest a very remarkable economic boom in *c.* 670–730. From the late seventh century, monastic churches were constructed at important centres, although they should be termed minsters, both because that is the contemporary term and also because it expresses the reality of a situation that was less rigid than the monasticism that prevailed from the tenth century.

Christianity meant a spread of education and literacy, and also provided new media for the Anglo-Saxon artist in the form of stone sculpture and manuscript illumination. The Lindisfarne Gospel, one of the great works of Northumbrian monasticism, illuminated between 689 and 721, revealed Irish influence in its script and ornamentation. Many of the decorative motifs used had their roots in pagan Saxon art, but others in the art of the Christian Mediterranean. One legacy of the culture was the Anglo-Saxon crosses, such as the Bewcastle and Ruthwell crosses. They probably served as funerary monuments or sanctuary markers. The principal carved decoration presented a series of sophisticated and literate scenes. The Ruthwell Cross bears, in runic lettering, a version of the Anglo-Saxon poem, *The Dream of the Rood*, a powerful account of the crucifixion as told by the cross.

It was this society that was attacked by the Vikings, who brutally sacked the great Northumbrian religious houses of Lindisfarne and Jarrow in 793–4. The limited availability of land for colonization in Scandinavia, and the attraction of England for raiding and settlement encouraged attack. English vulnerability to amphibious raids was especially serious, as the Viking longboats were effective ocean-going ships (in contrast to the Anglo-Saxon ships which were probably only coastal-huggers, although bolder claims have been advanced). In addition, due to their shallow draught, Viking longboats could be rowed in coastal waters and up rivers. Danish ships were first recorded in English waters in 789, and, from the 830s, Viking pressure increased markedly. Soon the Vikings came to conquer. Danish invaders took up winter quarters in Thanet in 850 and Sheppey in 854. The Danish 'Great Army' overran East Anglia in 865 and Yorkshire between 866 and 867. Edmund, the last Anglo-Saxon king of East Anglia, was killed.

Wessex was more successful: Egbert defeated a joint Viking-Cornish force at Hingston Down in 838, gaining control of

Cornwall; and his son, Aethelwulf, defeated the Danes at Aclea in 851. However, in 871, the latter's son, Alfred (871–99), was nearly crushed by the Danes and had to agree to pay tribute. The Danes then overran Mercia in 874. The defeated King, Burgred, fled to Rome, his successor, Ceowulf, paid tribute, and in 877 Mercia east and north of Watling Street became Danish.

A sudden attack on Wessex the following year led Alfred to flee to the Somerset marshes at Athelney, but he counter-attacked successfully to defeat the Danes at Edington. The Danish advance had been stopped, and a further Danish attack between 892 and 896 was unsuccessful. Victory at Edington was followed by a treaty leaving the Danes with the lands east and north of Watling Street – the Danelaw. Much, but by no means all, of this was to be an area of Danish settlement. This settlement was to be indicated by place names, with their typical endings of -by and -thorp, and material remains, although it is unclear how much of the population continued to be Anglo-Saxon. The likelihood is that Danish immigration was extensive, but patchy. Rapid acculturation ensured that the Danish and Anglo-Saxon populations were quickly co-assimilated. Norse/Norwegian settlers were more important around the Irish Sea.

As well as stopping the Danes, Alfred developed Wessex. He built a fleet, improved the system of military recruitment, and constructed a system of burhs (fortified towns). He also began minting good pennies, a clear sign of a well-established kingdom. Alfred also aimed at creating a more effective Christian polity. He produced a law-code, fostered an image of Christian kingship, patronized learning, and established schools in order to produce priests and laity who would be wise and just leaders and administrators. Seeking to sustain his image, Alfred commissioned a biography, *The Life of King Alfred* (893), from Bishop Asser. This stressed his suffering and endurance, presenting effective royal leadership in a markedly Christian light. Alfred's power and prestige were increased by the earlier destruction of the other Anglo-Saxon ruling houses at the hands of the Danes, and by Alfred's sensitivity in handling the Mercians. He presented himself as the champion of Christianity and all Anglo-Saxons against the pagan Danes, and was the crucial figure in the shift towards a new politics and a new country, England.

FIVE

THE OLD ENGLISH MONARCHY 899–1066

Although that was very much not the intention, the Danish invasions helped ensure that England developed politically and governmentally. It is important not to overlook the earlier, eighth-century expansion of Mercia, which involved considerable bureaucratic and fiscal skills, and the subsequent expansion of Wessex in the early ninth century before it was pushed back by the Danes. Furthermore, the Danes might have been successful and have extinguished Wessex. Nevertheless, their failure left the way open for the expansion of a stronger Wessex. A succession of able adult male rulers was also crucial in sustaining and strengthening the position of the house of Wessex and in creating the new state. Alfred's heirs, Edward the Elder (ruled 899–924), Athelstan (924–39), and Edmund (939–46), brought most of the area of modern England under their authority. This could be, was, and has been presented as a process of reconquest, the driving back of the Danes and the Norwegians, but it was as much one of conquest, in which the rulers of Wessex brought modern England under their authority. The legitimacy of the conquerors, however, rested in part on the notion of reconquest, which was appropriate in the sense that Christian territory was being regained. It also contrasted with the weakness of other Western European kingdoms.

Edward overran the Danish bases in eastern Mercia, conquered East Anglia, and built forts in the north-west

Midlands, including Manchester (919), to limit the danger of attack from the Norwegian kingdom of Dublin: the Norwegians had invaded the Wirral in 902. The defeated Danes were allowed to keep their lands, and the Danelaw retained distinctive features, including its own legal system, although the Danes were also quick to adopt Christianity. English Mercia was absorbed by Wessex in 918. In 927, Athelstan captured York and took over Northumbria.

This success was reversed after Athelstan's death, when Olaf II Guthfrithson, King of Dublin, gained York and the North Midlands. However, after the killing in an ambush in 954 of Eric Bloodaxe, the last Norwegian king of York, Northumbria (both Danish York and English Bamburgh) finally accepted West Saxon authority. Athelstan had employed the title *Rex totius Anglorum patriae*, although he was not crowned as such. Edgar (959–75) was the first to be crowned king of the whole English nation. This was crucial in the formation of the unified English nation. Probably as a consequence of the influence of Carolingian (the Frankish dynasty of Charlemagne) ideology, specifically the notion of a Christian empire, expressed by Jonas of Orléans and Hincmar of Rheims, which influenced Athelstan and Edgar, tenth-century Wessex moved towards a notion of kingship different from that of the amalgam of kingdoms epitomized by Offa's Mercia in the eighth century.

The period from Alfred to Edgar was that of the definition of an English state, one that did not require, nor was constrained by, precise ethnic or geographical borders. This was crucial because the history of the English owes much to that of the English state. Of the present-day area of England, Northumberland and Durham were only loosely attached, and Cumbria was not to be taken until the late eleventh century. Similarly, state formation in Scotland helped ensure that the English state would not extend across the entire island, either then or subsequently.

The expanding state, ruled by the house of Wessex, also developed internally. A law and order system, based on counties or shires and their subdivisions, hundreds, linked rulers and the free population. In the West Midlands, the formation of shires may have been intended partly to break up the former territories of Mercia and its satellite areas, so as to prevent Mercia's re-emergence. The county system offered decentralization, but was also controlled with sophistication through the use of writs. There was also a system of assessment for taxation and military service based on hides, the hide being the amount of land necessary to support a peasant family. The coinage was improved and frequently reminted. The management of the coinage by reminting from at least seventy mints of what was effectively a national currency permitted the adjustment of coin weights, with corresponding benefits to the rate of exchange and foreign trade. Society was increasingly monetarized – subjects paying taxes in coin, rulers spending money.

The Church was also closely linked with royalty. A close relationship between the house of Wessex and the archiepiscopal see of Canterbury was one result of the Danish attacks. Royal saint-cults helped raise the prestige of the ruling house. Under Edgar (959–75) and Dunstan, Archbishop of Canterbury (960–88), there was a reform of the monasteries, in reaction to the ninth-century decline. Canterbury, Sherborne, Winchester and Worcester all became monastic cathedrals, and important abbeys were founded or re-founded elsewhere. Monastic revival provided the context for literary and cultural revival, including manuscript illumination, stone carving and embroidery. The reform of the monasteries and the close association of the house of Wessex with the Church had a unifying impact.

Cultural activity again reflected a prosperous society, one that made a good recovery from the disruption of the Viking attacks. By the eleventh century, nucleated (village) settlement was widespread in lowland England. This reflected more settled farming systems, and the growth of local manorial lordship. Boundaries were delineated, and common fields organized. Royal taxation and the development of urban markets helped encourage economic growth in the countryside. Manorial names, such as Woolstone and Uffington (Wulfric's/Uffa's estate) in Berkshire, replaced some earlier topographical place-names. The foundation in the tenth and eleventh centuries of numerous local parish churches was linked to this nucleation, as well as to a greater popular interest in Christianity. In 1086, over 400 churches were recorded in Suffolk alone, although this figure was exceptionally high.

Hereditary tenure of land developed, alongside a closer definition of the status, rights and duties of *thegns* (gentry-like nobles); although it is unclear how far some of the developments of the tenth and eleventh centuries may have been anticipated earlier, but seem more evident in this period due to the nature of the surviving evidence. Thus, bookland, land granted in perpetuity by charter, had been granted to secular individuals since at least the reign of Offa.

Land was held in return for service in what was very much a service aristocracy: service to the king led to gains of land

and status. Alfred's biographer Asser referred to his 'noble followers and vassals'. The personal loyalties of the war band were given territorial form, regularity and aristocratic continuity in the tenth century. This process was not new, but was given a new range and political complexion by the extent to which statehood was being reshaped as Wessex became what was later termed the Old English monarchy. This was the first England, and the term can be employed without too much anachronism, although John was the first to use the title King of England; his predecessors were kings of the English.

Yet, at the same time, as with later Englands, this was very much a country dominated by one part, indeed more so because of its origins in the separate kingdom of Wessex. The Old English monarchy was still very much centred on Wessex. Alone among the tenth-century rulers, Athelstan spent much time in Mercia. Other kings spent most of their time in the four heartland shires of Wessex: Hampshire, Wiltshire, Dorset and Somerset. The precariousness of nationhood was indicated in 957 when the Mercians and Northumbrians renounced allegiance to Eadwig in favour of his brother Edgar, although the latter became King of Wessex as well on Eadwig's death in 959. The allegiance of Northumbria to whoever ruled at Winchester, the capital of Wessex, remained uncertain well into the eleventh century and both force and expropriation were used to further control.

Allowing for these limitations, there was an increasingly sophisticated system of administration. The king was linked to the localities by a system of officials: *ealdormen*, sheriffs, port-reeves and hundredmen. The strength of the monarchy was indicated by its role in urban defence and revival, and by the system in which groups of hides were responsible for the maintenance of sections of the defences of *burhs*. The administrative structure of the state placed a heavy emphasis on kingship, and administrative kingship was what distinguished England from France and Germany. The king's peace, the king's courts, the king's units, the king's taxes, all of which covered the kingdom as a whole, were not, for example, matched by the early Capetians in France.

Furthermore, the vitality of this system was such that it was continued by invaders, both Scandinavian and Norman. The degree to which, in particular, Henry I (1100–35) and Henry II (1154–89), the crucial moulders of medieval England, built their own administrative kingship upon Anglo-Saxon structures and practices was fundamental in giving English government a different shape and a different feel from that in France. In the latter, taxes were voted for the defence of localities more readily than for the needs of the kingdom. The roots of political centralism in England are thus more ancient and deeper than elsewhere. This should not lead to an underestimation of the regional outlook, but it is an enduring element in English history from the tenth century onwards. Furthermore, the most powerful agency for regional outlook, the shire, at once focused both long traditions of communal organization and the relationship between locality and monarchy.

Agriculture expanded. The permanent cultivation of common fields from the tenth century, and the production of wool and cloth, helped England to become wealthy by the standards of contemporary northern Europe, and also a tempting prize to foreign rulers. Cultivated land became increasingly important as a sign and source of wealth and power, in part replacing treasure. Economic growth, a monetary economy and wealth in silver made England both a tempting target for invaders, and also provided a basis for governmental development.

The century after Edgar's death in 975 revealed, however, that the governance and cultural life of England were still dependent on its political stability, and that this could be threatened by domestic division and foreign challenge. The creation of England – the replacement of the multiple-kingdoms by one kingdom – was only briefly reversed, but this creation helped ensure that problems of stability were more obviously national in scale. Furthermore, a single ruler, national taxation and a common coinage were not the same as a nation state: concepts and practices of national unity were limited. This was seen in the tenth century with the emergence of 'super ealdordoms'. Athelstan made Athelstan Half-King responsible for East Anglia, Essex and the East Midlands in *c*. 930, Eadred appointed an ealdorman for Northumbria, and Edgar another for (West) Mercia. The ealdordoms of East Anglia and Mercia were given to West Saxons, but there was the danger that they would become hereditary. Initially, they indeed remained within the families of the original appointees. Aethelred 'the Unready' broke this process and seems to have preferred to appoint lesser officials (high reeves) with smaller spheres of authority; but Cnut reverted to the system under Edgar.

The continuity of able adult leadership was broken with Edgar's death in 975. Both his sons were young. The elder, Edward, succeeded, but was unpopular and was murdered in 978 by supporters of his younger brother, and successor, Aethelred 'the Unready' (978–1016). Like King John (1199–1216), Aethelred may have been subsequently underrated, not least in Aethelred's case, because of the hostile tone of the relevant section of the *Anglo-Saxon Chronicle*. In fact, Aethelred made major efforts to improve the state's defences, but, like John, he lacked the ability to command or elicit trust, both crucial aspects of kingship in an aristocratic society. This limited his ability to deal with the return of the Vikings, now more threatening because the Viking lands had witnessed a measure of state formation: Aethelred probably faced larger armies than those that had attacked Alfred.

Soon after Aethelred's accession, the Danes started mounting major attacks, in one of which they defeated the Essex militia under Ealdorman Brihtnoth at Maldon (991). The stress on the loyalty of Brihtnoth's retinue to their lord in the poem inspired by the battle was an example of the sort of allegiance that successful lordship could elicit; a contrast to that received by Aethelred. Aethelred's attempts to buy the Danes off with 'danegeld', which began after Maldon, testified to the wealth and organization of the English state, and £137,000 was paid in 991–1012, a formidable sum for the period. However, the policy failed. A massacre of Danes living in England in 1002 provoked major attacks by King Swein of Denmark between 1003 and 1006. When Swein invaded again in 1013, resistance collapsed and Aethelred fled to Normandy. He returned when Swein died in 1014, but Swein's son, Cnut, continued the struggle.

After Aethelred died, England was divided, by the Peace of Alney of 1016, between his son, the energetic Edmund Ironside, and Cnut, the last receiving Mercia and Northumbria. Edmund, however, soon died, and Cnut became ruler of all England (1016–35). After his older brother,

Harold, King of Denmark, died in 1019, England became part of a Scandinavian empire. The achievement of the house of Wessex seemed completely buried and it is only in hindsight that Scandinavian rule can be seen as an interlude.

Cnut, however, did not create any administrative structures to weld his extensive Anglo-Scandinavian empire together. He sought to rule not as a foreign oppressor, but as a lord of both Danes and non-Danes. He was the king of a number of kingdoms, not a monarch seeking to enlarge one kingdom. Partly as a result, Cnut did not have to face rebellions. In England, he adopted the practices of the Old English monarchy, including its support for the Church and its practice of legislating for the whole kingdom, although he introduced a number of Danes into the aristocracy and divided the kingdom into a small number of earldoms. Under his successors, these earldoms were to become in effect autonomous and to play a role in the instability of the mid-eleventh century. An Anglo-Scandinavian aristocracy was being created, as England looked increasingly to Scandinavia. The Earldom of Wessex was given to Godwin, an English protégé of Cnut, who married a Danish princess and gave Danish names to four of his six sons, including Harold.

Cnut's succession was contested by his sons, Harold Harefoot and Harthacnut and, for a time, the country was divided between the two. Harold Harefoot became king of the entire country in 1037, but died in 1040; his half-brother and successor followed two years later without leaving any children. The stable and well-integrated aristocracy of the tenth century had been broken up by the troubles of Aethelred's and Cnut's reigns, leading to instability and a problem with what would later be termed 'overmighty subjects'.

The willingness in 1016 and 1035 to agree to partition, a technique employed on the Continent by the Carolingians, is as notable as the short-lived nature of both these agreements. No government in this period was all that effective in the localities, and power tended to rest with lesser and local individuals, who could have administrative functions but, whether they did or not, generally had considerable autonomy. The power that the monarch had over these individuals was a crucial issue. Rather than seeing this in terms of clear-cut administrative differences that, for example, distinguish the Old English monarchy from those in France and Germany, it is more appropriate to lay stress on political contingencies, especially in the case of invasion, and on the quality of monarchical leadership.

Yet, it is also appropriate to consider attitudes and patterns of political behaviour and identity. From the mid-tenth century, these seem to have made the English as a unit seem the norm. It is of course important to be wary of the nineteenth-century perspective of nationalism and state development. Then there was a tendency to trace the history of states and nations in that of peoples, and, in adopting a teleological (making future developments seem predestined) approach, to give less than due weight both to the tentative nature of such phenomena and to the absence of a clear causal relationship between peoples and states. Allowing for this, England was very different in 1042 to its situation prior to the ninth-century Danish invasions.

The house of Wessex was restored with Aethelred's surviving son, Edward 'the Confessor' (1042–66). His reign was a period of population growth and agrarian expansion. Wool exports to Flanders were of growing value, as the

English mastered the arts of sheep and corn husbandry, using the sheepfold, and also developed breeds of sheep with good wool.

The reign of the childless Edward was overshadowed, however, by the problem of the succession, which interacted with that of the powerful earldoms. Edward had been a refugee in Normandy and, after he came to the throne, his favour for Normans, such as Robert of Jumièges, whom he made Archbishop of Canterbury in 1051, exacerbated his poor relations with his father-in-law, Godwin. This led to a confrontation in 1051–2, in which Godwin rebelled and was exiled, but eventually returned and obliged Edward to restore him to favour. Leading Normans were then expelled.

Godwin died in 1053, but Edward's death on 5 January 1066 was followed by the election or recognition of Godwin's oldest surviving son, Harold, as king by the Witan, the great council of the realm. Earl of Wessex and, after the king, the largest individual landowner in the country, Harold had acquired considerable prestige from successful campaigning in North Wales against the ruler of Gwynedd. He claimed that Edward had granted him the kingdom on his death.

This claim was challenged by Duke William of Normandy, who argued that Edward had promised him the throne in 1051 and that Harold had acknowledged this claim in 1064. To meet the Norman threat, Harold initially concentrated his forces along the south coast. Contrary winds, however, prevented William from sailing. In September, Harold disbanded his forces and left for London. There he heard that the Norwegians under Harold Hardrada, King of Norway, supported by Harold of England's exiled brother, Tostig, had landed in Yorkshire. They defeated the local earls at Fulford

Bridge (20 September) and seized York, winning a measure of local support. However, Harold marched rapidly north and surprised and defeated Harold Hardrada and Tostig at nearby Stamford Bridge on 25 September.

After the winds changed in the Channel, William landed at Pevensey on 28 September. Harold pressed south in order to attack William before he could consolidate his position, but the English army was weakened by battle and fatigue. On 14 October 1066, although outnumbered by about 7,000 to 5,000, they had to fight again. Harold chose a strong defensive site on the slopes of a hill, but it was disturbed by advances designed to exploit real or feigned retreats by the Normans. After a long battle, the shieldwall of the English housecarls was broken and Harold fell.

The Anglo-Saxon claimant to the throne was now Edgar Atheling, grandson of Edmund Ironside, but he was weak and a mere totem figure. This helped William, as did the death of Harold Hardrada and Tostig at Stamford Bridge, and of Harold and two of his brothers at Hastings: the English force there consisted largely of the levies of Wessex, the East Midlands and East Anglia, of which the sons of Godwin were earls.

The victorious William crossed the Thames to the west of London and, as he approached the city, morale among the defendants crumbled. At Berkhamsted they submitted to William, and on Christmas Day he was acclaimed king in Westminster Abbey. The unification of England by the house of Wessex had ensured that it fell rapidly, unlike the more lengthy processes by which the Iron Age and Romano-British kingdoms had fallen to Rome and the Anglo-Saxons respectively. England had been conquered as a unit. Henry,

Archdeacon of Huntingdon, was to reflect in his *Historia Anglorum* (*The History of the English People*), written during the reign of William's youngest son, Henry I, that the identity of a sinful ancient Britain had been destroyed by successive invasions from the Romans on, as 'by a just and open judgment God determined to put an end to that people'.

SIX

NORMAN ENGLAND 1066–1154

The Norman conquest was a major discontinuity in English political, social, religious and cultural history; but there was no accompanying economic change. Furthermore, it is important to put political developments into context. There were no major changes in the environment, the major determinant of the health of an agrarian society. Climate fluctuations can be assessed by a number of methods, including the study of Oxygen 18 isotopes from the Greenland icecap. These indicate that, after a period when it became colder (*c.* 350–450), temperatures rose and were higher than those of Britain in the 1970s, by about one degree centigrade in the summer, until *c.* 1180. Even small climatic changes have major environmental effects. These include a higher tree line and the growth of crops, such as vines, further north than either in the late medieval period or in the 1970s. The retreat of the icecaps led to a rise in sea level in the Anglo-Saxon period. Climatic improvement was important to the establishment of new villages in previously marginal or unworked land. After *c.* 1300, however, there was a deterioration, leading to colder conditions, which persisted until a nineteenth-century rise in temperatures.

There were few defences for agriculture against harsh and unpredictable weather. This, however, was not the sole problem. There was also a shortage of fertilizer, and fields were left fallow for a year on a two-, three-, or four-year cycle, in order to maintain soil fertility. This was a characteristic feature of the open-field system, in which unhedged arable fields were split into narrow strips and communal supervision of cultivation was important. This was typical of the Midlands, but largely absent from upland areas, the southern counties, East Anglia, Kent, Devon and Cornwall, and the north-west, in all of which pasture was predominant. Communal supervision centred on rotation, as strips were grouped into furlongs which were the unit of crop rotation.

The localized nature of the agrarian economy was very pronounced. Soil types and drainage affected agricultural activity to a greater extent than in modern England, where their effects can be countered by fertilizers and agricultural engineering. Thus England was divided into a large number of local economies. These can be summarized geologically, for example as chalk or clay; or by relief, upland or lowland; or by climate; but the variations were far more numerous, for example between regions with short- and long-wool sheep. Different rural economies entailed varied field and settlement patterns, most simply the nucleated villages of arable lowlands as against the dispersed farmsteads of pastoral uplands, with obvious consequences, in terms of contrasting social and economic organization, and personal and communal experience.

This society grew considerably in the twelfth and thirteenth centuries, resuming the pattern of growth under the Old English state. The population increased, from a figure of about two million in 1086, although in a pre-census age all figures are very approximate. So also is any assessment of the prosperity of a society that ranged from powerful castles and fine stone-built churches to village houses constructed from wattle and daub, and chalk rubble.

Economic growth affected the socio-political arrangements created by William I (1066–87), a feudal world in which land was awarded to vassals in return for military service, and control over labour was fundamental to the working of land. There were important pre-Norman roots for feudalism, but it began to be systematized under William. Furthermore, Domesday Book's legal fiction of continuity in land tenure between Edward the Confessor's thegns and William the Conqueror's barons did not do justice to both profound discontinuity (the personnel changed dramatically) and, more specifically, a different understanding of terms and conventions.

Control over labour was not a matter of slavery, which became extinct in the early twelfth century, partly as a result of Church pressure, but more because of the availability of the alternative of the power of lords over their serfs (villeins). These were peasants who owed their lords often heavy labour services, as well as other obligations, such as the use of the lord's mill. Thanks to these labour services, the lords were provided with a workforce for their land, while the peasants – their tenantry – were allowed smallholdings for their own needs. The lords benefited from the peasantry through both rents and labour. The Norman Conquest helped to define earlier social trends and also was an important stage in the transformation of free peasants into semi-servile villeins. For example, according to Domesday Book, 44 per cent of the population of Berkshire were villeins, 31 per cent bordars (smallholders not yet depressed into servitude), 13 per cent slaves and 11 per cent cottars. However, areas of traditionally high levels of freedom, such as the Danelaw and Kent, seem to have preserved these levels after 1066.

The beginnings of Anglo-Norman feudalism can be seen, as if in a snapshot, in the land survey known as Domesday Book (1086). This was based on documentary evidence, such as taxation rolls, information from sheriffs, landowners and the hundred courts, and possibly visits. Domesday Book should not, however, serve to suggest that the situation was static. It is all too easy to assume that the frenetic pace of change in the modern period contrasts with an essentially static world, one kept constant by the role of agriculture, the rhythm of the seasons, and the belief in continuity. All were important, but they did not prevent change. Nor was change simply or solely a matter of general expansion until a fourteenth-century demographic, economic and social crisis that was followed by contraction, although this overall process can indeed be seen. Within this model, there was in fact also much change and development, as well as considerable variety.

Thus the establishment of Norman tenurial arrangements, itself a complex process, was at once followed by their transformation in response to new problems and opportunities, such as the spread of the money economy in both rentals and military service. Description in terms of a 'feudal system' should be avoided as it implies something altogether more coherent and purposeful than the reality warrants. Feudal bonds expressed mutual obligations of lord and vassal; land and protection being provided in return for (essentially) military service. Custom, law and God sanctified (and fixed) these ties, but while the resulting structure of social relations was somewhat sclerotic, it promised reasonable levels of stability and security when it was presided over by an effective king who could solve disputes between rival barons.

The initial relationships created by the allocation of land and services were rapidly tempered. Just as William had enfeoffed tenants-in-chief, the latter had enfeoffed their followers, leading to the formation of a system of feudal honours. This did not prove a readily reversible process. Links between lord and man became protected by custom and law, such that sub-tenancies were very difficult to recover.

This can be seen as an aspect of inflexibility, but it ensured that alternative ways to recruit support had to be developed. These were outside the feudal honour and led to both a weakening of feudal bonds and an increase in the fluidity of English society. More generally, there was a degree of flexibility absent in many contemporary societies, especially outside Europe. For example, although the Norman conquest brought a new ruling class from the Continent, there was no total caste-like exclusion of the English from landholding, as is often popularly depicted in for example legends about Robin Hood. Furthermore, again, although the Conquest brought major changes in the Church, both conquerors and conquered were Christian and this both tempered the process of conquest and aided long-term reconciliation. Lastly, the new ruling order was itself far from static. Indeed the relationship between monarch and feudal vassals was to be remade frequently in response to a rapid rate of political change and periodic crises, especially in the period 1087–1154. These crises made up not only the political history of the period, but also the background to a transformation both in England's relationship with the wider world and in her governmental system. Furthermore, these crises interacted with a marked lack of continuity among the leading men, with new leaders emerging under William I's sons and again under Stephen (1135–54). Much of this reflected the pressures of conflict: lords had a function as military leaders and those found wanting made way for others.

Continued Anglo-Saxon resistance to William the Conqueror after 1066, especially, but not only in the North, ensured both that the conquest was followed by more of a change in landholding than William might initially have intended, especially a dispossession of many (although not all) lesser thegns, and that the new regime had to be even more firmly based on force. The latter has left a clearly visible sign in the number of castles that date from the period, most famously the White Tower in the Tower of London.

Like Cnut, William claimed to be the King of the English. There was no attempt to destroy the kingdom and make England part of Normandy. William presented himself as the rightful successor to Edward the Confessor. However, a single Anglo-Norman ruling class was created with lands on both sides of the Channel. This elite was firmly based and there was a process of Normanization of the Church that resulted in the replacement of all but one of the English bishops by 1087. William had strong papal support, and fought under a papal banner (shown on the Bayeux Tapestry) in the conquest of England. This support was given partly over the issue of Harold's alleged perjury, and partly because of William's pledge to get rid of Archbishop Stigand, whose holding Canterbury in plurality with Winchester was regarded as scandalous. Stigand was indeed deposed in 1070. St Wulfstan of Worcester (1062–95) was the last English bishop. There was far less assimilation than there had been under the Danish kings between 1016 and 1042. The new ruling class was more comprehensively established and there was a change in Church leadership that was far more sweeping than that under Cnut.

There was also far more resistance to William than there had been to Cnut, although, in part, this was because Cnut's succession to the throne had followed years of conflict. There were major rebellions, especially between 1067 and 1069. The response was harsh, particularly in the north where a rising in 1069 was suppressed with a brutal 'harrying' in which systematic devastation created much hardship. Norman ruthlessness, a lack of coordination and effective leadership among the English rebels, and an absence of consistent Scandinavian support all left William in fairly firm control of England by 1076, although this was not achieved north of the Tees until later: the 1080s in Durham and the lower Tyne valley, and the early eleventh century in Northumberland. Castles entrenched the new order. They were very different to the characteristic feature of Anglo-Saxon fortification, the *burh* or fortified town, and this symbolized the way in which the country had to be held down, rather than defended from outside, although, under the Normans, the latter remained important, against both the Scots and the Scandinavians.

Early castles were generally motte-and-bailey earth-and-timber constructions, thrown up in a hurry (although still requiring many man-days to construct) and able to give protection against local discontent. Many from the reign of William II onwards were replaced by stone works, powerful means and symbols of control. Although numerous castles fell into disrepair and ruin or were destroyed and built over, especially in urban areas, surviving examples provide ample illustration of how they literally towered over and commanded the surrounding countryside. This was true both of frontier areas and of more settled regions.

Castles were matched by the great stone-built cathedrals of the period. The Romanesque style had probably arrived in England before the Conquest, as Edward the Confessor employed Norman architects for Westminster Abbey in the 1050s, but it became far more pronounced thereafter. The monumental architecture seen, for example, in Durham, Ely and Peterborough cathedrals, with their thick walls, long, rhythmic naves and massive columns and arches, was a counterpart to the attempt by foreign prelates to discipline the English lesser clergy. The nave of Durham Cathedral, begun in 1093, completed in 1128, and vaulted between then and 1133, is a prime example of the inventiveness of English Romanesque style. It also symbolized the power of the Norman Church in the spiritual geography of England: the remains of the great Northumbrian holy man St Cuthbert were translated into the new cathedral in 1104. This was part of a process that also saw the movement of episcopal sees, for example from Dorchester-on-Thames to Lincoln.

More generally, the Conquest led to a reassertion of episcopal authority, a further expansion of the parish system at the expense of the older minster system, and monastic revival as part of a new monastic structure firmly linked to developments in northern France. By 1087, only eight religious houses had English heads, and most of them were soon to be replaced by foreigners. The ninth-century Danes had killed clerics, but not taken over the Church, which had thus remained as the centre of English culture and consciousness. The Norman challenge was far more pronounced. The cultural transformation of the Church was symbolized by the withering away of writing in Old English. The last version of the *Anglo-Saxon Chronicle*, written up intermittently at Peterborough after the Conquest, ceased in the mid-twelfth century.

Yet it is important not to see this period simply in terms of conflict, nor to overlook a wider perspective. The latter is presented by the Gregorian reform movement in the later eleventh century (named after Pope Gregory VII), and the attempt throughout Catholic Christendom to impose standards and control activity from Rome. This led, for example, to efforts to enforce clerical celibacy and to end the clerical dynasties that were important among the parish clergy. It also led to the reform of existing monastic orders and to the foundation of new orders.

England would have been exposed to such pressures even had there been no Norman Conquest. For example, the spread of new orders, such as the Austin Canons, Premonstratensians and Carthusians, was facilitated by the Conquest, but the most important new order, the Cistercians, was also established in the part of Wales that avoided Norman conquest, as well as in Scotland. Similarly, the reforming aspirations of the first two post-Conquest Archbishops of Canterbury, Lanfranc and Anselm, both Italians, were furthered by the Conquest, but similar demands would have arisen anyway.

Large-scale Norman foundation of new religious houses in England was not immediate. William I founded Battle Abbey to atone for Christian blood shed at Hastings, but most Norman lords channelled revenue from English lands to religious houses in Normandy. Their spiritual roots were still in their original homeland. It was only the following, more emphatically Anglo-Norman generations that established new religious houses in England in large numbers. The wave of new foundations began several decades after the Conquest and this fitted in with the advent of new forms of monastic spirituality.

There was also continuity. The first Norman abbots of St Albans, Malmesbury, Evesham and Abingdon were inclined to slight, or at least to doubt, the Anglo-Saxon cults they found at these monasteries, and Lanfranc had to be persuaded by Anselm that St Alphege (Aelfheah), killed by the Danes in 1012, was worthy of veneration. Nevertheless, he then commissioned a life of Alphege from the English monk Osbern of Canterbury. Ailred (c. 1109–66), son of a Hexham priest, became successively abbot of the Cistercian houses of Revesby and Rievaulx, and composed both a eulogy of St Cuthbert and a life of Edward the Confessor, whose body was ceremoniously translated to Westminster in 1163.

The Conquest also caused English monasteries to produce writings authenticating their holdings of land and the credentials of their saints. Monasteries 'manufactured' pasts for themselves as a defence against secular powers and Church reformers who might, respectively, strip them of land and question the status of native saints. Thus, the Conquest generated a burst of 'native' historiography.

In addition, an Anglo-Norman identity was constructed in the early twelfth century by writers who were half-English, half-Norman, such as William of Malmesbury and Orderic Vitalis, or English, such as Eadmer and John of Worcester. With works such as Geoffrey of Monmouth's *Historia Regum Britanniae* (c. 1135), there was a measure of celebration of the pre-Norman past that offered a degree of continuity for notions of English national identity, although there was an important Welsh element in Geoffrey's *Historia*. The Normans soon identified with the traditions of their conquered land.

This does not appreciably lessen the discontinuity and tension caused by the Conquest. To employ a doubtless inappropriate modern analogy, an emphasis on the need throughout Europe to respond to the strains of a post-industrial society does not lessen the difficulties created by the process of European unification. Furthermore, although there was a measure of continuity, there was also in the twelfth century a new sense of Englishness that reflected the impact of changes after the Conquest.

Much of the reign of William I (1066–87) was spent in establishing and enforcing the new regime. William also had to face the threat of Scandinavian invasion, for example attacks in 1069, 1070 and 1075, and the threat of invasion between 1085 and 1086, as well as opposition from discontented Normans, as in 1075. William brought over a large army to deal with the threat of invasion in 1085–6, and the problems involved in maintaining it may well have prompted the making of Domesday Book in order to ascertain his overall resources. Furthermore, the territorial interests of the Duchy of Normandy, and its disputes with expansionist neighbours, the kingdom of France and the county of Anjou, began a process of commitment to Continental power politics that was to last for centuries. Until the fall of Calais in 1558 the rulers of England continually thereafter held part of the Continent, and this brought frequent conflict. Indeed, William I died as a result of injuries sustained when thrown by his horse in the French town of Mantes, which he had burnt as a result of a border conflict, the first of five monarchs (himself,

Henry I, Henry II, Richard I, Henry V) who were to die in France while struggling to protect or strengthen their position.

Again, it is necessary to be careful not to assume that the history of England without the Conquest would not have involved war on the Continent. The Anglo-Saxon state had been involved in Continental diplomacy, although that had not entailed war. There had been conflict with other powers in the British Isles as well as with Scandinavian invaders, but the latter had simply been in response to attack. Without the Conquest, it seems likely that England would have remained a major player in Scandinavian politics. Some of the rebels against William I turned to Scandinavia for support, and cultural and trade links were still significant in 1066. Possibly an independent Anglo-Saxon England in the eleventh and twelfth centuries could have gone on to conquer Wales and unite in some way with Scotland, creating an effective Britain. Equally, this might have entailed war with France had the latter supported opposition in Wales and Scotland. Yet, there might have been no need for this if the English rulers had not pursued territorial interests of their own in France, as the Normans were to do.

It is therefore difficult to avoid the conclusion that the crucial legacy of the Conquest was continual confrontation on the Continent, leading to repeated conflict. The net effect was damaging. It may well have encouraged governmental development, in order to raise the necessary funds, and the eventual creation of Parliament in order to obtain political and financial support for war in France, but this more effective state was bought at a heavy cost, not only in men and treasure but also in a political system, society and culture for which war continued to be crucial.

This development might have been cut short by William I's arrangements for his successors. As yet, there was no clear preference for male primogeniture (succession by the eldest male child) over partible inheritance (division among heirs). William left Normandy to his eldest son, Robert, who was in rebellion when William died, and England to the second, William II. The latter was known from his red face or hair as Rufus (1087–1100); according to Orderic Vitalis, his hair was yellowish. The allotment of inheritance (Normandy) to the eldest son, and of acquisition (England) to the next, was entirely in keeping with contemporary practice. However, such division was unwelcome not only in the ruling family but also to nobles with estates on both sides of the Channel. Rufus tried to reunite the inheritance, and, after some fighting, Robert pawned Normandy to Rufus in 1096, in order to raise funds to go on the First Crusade.

Rufus was a vigorous ruler, with a high reputation in knightly circles. In 1092, he occupied Cumbria and created a town and built a castle at Carlisle. He was also successful against Norman rebels and the French. However, Rufus became unpopular with the Church. He did not support ecclesiastical reform or papal authority, left bishoprics vacant in order to enjoy their revenues, and clashed with Archbishop Anselm of Canterbury, who left the country in 1097. Rufus' death in the New Forest was a matter of controversy, but was probably the result of a hunting accident.

Rufus was succeeded in England by his capable younger brother, Henry I (1100–35). Henry rushed to seize the Treasury at Winchester: at this stage, London was not the capital of 'England', and the ancient capital of Wessex remained important. Henry, however, had to face a renewal of family conflict, because Robert, who had taken part in the capture of Jerusalem in 1099, returned to Normandy in 1100, and in 1101 invaded England. Henry persuaded him to renounce his claim to the throne, but relations between the two brothers continued to be difficult. Henry invaded Normandy in 1105, and, in 1106, defeated Robert at Tinchebrai and conquered the Duchy. Robert was imprisoned until his death in 1134. This, however, was not the end of Continental warfare, because the situation in Normandy proved difficult to stabilize. Robert left a son, William Clito, around whom resistance crystallised until his death in 1127. Henry faced both frontier disputes and rebellions. Nevertheless, he brought the neighbouring principalities of Brittany and Maine under control and defeated Louis VI of France at Brémule in 1119.

This focus on Normandy greatly affected the government of England: it had to pay much of the bill and, also, face an absent monarch. As a consequence, the administrative development of the Old English state in the tenth century was resumed, although the government scarcely seemed benign to many of its subjects: indeed the *Anglo-Saxon Chronicle* presented it as predatory.

Much of the governmental machinery of the Old English monarchy was maintained and, in particular, government remained 'public' to a far greater extent than in France. For example, the sheriffs remained dismissable royal officials. When in 1086 at Salisbury, William's vassals renewed their oaths of allegiance to the king, so also, importantly, did their vassals. Minting was almost entirely a royal monopoly in England – a legacy of the Old English state – unlike in France, where the disintegration of public authority put it in the hands of a large number of secular and ecclesiastical powers. While France was little more than a confederacy of princely courts, England had not fragmented. Within the context of what was possible in the period, a powerful state had been created and sustained. In England, it proved possible to control and regulate feudal lordship, and the latter encouraged the development of English law. The expansion of royal judicial activity under Henry I, and the appointment by the crown of local and itinerant justices, were signs of a sophisticated and settled administration. The Exchequer provided a regular and methodical collection of royal revenues and control of expenditure. New ideas and methods, notably the abacus, were employed. Written records became more common, and that itself was important to the development and consistency of government.

Stability, however, was threatened by the succession. Henry had over twenty bastards, but his sole legitimate son died in the wreck of the *White Ship* in 1120. Henry therefore turned to his daughter, Matilda, who, in 1128, married Geoffrey Plantagenet, heir to the Duke of Anjou. When Henry died in 1135, however, the throne was seized by Stephen, Count of Blois (1135–54), son of William I's daughter Adela. His reign was almost as disastrous as that of Aethelred the Unready. Stephen was unable to maintain control in England and in 1139 Matilda invaded. In the subsequent conflict Stephen had much of the South-East under his control, and Matilda the South-West. Much conflict occurred where these two zones met. Matilda captured Stephen at the battle of Lincoln in 1141, but, again, this did not bring stability. She alienated London, was defeated at Winchester by Stephen's wife Matilda, and had to exchange Stephen for her captured half-brother, Robert of Gloucester. Stephen's capture was arguably decisive in the long run, because it led to his former supporters in Normandy starting to come to terms with Geoffrey of Anjou who eventually occupied the whole duchy. There was no possibility of England under Stephen reoccupying Normandy, so the cross-Channel lordships could only be reconstituted if Normandy, under Geoffrey or his son, took over England.

Civil war was accompanied by the collapse of government authority. Prominent nobles, such as John the Marshal in Hampshire and Wiltshire, used the civil war to pursue their own interests and build up local power. Many castles were built. Stephen's reign acquired a reputation as a period of anarchy when 'Christ and his angels slept'. Although Stephen was successful against Matilda in England, in 1144 Geoffrey completed the conquest of Normandy, and in 1152 his heir, Henry, invaded England. The nobility on both sides wanted peace, and their lands on both sides of the Channel, rather than partition. In 1153, they obtained the Treaty of Westminster, by which Stephen was to remain king, but to adopt Henry as his heir.

Stephen died within a year, and the first of the Angevin dynasty, Henry II (1154–89), came to the throne. The readiness with which power flowed back to the crown once Henry came to the throne illustrated the desire of most nobles for peace and stability. The events of Stephen's reign, including Scottish attacks in the 1130s and Geoffrey's conquest of Normandy, encouraged an identification by the Normans in England with both England and the English past.

SEVEN

MEDIEVAL ENGLAND 1154–1485

England was now part of an even larger European empire. Henry II (1154–89) inherited England and Normandy from his mother, and Anjou, Maine and Touraine from his father, and obtained control over much of Central and South-West France through his marriage in 1152 to the imperious Eleanor of Aquitaine, the divorced wife of Louis VII. Furthermore, Henry used his power to resolve inheritance disputes in his favour, gaining control of Brittany and more of Southern France. This made Henry one of Europe's leading monarchs. Within France, he was more powerful than his suzerain (feudal lord) for his French territories, the King of France.

This was not the limit of Henry's expansionism. He also pushed back the Scottish frontier, retrieving Cumbria and Northumbria, which had been lost in Stephen's civil war, campaigned in Wales, and intervened in Ireland (1171). In short, his reign indicated the absence of fixity in international boundaries and relations, and the powerful sense of volatility, opportunism and opportunity that was so important in the politics of the period. Force and legitimacy were uneasily related, as in Henry's relations with France and Scotland, and his policy in Ireland, where he made much of the rights granted by a papal bull in 1155.

Force and legitimacy certainly played a major role in Henry's relations with the Church. He is best remembered today for his quarrel with Thomas Becket, Archbishop of Canterbury, which led to Becket's murder in 1170. Becket was initially a friend of Henry, but he made a stand on the right of clerics to trial in Church courts, an issue that fused issues of sovereignty, such as the freedom of appeal to the Papal government, and finance, for justice involved money. Becket fled the country in 1164, when Henry turned the resources of royal judicial power against him. He returned in 1170, but was unwilling to abide by the spirit of compromise that was necessary for successful Church–State relations. Henry's outraged explosion, allegedly with the words 'Will no one rid me of this turbulent priest?', was taken at face value by four of his knights who hacked Becket to death in his cathedral. Henry had to do penance, Becket was canonized, and his shrine at Canterbury became a major centre of pilgrimage. Restrictions on appeals to Rome were lifted and the basic immunity of criminous clerics from lay jurisdiction was confirmed, but, in practice, senior clerics had to continue to seek the support and co-operation of the king.

Henry's attempt to define and limit the legal rights of clerics was part of his general policy of systematizing the law and increasing royal judicial powers. The standardized common law, which replaced pre-Norman regional customs, gained in strength and helped to consolidate England. The enforcement of justice improved, and this both contributed to and reflected royal power. Land actions were begun by royal writs, and law and order enforced by royal justices itinerant. English common law had links with what was going on abroad, but was also a distinctive unity, and that at a time when Roman law was coming back into fashion on the Continent.

It has been argued that English common law was especially suited to the protection of rights and liberties, and that it encouraged a respect for the autonomy of individual thought and action. In combination with the early emergence of an institutional monarchy, this has been seen as particularly responsible for the character and continuity of English political society. The access of the political nation to the king's law helped contribute to the identity and coherence that were to give the English a system of government possessing great continuity. It helped ensure that the group of knightly families that was subsequently to develop into the gentry could have a relationship with the Crown instead of one solely with provincial magnates. This was important given the role of the gentry in the political, social, economic and religious history of the country. Their energies could be harnessed to the creation of a political world that was at once both national, in that it was centred on the Crown and its relationship with landowners, and local, in that it contributed to the growth of a county government at once serving central governmental interests and yet also able to resist autocracy.

Under Henry II the collection of royal revenues improved and the processes of government became more effective and regular. Regular record-keeping began: the Exchequer Pipe Rolls continuously from early in Henry's reign, and the Close and Patent Rolls, the letters enrolled under the Great Seal, from just after 1200. The processes of government were less dependent on the personal intervention of the monarch than had been the case under the Normans.

The expansion of government activity required increasing numbers of professional administrators, a group that developed under Henry I. These *curiales* were mostly 'new men' who were resented by better-born nobles. This was one reason why the development of government created tension.

More generally, arbitrariness on the part of successive rulers, made law and justice seem far from co-terminous. Tenants-in-chief were very much at the king's will, and the greater coercive power of government made it a formidable instrument of tyranny. This was one reason for the popularity in some quarters of Becket, who had stood up to royal power, as also later of the less saintly and more mythical reputation of Robin Hood. Royal government aroused immense resentment, in part because bureaucratic principles of impartial government were slow to develop. Royal will, instead, remained supreme. Between 1207 and 1208, King John wrote, 'It is no more than just that we should do better by those who are with us than by those who are against us'. Such an attitude required the skilful management of factional politics.

Three of Henry's five legitimate sons predeceased him, and he was succeeded by his third son, Richard I, the Lion Heart (1189–99). Richard had acquired considerable military experience in suppressing rebellions in Aquitaine and was a warrior king who spent even more of his reign abroad than Henry had done. This activity was not, however, devoted to campaigning in Wales, Scotland or Ireland. Instead, Richard was a key participant in the Third Crusade. After capturing Acre, he defeated Saladin at the battle of Arsuf (1191), but narrowly failed to reach Jerusalem. Imprisoned in Germany on his way back (1192–4), his absence was exploited by his younger brother, John, and more seriously by Philip Augustus, King of France (1180–1223) and a determined and skilful opponent of the Angevin empire. Richard was ransomed for 150,000 marks, a vast sum that was a tribute to English wealth and in particular to the spread of commerce that led, for example, to the creation of numerous urban markets and the expansion of towns. The payment of the ransom was also a tribute to the administrative calibre of the government of England.

Richard spent most of the rest of his reign in France, recovering what had been lost during his absence, a process that led to his death in a siege. Although primarily a warrior, Richard was also a reasonably effective monarch with considerable political skill. Nevertheless, his wars were costly and Richard's quest for money led him to resort to unpopular expedients of dubious legality, for example his insistence in 1198 that charters be renewed under his new seal, an expensive process. The chronicler Ralph of Coggeshall was impressed by Richard's early years as king, both his crusading and his rule in England, but then discerned a marked deterioration, such that he saw Richard's death as divine punishment and the famine of the 1190s as a consequence of divine anger at his war with France. This critical judgement was matched by other chroniclers.

Having no legitimate children, Richard was succeeded by his brother John (1199–1216). Although chroniclers approved some of his early policies and his early personal conduct, John was not to be equal to the challenges of his reign. A tough and nasty individual, naturally avaricious and suspicious, who lacked skills of man-management and did not improve with adversity, John did not have the personal prestige that might have helped him respond more successfully. John's lack of prestige was summed up above all in the epithet 'softsword'. Nothing would have raised his standing more than an ability to win battles.

However, he also faced a difficult situation, not least because of pressure from Philip Augustus and the growing strength of

French resources. John harmed his position by his tactless handling of his French vassals, which was exacerbated by accurate rumours that he had been responsible for the death in 1203 of his nephew, Arthur, Duke of Brittany. Philip Augustus's rapid conquest of Normandy and Anjou between 1203 and 1204 ensured that, for most of the remainder of his reign, John was focused on the recovery of his lost dominions. He jeopardized his position in England for this goal, although it is unclear whether he would not have found another way to offend opinion in England had there been no war with France. John's efforts to raise funds, and the intrusive and aggressive nature of his government, aroused opposition, while a dispute over an election to the archbishopric of Canterbury led to a quarrel with a very determined adversary, Pope Innocent III. In 1208, Innocent laid England under an interdict. All church services were suspended and in the following year John was excommunicated. Continental losses accentuated the focus on England. Other than Stephen, who had faced civil war, John was the first ruler since 1066 to spend the majority of his reign in England.

John was able to buy his peace by making England a fief of the papacy in 1213, but his other enemies were more intractable. John's attempt to regain his French lands ended in failure when his allies were defeated at Bouvines in 1214. This encouraged his domestic opponents to rebel, a rebellion that revealed the extent to which John had lost support among the baronage. By 1215, John had alienated almost everyone who mattered among the nobility and hence had deprived himself of a faction to manage. That year, he was forced to accept the terms of what was later to be called Magna Carta, in order to bring peace. Magna Carta was an indictment of John's government and a demand for a better future. John's use of feudal, judicial and other governmental powers was condemned in Magna Carta's definition and limitation of royal rights. Magna Carta was in effect an enormous list of everything that was wrong with government as John applied it, and covered practically everything, hence later calls for its confirmation. Baronial liberties were protected and freemen were provided with some guarantees against arbitrary royal actions. The crown alone would not be able to determine its rights. Magna Carta also says something about the acceptable side of Angevin government: the rebels wanted ready access to royal justice.

A sense of political community headed by the king but to which he could be held accountable lay behind Magna Carta and also the other political and constitutional developments of the century: the reissues of Magna Carta, the baronial movement towards the close of Henry III's reign, and the criticism of Edward I in the 1290s.

Forcing rulers to accept limitations was always, however, problematic, for the effectiveness of a settlement like Magna Carta depended on royal willingness to change attitudes, or on the ability to force the ruler to do so. John's unwillingness to implement the agreement led his opponents to offer the throne to Philip Augustus' son, Louis. French intervention was a logical consequence of the post-Conquest cross-Channel nature of the English monarchy. England drifted into a serious civil war, and John died while on campaign in 1216, shortly after the quicksands and tide of the Wash had claimed a valuable part of his baggage train. His reputation, mixed when he became king, markedly deteriorated both during his reign and over the following decade. Many believed that he went to hell.

John's son, Henry III (1216–72), was a more acceptable monarch: as a child of nine he was no threat. Helped by victory in war, especially the battle of Lincoln and Hubert de Burgh's naval victory off Dover, both in 1217, Henry's supporters drove Louis to abandon the struggle that year. Yet regaining control of England was not enough. Just like his father, Henry III was determined to drive the French from their conquests. There was repeated failure. The disastrous 1242 Poitevin campaign damaged Henry's reputation and finances, and, in the Treaty of Paris of 1259, Henry finally accepted losses that left him with only Gascony in south-west France.

Failure abroad was matched by uncertainty and discontent at home that eventually led, as with John, to a breakdown in royal power. During Henry's minority, the idea developed of restricting a ruler through written regulations and insisting that he seek the advice of the nobility. 'Great Councils' were summoned to win baronial consent and thus co-operation. Magna Carta was reissued. Henry's unpopularity was due to his granting favour to friends and advisers who were not members of the English elite and many of whom were foreign, especially his Poitevin half-brothers, kinsmen of Henry through his mother's second marriage. The barons attacked the evil counsel which the king was receiving from aliens but avoided criticizing the king directly. They sought to restore their own role at the heart of royal government as Henry's natural counsellors. Furthermore, governmental financial pressure, and misrule and corruption by royal officials aroused anger and disquiet. In his *Chronica Majora* (1236–59), Matthew Paris, a monk at St Albans, complained about the abuses of Henry's court and his foreign favourites.

Like his father, Henry proved unable to sustain acceptable relations with his leading subjects. By the Provisions of Oxford of 1258 and of Westminster of 1259, the barons sought to take power out of Henry's hands, and thus to enforce their own conception of good kingship. War broke out in 1264 and many of the barons, under the king's brother-in-law, Simon de Montfort, Earl of Leicester, defeated Henry at Lewes. However, they were to lose decisively at Evesham in 1265, not least because quite a number of the barons stayed loyal, while others were alienated by Montfort. Royal authority was restored, although, in the face of continued baronial opposition, this took two years, and Henry thereafter took pains to adopt a more careful attitude.

It is possible to trace the development of constitutional mechanisms for dealing with kings who threatened the vital interests of the nobility. Magna Carta was an attempt to compel John to subject himself to his own law, with rebellion as the enforcement mechanism. During the crises of Henry III's reign, the barons built on Magna Carta, but this time they tried to subject the king to a council of barons. In 1258–9, the barons hoped they were setting up machinery for twelve years. Several efforts were made to attempt arbitration in order to avoid armed enforcement. The reign of Edward II (1307–27) was to see the evolution of deposition, as well as the formulation of a clearer distinction between the person of the king and the institution of the crown. Such a subtle distinction had not been established in John's reign.

English national feeling can be seen under Richard I and John, but it developed markedly in Henry III's reign, creating new pressures that were accentuated by defeat abroad. Much of this national feeling was focused on hostility to foreigners from those who saw themselves as native born. In 1258, this hostility was central to the attempt to limit royal authority. Many foreigners were expelled and royal castles were mostly entrusted to Englishmen. In 1263, there was a renewed burst of anti-alien and anti-governmental activity, in part a response to the deployment of foreign troops by Henry's heir, Edward. There was comparable agitation in the Church. Hostility to papal taxation led to a series of clashes. In the 1230s, there was a considerable display of hostility to foreign elements in the Church, leading, for example, to attacks on tithe barns owned by alien priories – priories whose mother houses were foreign monasteries, such as Cluny. There was a widespread movement in 1231 against alien absentees, especially Italians, and in 1257 and 1258 English bishops met to oppose the claims of the papal nuncio.

Such opposition was part of a more widespread antagonism throughout society to strangers. It was a consequence of a gradual coalescence into communities that created mental borders. This process was crucial in the growing definition of parochialism and nationalism.

Henry III's son and successor, Edward I (1272–1307), was a warrior king: impressive as ruler, general, administrator and legislator, a dominating personality and determined monarch, firm in the defence of his rights, strong and pre-emptory in the maintenance of his dignity. The victor of Evesham, he was on his way back from the crusades, in which he had had some success, when he heard of his father's death. However, Edward did not return to England until 1274, an indication of the ability of government to continue without the king's personal supervision. In many respects, this was a sign of a much-developed state, although Cnut and Henry II had also been able to leave England for long periods. Edward I's trouble-free succession after the turmoil of his father's reign illustrated the strength of both the dynasty and the institution of monarchy. Also, it seems that new kings inherited the good will and co-operation of the baronage as of right; a new reign being seen as a fresh start.

England in 1272 was a prosperous country and an effective state. The increasingly market-orientated nature of part of the agrarian economy produced more wealth for taxation. About 30–40 per cent of all grain grown was marketed. This also helped provide for a growing urban sector. Furthermore, the growth of commerce fostered urban development. Numerous markets were founded, particularly in the thirteenth century.

English wealth was expressed in good silver coinage, with major recoinages in 1247–8 and 1278–9. The substantial yields of royal revenues, especially judicial eyres (circuit courts conducted in each shire by itinerant royal judges), were visible in Henry III's rebuilding of Westminster Abbey, and at royal palaces such as Clarendon. The wealth of the country was indicated by such works as the new cathedral of Salisbury, completed, except for the spire, between 1220 and 1260. Surviving records suggest that the south was the wealthiest part of the country. The new tax valuations required for the lay subsidy of 1334 indicated that the five wealthiest counties per square mile were, in order, Middlesex, Oxfordshire, Norfolk, Bedfordshire and Berkshire. Winchester, the Old English capital, lost out to London, a city that was also the most dynamic and important commercial centre in the country.

Edward I was a durable personality, with more judgement, strength of will and military ability than Henry. After establishing himself in Gascony and England, Edward subjugated North Wales, a task completed in 1282 and cemented by a series of expensive and powerful castles. English common law and the shire system was introduced in the conquered regions. Edward had less success with Scotland. The strength of the Scottish monarchy indicates that the development of an effective state did not require Norman conquest, and raises the question as to how the Anglo-Saxon state would have changed without such an invasion. In Scotland, there was considerable Normanization of government in the twelfth century, but as a result of the peaceful introduction of Norman lords invited in by rulers, especially David I (1124–54), not as a consequence of conquest.

In 1286, Alexander III of Scotland died, to be succeeded by a young grand-daughter, Margaret, the Maid of Norway. Edward I saw this as an opportunity and in 1289 secured the Treaty of Salisbury by which the marriage of Margaret and the future Edward II was agreed, a dynastic union that prefigured the one that was to occur in 1603. Margaret, however, died en route for Scotland in 1290, leaving a number of claimants. Edward I was asked to adjudicate, had his overlordship over the crown of Scotland recognized by the claimants, and declared John Balliol king. However, his subsequent interference in Scottish government was unacceptable. With tension rising, Edward invaded Scotland in 1296, storming Berwick, defeating the Scots at Dunbar, and accepting Balliol's surrender of the kingdom. The precariousness of this achievement was shown in 1297 when William Wallace rebelled and defeated the English at Stirling. The following year, Edward defeated Wallace at Falkirk, but it proved difficult to subjugate Scotland. There was a very important French connection behind Scottish resistance. Edward did best when he only had to fight on one front. He came nearest to victory in Scotland in 1304–5, when the French were too preoccupied in Flanders to be of any help to the Scots. Wallace was captured and executed in 1305, but in 1306 Robert Bruce rebelled, and in 1307 Edward died at Burgh-on-Sands on his way to campaign against him.

Scotland was an apparently intractable problem when Edward II (1307–27) came to the throne; he made it a disastrous one. Edward II lacked his father's military ability and ambition, and the less intense pace of English military pressure helped Bruce to consolidate his position. In 1314 he captured Edinburgh and crushed Edward II at the battle of Bannockburn. In 1318 Berwick fell, and in 1319 the Scots ravaged Yorkshire. English counter-attacks were unsuccessful, and in 1328, by the Treaty of Edinburgh, Scottish independence was recognized. A state based on the hegemony of the English crown over the British Isles was not to be created.

In the meanwhile, long-standing domestic political problems had flared up again. The cost of war placed a major strain on relations between the king and the political nation. These also affected the response to the extensive reform of law and administration that Edward I carried through by a series of statutes between 1275 and 1290. Edward's relations with the nobility were very tense in the 1290s, and the issues of taxation and financial grievances came to play a major role. The clergy and the merchants were also alienated. There was a political crisis in 1297, with many of the nobility resisting very high taxation to pay for war and deeply unpopular demands for military service. Edward I's reign was very important for the development of Parliament, especially for the concept of representation, which was outlined in the writs summoning representatives of the clergy, counties and boroughs to the 1295 Parliament. They were instructed to appear with authority to give advice and consent on behalf of the communities they represented. The use of parliamentary pressure to influence government policy in response to royal demands was seen for example between 1300 and 1301, when tax demands were countered by requests for an enquiry into the boundaries of the area under forest jurisdiction.

The situation was exacerbated under Edward II. He had to face major difficulties but made them worse by his own political incompetence. Edward's inability to deal with the Scots stemmed in part from his quarrels with his barons, notably over the arrogant Piers Gaveston, a Gascon who may have been his lover as well as his brother-in-arms. Edward I had banished Gaveston, but his son recalled him, made him Earl of Cornwall, and gave him considerable wealth and a prominent role. Edward's favour for Gaveston led to a political crisis and in 1311 he was forced to accept Ordinances limiting royal power. The following year, Gaveston was murdered by nobles opposed to Edward, a step the king never forgave. Thomas, Earl of Lancaster, the king's cousin, dominated the government, until Edward defeated him in battle at Boroughbridge in 1322. Lancaster was then executed and the Ordinances repealed, but Edward remained distrusted and unpopular, not least because of his favour for the Despensers, father and son.

Edward failed to conform to contemporary expectations of kingship. Lacking dignity, he also had unroyal tastes, such as digging ditches and boating. Furthermore, the monopolization of royal patronage by favourites exacerbated aristocratic discontent. This was exploited in Edward's last years by his wife, fiery Isabella, daughter of Philip IV of France. With her lover, Roger Mortimer, she overthrew Edward in 1326. His regime had become very narrowly based and deeply unpopular. No one was prepared to fight for Edward. He was deposed in favour of his son in 1327 and brutally murdered in Berkeley Castle, supposedly with a red-hot poker inserted in his anus in order to leave few incriminating marks on his body. Assuming that William Rufus died accidentally in 1100, Edward II was the first king to be murdered since Edward the Martyr had been killed at Corfe in 978. Within 160 years another three – Richard II in 1400, Henry VI in 1471, and Edward V in 1483 – were also to be murdered, a testimony to growing instability.

Edward II's deposition testified to the role of new and sophisticated political concepts, because the community of the realm in Parliament was deliberately involved in order to help legitimate what was misleadingly presented as an abdication. The killing of Edward II was a consequence of the new constitutional instrument that had evolved to deal with kings who ruled tyrannically and threatened the vital interests of the nobility. As later with Richard II, there was a need to neutralize deposed kings as a focus for rebellion.

Isabella and Mortimer ruled for the first years of the reign of Edward III (1327–77), but, when Parliament met in Nottingham in 1330, Edward and his friends entered the castle through an underground passage and seized Mortimer. He was hanged and Isabella was confined in Castle Rising. Edward III possessed the ability and determination to restore royal prestige and authority, to avenge his father's humiliations, and to reassert the position of his dynasty in France. He was also notably effective in his dealings with the barons, and was far more successfully married than his father. Apart from his mistress late in his reign, Edward had no favourites, and he brought many of the leading barons into the royal circle as Knights of the Order of the Garter, which he established in 1348.

The resumption of war with Scotland brought short-term successes, including victory at Halidon Hill in 1333 and the installation of a client ruler, Edward Balliol, in 1334, but none proved lasting. Furthermore, Edward soon concentrated on France where the end of the male line of Philip IV led Edward in 1337 to challenge Philip's nephew, Philip VI, and claim the throne. There were spectacular successes, including the naval victory at Sluys in 1340, and land victories at Crécy (1346) and Poitiers (1356) in which English longbowmen defeated larger cavalry armies. This stage of the war was ended by the peace of Brétigny of 1360 by which Edward realistically renounced his claim to the French throne, Normandy and Anjou, but was recognized as Duke of the whole of Aquitaine, as well as ruler of Calais, which had been captured in 1347. This, however, was not a stable settlement. War was resumed in 1369 as a result of French encouragement of opposition to Edward in Aquitaine. Edward reasserted his claim to the French throne, but the war went badly both in Aquitaine and at sea and, by the time of the Truce of Bruges (1375), England held little more than Bayonne, Bordeaux and Calais.

Much of the cost of the war was met by the depredations of English forces in France, but there were also formidable costs to be met in England. Even in the early years of the conflict, when it had gone reasonably well, there were serious complaints, both about the cost and about Edward's failure to elicit sufficient support for his policies. Between 1339 and 1341, there was a political crisis built up from opposition to war taxation and parliamentary hostility to the conduct of government. Renewed criticism of tax demands were expressed in the Parliaments of 1343, 1344, 1346, 1348 and 1352.

This financial demand pressed on a society in crisis. Strains and difficulties can be discerned in all periods, but if any period of English history deserved the description crisis it was most appropriate for the fourteenth century. The most striking cause was the Black Death, an epidemic, probably of bubonic plague, which killed about 40 per cent of the population between 1348 and 1351, greatly disrupted the economy and contributed to a serious loss of confidence. Mortality in towns was probably much higher than average. In contrast, only 25 per cent of aristocrats died.

Yet the Black Death was only part of a wider crisis. Aside from epidemic disease, there were problems arising from an inability to sustain earlier expansion and from a downturn in the climate. Earlier expansion had led to the cultivation of marginal lands and had put pressure on the agrarian economy, not least because of a lack of sufficient manure. In the fourteenth century, the climate became colder and wetter, and also more erratic, with both floods and droughts. This hit the viability of much agriculture, particularly of clay lowlands which were liable to become waterlogged. Agricultural problems affected the population before the onset of the Black Death. Thanks to bad weather, harvests failed in 1315, 1316 and 1322, probably causing many deaths by progressive under-nourishment as well as by actual starvation. A study of Halesowen has suggested that about 15 per cent of male residents died in the famine.

The dramatic impact of the Black Death greatly aggravated the situation and this was sustained because plague now became endemic until the seventeenth century and held the population down until the start of the sixteenth century. The population did not increase strongly until the mid- to late sixteenth century. As a result, demand for food fell, while the cost of labour rose as its availability fell. This encouraged a shift to the more profitable keeping of sheep for wool, an activity that required less labour. The net effect was an abandonment of many villages and in the Midlands small settlements subsidiary to villages tended to contract and end up as farms. These changes were achieved without any of the social welfare of modern Britain, and in a difficult political context. Furthermore, there was also resistance to change in the rural economy. Lords sought to prevent peasants from exploiting the scarcity of labour by demanding higher wages. The Statute of Labourers of 1351 sought to fix low, pre-plague labour rates. Yet the ability of legislation to constrain socio-economic changes was limited. The development of an active land market and of agricultural production for market accentuated the pace of change.

The task of implementing the legislation conferred more functions on the commissions of the peace (the Justices of the Peace for each county) and helped to make them more central in the localities. More generally, the early decades of Edward's reign were fundamental in the evolution of Justices of the Peace, and were also important in the development of assize circuits and in the growth of judicial activity. The law became more insistent as a means by which disputes between the propertied were handled. However, although legal strategies for the resolution of disputes did become very prominent, recourse to the law remained only one tactic in a repertoire of measures employed against opponents. Few legal cases ever came to judgment, and the law tended to be used to harass opponents, sometimes with calculated violence in support. Much of the resolution of disputes appears to have relied on arbitration, involving the services of other members of the gentry community or noblemen, although such arbitration may have been a means for the powerful to exert influence as much as, or indeed far more than, even-handed justice.

While tension built up in rural areas, there were also growing problems in parliamentary management and, more generally, a loss of confidence in Edward III's regime in the 1370s. Parliament became the focus of discontent. During Edward's reign, the representatives of the counties (the Knights of the Shire) and boroughs became a fixed part of Parliament and began to meet as a separate assembly, the embryonic House of Commons. Parliament served as a means for eliciting support and funds for royal policies. The need to fund substantial amounts of war expenditure was crucial, as the king could only be independent of Parliament if war was avoided. The development of corporate identity and continuity also affected the freedom of political manoeuvre that monarchs enjoyed. A 1362 statute stated that Parliament must agree to all taxation of wool. The crown's freedom of manoeuvre was also lessened as it became more dependent on grants of taxation and less able to subsist on land revenues and prerogative rights.

After problems about agreeing taxation at the Parliaments of 1372 and 1373, the 'Good Parliament' of 1376 witnessed a sustained attack on the personnel and policies of the government. Taking the initiative, the Commons elected their first Speaker and two key officials were among those impeached (prosecuted). The Commons were only able to act effectively because the peers failed to stand together; some were disaffected. Edward was weak by the close of his reign: he may have suffered mentally from the effects of a series of strokes. His extravagant and unpopular mistress, Alice Perrers, served as a focus for tension. More generally, by the 1370s, Edward's regime was in serious difficulties.

There was also growing tension in Church matters. Hostility to foreign ecclesiastical jurisdiction and to the movement of funds abroad led to fourteenth-century jurisdiction designed to establish limits on papal rights: the Statutes of Provisors (1351) and *Praemunire* (1353). Anti-clericalism was exploited by the Lollard movement, which was inspired by John Wycliff, a radical Oxford theologian who died in 1384. He called into question certain fundamental tenets of the Catholic faith, including transubstantiation (the doctrine that the priest's blessing turns the communion bread and wine into the body and blood of Christ); the need for priestly intercession between God and man; and papal temporal authority. Emphasizing the authority of Scripture, Wycliff advocated lay reading of the Bible, which at this time had not been translated into English, and also condemned the wealth of the monastic orders.

The Peasants' Revolt of 1381, however, was the outburst that has most aroused subsequent interest. Poll taxes designed to fund the war with France and to shift the tax burden from property taxes to a wider circle of payers led to high rates of evasion and to localized rioting in 1379, and the process culminated in the Revolt. This also reflected the exploitation by the lords of their seigneurial powers, a blow to the livelihood as well as the self-esteem of peasants. For the peasants, conditions should have been improving, and to some extent were in what was an increasingly fluid society, but progress was artificially restricted. Other factors included failure in war, which led to French raids on the south coast, as well as the disruption to the normally lucrative East Anglian cloth industry produced by economic problems, and a strong measure of anti-clericalism. This reflected and contributed not only to specific opposition to aspects of ecclesiastical conduct, but also to a more widespread sense of alienation and a lack of confidence in the ruling order and its legal system. The 1381 revolt was not an isolated episode; resistance to landlords was common and often violent. Aside from assaults on officials, such as reeves and stewards, there was also a refusal to accept the dictates of the manorial economy, for example by performing customary services or taking up holdings.

Yet, at the same time, there was also a considerable element of conservatism in the Peasants' Revolt, including appealing to ancient precedents and attacking seigneurial and governmental innovations. An important source of antagonism – in addition to the Statute of Labourers and the Poll Tax – seems to have been the efforts of some lords to reimpose labour services and other features of villeinage which had fallen into disuse. These were viewed as dangerous novelties, enacted contrary to customary practices. The fundamental conservatism of the Revolt was to be shown by the reaction of the rebels to Richard II at Smithfield: their respect for kingship enabled Richard to defuse the rising at its most dangerous moment.

The Peasants' Revolt was not a breakdown of authority in a frontier or distant region, but a crisis at the centre of power. Furthermore, the revolt was not an episode of mindless violence, but one in which the participants had recognized and selective goals and were organized. The rebellion began in Essex and spread throughout Southern England, being especially strong in Kent and East Anglia, but also leading to disturbances in Sussex, Yorkshire, Winchester, Somerset and Cornwall. The destruction of manorial records reflected the hostility of villeins to the private jurisdiction of their lords. This was a rejection of what was seen as unjust lordship. The Chief Justice, Sir John Cavendish, who had enforced the Statute of Labourers, was killed at Lakenheath in Suffolk. Led by Wat Tyler and a priest, John Ball, the rebels marched on and occupied London with the help of dissatisfied Londoners. The Tower of London was seized and royal officials, including Simon Sudbury, who was both the Chancellor and the Archbishop of Canterbury, murdered. The rebels, however, did not wish to take over the government, but rather to pressurize Richard II (1377–99) into far-reaching changes in their conditions. On 15 June 1381, Richard met the main body of the rebels under Tyler at Smithfield. Believing that Tyler was threatening the king, the Lord Mayor, William Walworth, lunged forward and killed Tyler. As fighting was about to break out, Richard averted the crisis by promising to be the rebels' leader. Once they had dispersed to their homes Richard revoked the charters of freedom that had been given and punished the rebels. John Ball was tried and executed.

As he grew older, Richard came to want to rule as well as reign, but the nobles who had dominated his minority were unwilling to yield authority and were suspicious of the favourites patronized by Richard, especially Michael de la Pole, a merchant's son whom he made Chancellor and Earl of Suffolk. At the 1386 Parliament, Richard was pressed by a group of leading nobles, known later as the Appellants, to dismiss the Chancellor and the Treasurer and, when he refused, was threatened with deposition. A commission of nobles was appointed, with powers to reform the royal household and the realm. Richard had this declared illegal, but his principal supporter, Robert de Vere, Earl of Oxford, was routed at Radcot Bridge in December 1387. The 'Merciless Parliament' of 1388 condemned Richard's leading supporters for treason and several were executed. Richard was deposed for a few days, and reinstated only because the Appellants could not agree on a successor.

In 1389, Richard was able to appoint a new set of ministers and in the early 1390s he ruled in a more conciliatory, but still assertive fashion. Tensions persisted and, in 1397, Richard gained his revenge on the Appellants. A packed Parliament convicted them of treason and annulled the acts of the Merciless Parliament. Richard followed this up by extorting forced loans and blank charters from people who were terrorized by his army of Cheshire guards. In 1399, he deprived his cousin, the exiled Henry Bolingbroke, a former Appellant, of his inheritance from his dead father, John of Gaunt, Edward III's fourth son. If such a prominent noble was not safe, who was? That May, Richard led an expedition to Ireland, but in July Bolingbroke landed at Ravenspur in Yorkshire. Richard's unpopularity and political folly had left him with an overly small power base. Too few people had an interest in preserving his regime; too many an interest in ending it. Richard returned from Ireland, but was outmanoeuvred, captured and forced to abdicate in favour of Bolingbroke, who became Henry IV (1399–1413). Imprisoned in Pontefract Castle, Richard was killed in 1400 in order to end a focus for disaffection; his supporters had already tried to murder Henry in Windsor Castle.

The brutal end of the Plantagenet line had been eased by a show of legality: Richard had resigned the crown and Henry was persuaded not to claim it by right of conquest. Parliament played a major role in the transfer of the crown. Nevertheless, the removal of Richard, like the earlier crises of his reign, was a proof of the instability produced by royal claims to exercise the prerogative as the monarch thought fit and for the benefit of those whom he wished to patronize, and the claims of some of the magnates to ensure that they were consulted. To guarantee the fidelity of their dependants, magnates required access to the benefits of court favour, for an economy of patronage was important to this socio-political world, a process that was accentuated by the agrarian depression of the late medieval period. Many nobles were loyal, but not all; the stakes in the struggle for access to power were great, and this helped to exacerbate both disputes in Parliament and factional competition. The nature of magnate power had changed with the spread of so-called Bastard Feudalism, in which lords rewarded their followers and retained their services with an annual payment of money, rather than with land. This reflected the extent to which land was now a commodity, the landlord–tenant relationship increasingly separate from that of lord and man. Land therefore could not so readily serve as the basis of a retinue, or as the source of military power. Feudal relationships became less relevant politically, as feudal control, whether of the king over his magnates as tenants-in-chief, or of the latter over their tenants, declined. Retaining offered, in the form of the affinity or group of retainers, the possibility of a more flexible structure of control and strength. Bastard Feudalism and the affinity were defined by the association of men in mutual (but flexible) bonds of fidelity. Political reciprocity, essentially protection in return for some form of service or support, lay at the heart of the relationship. This form of patronage and clientage was not necessarily a cause of civil conflict, but, in the event of a breakdown in relations between monarch and magnates, or in the ranks of the latter, it made it easier for the magnates to mobilize and sustain their strength. They could equally easily lose it, as retainers deserted them for another lord with more to offer.

Richard II's maladroit handling of the situation, his unwillingness to search for compromise in the late 1390s, ensured that the throne itself became the subject of contention. Once one monarch had been deposed, it was impossible to prevent attempts to repeat the process, although a king still had to rule 'badly' to warrant deposition. To take the field against the king remained a supremely risky enterprise and barons would only act in extreme circumstances, as Thomas of Lancaster did against Edward II and Henry Bolingbroke against Richard II. Edward II had eventually been removed to make way for a government claiming to rule on behalf of his heir. Henry IV did not have so clear a claim to the throne, although his position was eased by Richard's childlessness.

Violence played a central role in the politics of the following century. It was also a key feature of medieval society; incessant poverty and insecurity helped to lead to competitiveness and a high level of quarrels and violence. In the 1270s, Devon had an average rate of over thirty-six killings per annum, and there was also a high rate of robbery. The many moated sites of the fourteenth century were possibly a product of an insecure society. Neither religious teachings and sanctions, nor secular administration, nor the strenuous efforts made throughout society, at all levels, to contain violence and promote conciliation, by both formal and informal means, could restrain the high crime rate; and, though the circumstances were different, it is scarcely surprising that the same was true of political violence. However, much of this violence, especially political violence, was carefully calculated for particular ends, and this perhaps made it less random and terrifying than the figures might suggest.

Political issues and problems frequently come first in any account of the fifteenth century, a period when Henry V's invasion of France from 1415 led to hopes and plans that crashed into ruin under his successor, Henry VI, and the latter's reign was, in turn, best known for what were to be termed the Wars of the Roses. Important as these were, it is also necessary to note the continued impact of the fall in population and economic problems of the fourteenth century. Farmhouses, barns, ditches, fences and walls fell into disrepair, and soil improvement through marling appears to have declined. There was not the manpower to weed effectively. It was difficult to find occupants for vacant holdings, and there were shortfalls of rent. Many rural settlements were deserted. These problems hit urban life. The trade of most markets and fairs fell, and there was a shortage of coin in circulation. Difficulties in rural hinterlands led to the decline of towns such as Canterbury.

Yet, there was prosperity as well. The fall in population brought advantages to peasants able to exploit demands for labour, and they were helped by the decline of serfdom. Villeinage withered away as lords commuted services into fixed money rents. Hired workers were found to be more productive. The growth in pastoral farming produced more meat for eating and also wool. Wool exports declined steeply as the wool was now made into cloth. This was exported, bringing much prosperity, particularly to East Anglia and London, but also further afield, for example to Berkshire. The pre-plague population of Colchester – 3,000–4,000 – doubled by the early fifteenth century. Communications improved. Fords at major crossing points were replaced by bridges which increasingly rested on stone arches and were able to accommodate carts.

The relative wealth of the South-East was considerably accentuated in this period. The nature of this prosperity can be seen today by visiting cloth towns such as Lavenham and Long Melford, with their impressive churches. Several foreign visitors commented on the wealth and prosperity of England as a whole, not just London and the court, although few foreigners reached the north. This relative prosperity, certainly an improvement on the situation in the thirteenth century, helped underwrite not only the ambitions of Henry V but also, more generally, late medieval government and the political system. London played a major role in the Wars of the Roses.

Rich and poor alike had to contribute to the conflicts of the fifteenth century. Henry IV (1399–1413) faced a serious rebellion in Wales led by Owain Glyn Dŵr (Owen Glendower) as well as the problem of a pseudo-Richard II and opposition from the Percies, a mighty magnate family who wielded great power in the North and had helped Henry depose Richard II. Henry defeated and killed the Percy heir, 'Hotspur', Sir Henry Percy, at the battle of Shrewsbury in 1403, but Hotspur's father, Henry, 1st Earl of Northumberland, rebelled again in 1405 and 1408 before being defeated and killed on Bramham Moor in 1408. This warfare overshadowed the reign, but, looked at differently, it represented the consolidation of a new dynasty. Henry was reasonably successful in this and also lucky and skilful in foreign policy. It was particularly helpful that Henry was able to take possession of the heir to the Scottish throne, the future James I, who was captured by English pirates in 1406.

To a certain extent, his success contributed to the domestic stability of England during the reign of his eldest son and successor, Henry V (1413–22), a young and vigorous warrior-king. In 1414, Henry crushed a conspiracy organized by the Lollard Sir John Oldcastle. The king, like Richard II before him, was much associated with religious orthodoxy. The following year, on the eve of Henry's invasion of France, a conspiracy to overthrow him in favour of the Earl of March was betrayed to him by March himself.

Invading Normandy in 1415, Henry captured the port of Harfleur, and, thanks largely to his longbowmen, smashed a larger French army at Agincourt. Between 1417 and 1419 he conquered Normandy and laid claim to the French throne. Henry's success led the weak Charles VI of France to betroth his daughter Catherine to Henry, and, by the Treaty of Troyes of 1420, recognize Henry as regent during his reign. Henry and her heirs were to inherit France on Charles' death. Charles VI's son, the Dauphin, refused to accept the treaty and Henry had to fight on. In August 1422 he died, possibly of dysentery, while besieging Meaux. Henry left France south of the Loire unconquered, and Parliament critical of the likely cost of the war, and, also, unhappy with the idea that England should have to pay for the assertion of Henry's control over his French subjects.

Henry V's reign epitomized the unpredictability of events and the difficulty of assessing England's likely relationship with the wider dynastic polity that it was part of. Under Richard II and Henry IV, England had been overwhelmingly the key dominion among the monarch's territories, but Henry V really wished to be accepted by Frenchmen as their ruler, the heir of St Louis; not as a conqueror. The quest for the crown of France was an attempt to usurp, but also absorb, the leadership of Christendom, in so far as it was held by the French. This played a role in the anxiety of Parliament about keeping the two crowns separate and not becoming a satellite of France. In 1421 the Commons approved a petition that the Crowns of England and France should in perpetuity remain separate and independent. This was a repetition of an Act of 1340, after Edward III took the title. The French ambitions of successive monarchs was a very different challenge to English identity from that posed under the Normans, because after 1066 English consciousness was represented by the defeated Anglo-Saxons, while in the fifteenth century there was a stronger sense of English identity among the landholding elite than among their Norman and Angevin predecessors and, in Parliament, a body to give this sense institutional focus. The Continental involvement of the rulers may have lessened the identification of monarchs with England, but it also forwarded the development of a 'national' state. The Hundred

Years War encouraged xenophobia, royal war-propaganda, military service, national taxation, the use of the vernacular, and the expansion of the role of Parliament. In its early stages, Parliament was no different, to any great extent, from its Continental counterparts, but the frequent need to raise taxation to pay for warfare led to Parliament becoming more powerful. This was not inherently a cause of instability. Instead, Parliament provided an opportunity for the peaceful restraint of governmental aspirations and, more generally, for the conciliation of royal with group and provincial interests.

Henry V's nine-month-old son, Henry VI (1422–61, 1470–1), became king. Initially, his forces in France, under the direction of the Regent there, his uncle John, Duke of Bedford, had some success, including an important victory at Verneuil in 1424. However, the Treaty of Troyes had set a benchmark for success that could not be met and thus helped ensure that force, not a compromise peace, would settle the issue. A charismatic French peasant, Joan of Arc, inspired Charles VI's son, Charles VII, and, in what was to be the turning point of the conflict, broke the English siege of Orléans in May 1429. Patriotism along English lines was created in France under the pressure of war. Although Joan was captured and burned as a witch, the impetus had been lost. In 1435, Henry was abandoned by the powerful Duke of Burgundy, who had been a crucial ally, and Bedford died; in 1436 he lost Paris, and in 1444 Maine. In 1449–51 Charles conquered Normandy and Gascony, and in 1453 a counter-offensive in Gascony was smashed. France had gone. Calais was held until 1558, and the Channel Islands were still under the British crown, but a theme that had been insistent in English history since 1066 was now cut short. From 1453 until 1603 England was a unitary kingdom, although rule extended over Wales and part of Ireland.

Defeat led to a crucial loss of prestige, and was followed by crisis at home. What was to be termed the Wars of the Roses was the lengthiest period of civil conflict in English history: 1455–71 and 1483–7. The severity of this conflict has been minimized (as has that of the civil war during Stephen's reign) by arguing that conflict was far from continuous, that by contemporary Continental standards, England was not particularly violent, and that the damage and disruption caused by the war should not be exaggerated. An agrarian society was better able to stand disruption than a modern industrial counterpart, while, in part, conflict in the localities was a continuation and accentuation of already high rates of localized violence. All of this is true, and it is clearly unrealistic to judge England in the 1450s–80s by the standards of its twenty-first-century descendant. Yet, it is equally the case that there had been a decline from the situation in say the 1420s. Furthermore, civil violence was disruptive to domestic trade; there was much destruction, as well as the diversion of resources to warfare; and the institutions and processes of government and law, including the monarchy itself, were fatally entangled with violence and bitter partisanship. As such, there was a crisis in legitimacy. It is interesting to note, however, that the response was not to seek either a new shape for England or constitutional change. After its advances over the previous century and a half, Parliament did not play a significant independent role. Nor was there any process akin to that by which the Dukes of Burgundy had acquired semi-statehood within France. There was foreign intervention in the Wars of the Roses – by the rulers of both France and Scotland – but it was designed to help one or other claimant, not to remould English political space. Again, the contrast with the relative plasticity of political boundaries and dynastic units across much of Europe is apparent. Henry V's ambitions in France had suggested that a comparable process could take place there. The severity of the domestic crisis of the Wars of the Roses and the fact that it led to so little political change are both worthy of note. This might lead to the suggestion that the crisis was not all that serious, but alternatively it can be argued that it reflected the limited possibilities for change. Indeed, a new ruler was the sum total of what was possible.

The calibre of the monarch owed much to his ability to take command of a political situation made complex by competing aristocratic factions. Henry VI was not up to the task and unable to intervene intelligently and to resolve disputes. Henry was apt to mess up sensible arrangements made for him by intelligent subordinates. The surrender of Maine to the French was Henry's own idea, and was carried through at his insistence. The chaos that descended upon northern England in the 1440s was largely due to Henry's promoting the Percies at the expense of the Nevilles in Cumberland, quite unnecessarily. The contrast with the heroic image, political adroitness and skilful determination of his father was striking. In Richard, Duke of York, Henry faced a member of the royal family who felt that his status entitled him to more recognition. Henry VI's lengthy minority was unsettled, with factional struggles between leading nobles, especially his uncle, Humphrey, Duke of Gloucester, and great-uncle, Cardinal Henry Beaufort, and a waning of royal power in the localities. Force, and the threat of force, came to play a greater role in local and national politics than had been the case under Henry V, and local disputes came to affect the Court as aristocratic feuds, such as that between the Percies and the Nevilles, transmitted tension and animosity both ways.

The political crisis became more serious in 1450 with a major breakdown in order in London and the South-East. The unpopular chief minister, William de la Pole, 1st Duke of Suffolk, who had been criticized in Parliament the previous year, was impeached there, banished and then murdered on a boat in the Channel. In June 1450, the outbreak of Cade's Rebellion in Kent reflected anger about extortion by manorial officials and about the loss of Normandy, widespread hostility to the government, and its inability to control areas near the centre of government. The rebels beat a royal army at Sevenoaks, seized London, and killed unpopular officials, before being driven out by the citizens and defeated. The crisis was more serious than that of the Peasants' Revolt, because of the concatenation of aristocratic and popular discontent. The loss of France ensured that the aristocracy no longer had a useful foreign outlet for their aggression. Cade was keen to have it thought that the Duke of York was behind him, and York used the rebellion to return from Ireland and demand changes in government. In 1453, a mental and physical collapse by Henry led to York becoming Protector, but the birth of a son to Henry ruled out his chances of succeeding by hereditary right. The king's partial recovery in the winter of 1454–5 gave the court party, under Edmund Beaufort, Duke of Somerset, the opportunity to turn against York.

This led to hostilities. In 1455, the Duke of York clashed with Somerset at the first battle of St Albans, killing Somerset and capturing Henry. This did not bring stability and in 1457 York lost control of the government. Fighting became more frequent from 1459. In 1460, York defeated the Lancastrians at Northampton, captured Henry again and claimed the throne, a step that made it impossible to restore order on the basis of compromise. Henry's unpopular queen, Margaret of Anjou, was not prepared to see the disinheritance of her son, and York was attacked, defeated and killed at Wakefield on 29 December 1460. His severed head was contemptuously adorned with a paper crown.

In a fast-moving situation, the Duke of York's ambitious and able eldest son, Edward, next claimed the throne, as Edward IV. Margaret defeated Richard Neville, Earl of Warwick, 'the King-Maker', a key Yorkist, at St Albans on 17 February 1461, but London defied her. At Towton on Palm Sunday, 29 March 1461, the Lancastrians were soundly defeated during a heavy snowstorm in the largest and bloodiest battle ever fought in England. The thoroughness of Edward's victory established his position, although it was not until 1464 that the Yorkists were established in Northumbria. Captured in 1465, Henry was sent to the Tower.

Edward IV was able to restore a measure of order, but by 1469 he had fallen out with Warwick. They clashed over diplomacy, and, more pointedly, over Edward's favour for the Woodvilles, relatives of the Queen who challenged Warwick's position at court: the very fact that Edward had married Elizabeth Woodville in the first place shows that there were limits to Warwick's dominance. After defeating and capturing Edward at Edgecote on 26 July 1469, Warwick seized power, but he could not maintain his authority, and in 1470 he fled to France. There, in one of the most striking volte-faces of the period, Warwick was reconciled with the exiled Margaret and committed himself to Henry's restoration.

With French help, Warwick and his son-in-law, Edward's disloyal brother, George, Duke of Clarence, invaded in 1470. Edward was deposed and forced to flee into exile, and Henry VI was restored. In turn, Edward invaded with Burgundian assistance in 1471, defeated and killed Warwick in thick fog at Barnet, and defeated Margaret at Tewkesbury. Henry's son was killed on the battlefield, and Henry, imprisoned in the Tower of London, was murdered. These victories and killings weakened Lancastrian prospects and helped return a measure of stability, but there were still tensions. Distrust led in 1478 to the killing of Clarence (who had betrayed Warwick in 1471), supposedly drowned in a butt of malmsey wine.

Edward died at forty in 1483, too early to leave his elder son, Edward V, as an adult successor. Unlike in 1422, when the far younger Henry VI had been left to grow up as king while a strong regent directed affairs, there was a seizure of the throne. Edward IV's surviving brother, Richard, Duke of Gloucester, fearful of a Woodville takeover, moved swiftly. He seized power in April 1483, declaring his nephews, Edward V and Richard, Duke of York, bastards, and sending them to the Tower. They swiftly disappeared, and, given Richard's character and situation, were probably murdered.

Richard III (1483–5) was an able political operator and an effective lieutenant in the North during the latter half of his brother's reign, but his seizure of the throne divided the Yorkists, and he had only a slender base of support. This was shown in October 1483 when the Woodvilles and Henry, Duke of Buckingham, who had played a major role in Richard's seizure of the throne, rebelled. Richard swiftly crushed the rebellion, but was unable to consolidate his position before the next challenge was mounted in 1485. The challenger was Henry Tudor, the Lancastrian claimant. Invading through Wales, with the help of French and Scottish troops, Henry had little support in England, but Richard was similarly bereft, as was to be shown on the battlefield of Bosworth when he was abandoned by much of his army and subject to the swing of the Stanleys to Henry. Richard was killed in the battle. His only son had already died the previous year, and the earlier killings among the Yorkists helped Henry establish his position as Henry VII (1485–1509). His marriage in 1486 to Elizabeth of York, Edward IV's daughter, helped to unify the two factions, a process symbolized by the replacement of the white rose of York and the red rose of the Beauforts (and maybe of Lancaster) by the Tudor rose, and also masked Henry's very thin claim to the throne. Death on the battlefield throughout the period had also helped lessen the size of the political elite.

Bosworth is popularly seen as the end of the Wars of the Roses, but there was still conflict and conspiracy. Rebellious Yorkists and hostile foreign rulers supported the cause of two impostors, Lambert Simnel and Perkin Warbeck, who claimed, respectively, to be Clarence's son (then, in fact, held in the Tower) and the younger of the two princes who had disappeared into the Tower in 1483. Simnel was defeated at Stoke in 1487, a hard-fought battle with more combatants than Bosworth, and given a job as a turnspit in the palace kitchen. This was the last battle in the Wars of the Roses and had it gone the other way might well have led to a new Yorkist order. Conspiracies continued, Warbeck was not hanged until 1499, and Henry VIII (1509–47) was to be worried about possible claimants to the throne, but, in so far as divisions are valid, Stoke did bring to an end both the Lancastrian dynasty and a period of disorder that had begun in 1450 or 1455.

The extent to which this was the close of 'medieval' England is far more dubious. Indeed, scholars have long sought parallels between the policies of Edward IV, Richard III and Henry VII and referred to this as a period of 'new monarchy', although it is unclear how far there was much more than the re-establishment of royal power after a period of disruption. If the novelty of 'new monarchy' can be doubted, so also can be that of the early Tudors. To turn to signs of discontinuity and new beginnings, it is more appropriate to consider the ecclesiastical and religious changes from the 1530s (Henry VIII's break with the Catholic Church and Edward VI's embrace of state Protestantism), the opening of England to a new wider trans-oceanic world, and the major demographic and socio-economic shifts that stemmed from population rise and economic change in the sixteenth century.

At the same time, it is necessary to give due weight to long-standing developments that were important to the character of English society and politics. These included the development of the vernacular (the English language), the growth of Parliament, the role of the common law, and the increased flexibility of English society. The last has led to claims that, at least since the thirteenth century and possibly from far earlier, England was distinctly and distinctively less stratified than elsewhere in Europe.

The rise of the vernacular lessened the role of both Latin and Anglo-Norman, the French spoken in England. The use of

French declined from the early twelfth century, but it became fashionable again, more than ever before, in the thirteenth. Nevertheless, in the thirteenth century, the English language was increasingly identified with an English people and nation, and, from the fourteenth century, English became more important, not least in literature. Laurence Minot used English for his vigorous poems of the 1330s and 1340s which stressed the unity of the English and their triumphs over the French and Scots. Geoffrey Chaucer's *Canterbury Tales* (*c.* 1387–1400) and William Langland's *Piers Plowman* (different versions, 1362–92) were written in English.

The development of the vernacular also had a political aspect. At the start of the Hundred Years' War, the aristocracy of England was international in outlook and French was the language at court and of anyone with upwardly mobile aspirations. However, as politics drove the two realms into a long war, it became awkward that high society in England aped French style, manners, and customs. The government also manipulated patriotic characteristics and deliberately harnessed linguistic awareness. In 1344, it was claimed before the House of Commons that Edward III had information that Philip VI was 'fully resolved . . . to destroy the English language, and to occupy the land of England'. As the lower classes spoke English anyway, it was only a shift by the upper classes that was at issue.

The official switch of tongue gathered pace from the 1350s. In 1356, proceedings in the London Sheriffs' courts switched to English. In 1362, a statute decreed that court proceedings be in English, with the record kept in Latin. In 1363, the Chancellor addressed Parliament in English, and in 1373 likewise the Convocation of Canterbury. The earliest parliamentary petition in English was in 1386. Henry V switched himself in 1417, a significant year given the developing conflict with France. From 1420, chancery clerks were pushing English as the official language of government.

Distinctiveness was also seen in the Perpendicular, a native architectural style of the fourteenth and fifteenth centuries, and in a distinctive style of English music. England was part of an international cultural world, but it was increasingly far less dependent on Continental, especially French, influences.

The Common Law was another aspect of English distinctiveness. From the twelfth century this was true of both the content of the law and the way in which it was administered. The legal system reflected the particular imprint of interested monarchs, especially Henry II and Edward I, and the nature of what was, by contemporary standards, a sophisticated administrative system that owed much to the strength of Norman and Angevin monarchical power. English Common Law had links with what was going on abroad, but was also a distinctive unity, and that at a time when Roman Law was coming back into fashion on the Continent; it did so later in Scotland. It has been suggested that English Common Law was particularly suited to the protection of rights and liberties, and that it encouraged a respect for the autonomy of individual thought and action. In combination with the early emergence of an institutional monarchy, this has been seen as particularly responsible for the character and continuity of English political society.

EIGHT

TUDOR ENGLAND 1485–1603

The society of sixteenth-century England can be seen more readily than that of the previous century. Partly thanks to printing, a rise in literacy and population, more extensive governmental activity, and the nationalization of the Church, records, both private and state, are more copious. There are also more surviving buildings, especially secular buildings, and also more of the material culture, the world of things. As a result, Tudor England seems closer to us. The use of the English language was a fourteenth- and fifteenth-century development that was pushed further under the Tudors when it became both the language of authority and of a culture that still echoes today, in large part thanks to the oft-seen and cited plays of William Shakespeare (1564–1616). In addition, thanks to more lifelike and more numerous portraits, for example by Holbein, we can see portraits of the people as we cannot see their fifteenth-century predecessors.

Yet, as so often with the past, a suggestion of common humanity should not blind us to difference. Both the facts and details of life, and the attitudes of the period, were totally different. This was a world that was shadowed by a world of spirits, good and bad, and these spirits were seen and believed to intervene frequently in the life of humans. This belief brought together both Christian notions, in particular providentialism, a conviction of God's direct intervention in the life of individuals, the intercessory role of saints, sacraments, prayer and belief, the existence of heaven, purgatory, hell and the devil, and a related and overlapping group of ideas, beliefs and customs that were partially Christianized, but also testified to a mental world that was not explicable in terms of Christian theology. This was a world of good and evil knowledge and magic, of fatalism, of the occult, and of astrology and alchemy. Furthermore, such beliefs were not marginal, nor held only by the poor.

This fearful world could be only partially countered by Christianity and, indeed, other forms of white magic, but the very sense of menace and danger helps to account for the energy devoted to religious issues in the sixteenth century and the fears encouraged by changes in Church belief and practice, for example the despoliation of shrines and ending of pilgrimages. The true path of Christian virtue and salvation was challenged not only by false prophets laying claim to the word of Jesus, but also by a malevolent world presided over by the Devil. Witches were prominent among his followers.

Concern about witches gained a new prominence in the sixteenth century, and bridged elite and populace, and Church and State; although there was a contrast between the category of witchcraft imposed by the law and less defined traditional religious and folklore beliefs. The frequency of curses in disputes and the concern to which they gave rise focused attention on the power of bewitchment. Accusations of witchcraft arose from a range of causes, including refusals to give charity, but fear of real evil was the core. It was believed possible to cause harm to person and property using magical means, as part of a rejection of society and Christianity.

These beliefs were not swept away by the Renaissance, the Reformation or the supposed onset of the modern age. Indeed, they did not decline in impact until the eighteenth century.

Belief in prediction, astrology, alchemy (Henry VI's advisers had turned to it in 1456), and the occult indeed were especially strong in the early seventeenth century, as was fear of witchcraft. James I (1603–25) wrote against witches and was believed to be the target of their diabolical schemes, although he later recanted. James's writings were an aspect of the way in which news of witches was spread in the new culture of print, in learned treatises, chapbooks, printed ballads, and engravings. Acts against witchcraft were passed in 1563 and 1604.

The Protestant Reformation with its emphasis on a vernacular Bible ensured that good and evil became more literary and less oral and visual than hitherto, but that did not diminish the need for people to understand their world in terms of the struggle between the two; indeed it may even have encouraged it. Protestantism had little time for sacred places, such as holy wells, but did not lessen the sense of direct providential intervention, and of a daily interaction of the human world and the wider spheres of good and evil. Evil, malevolence and the inscrutable workings of the divine will seemed the only way to explain the sudden pitfalls of the human condition. Fatal accidents and tragic illnesses snuffed out life with brutal rapidity.

This remained the case in the sixteenth century. There were still virulent outbreaks of the plague, as in 1499–1500, 1518, 1538 and 1563. Nevertheless, there was also a major rise in population. Prior to the first national census in 1801, all figures are approximate, but the population of England seems to have increased from under 2.5 million in 1500 to over 4 million by 1603 and about 5 million by 1651. The impact of this change was accentuated because it followed a period of stagnation after the Black Death and preceded another that lasted until the 1740s.

The analysis of past population trends is far from easy, but it has been the subject of much research for several decades, including the development of family reconstitution studies and the methodical analysis of parish registers. It seems clear that the increase in population was due largely to a fall in mortality, not least the retreat of the plague which became less frequent. A rise in fertility, stemming from a small decrease in the average age of women at marriage, was probably also important. The absence of artificial contraceptives (although, thanks to coitus interruptus, not of contraception), and general abstinence from sexual intercourse before betrothal, ensured that the average age of marriage was crucial to fertility. Infanticide was employed as a form of post-birth contraception: action in 1624 against the concealment of the deaths of newborn children was specifically aimed at unmarried mothers. There may have been awareness of the capacity of ergotism, poisoning through eating cereals affected by the ergot fungus, to act as an abortifacient.

The rise in population affected the structure of society. It led to 'over-population' as far as the distribution of resources was concerned, certainly in comparison with the fifteenth century. This encouraged a persistent rise in prices. The demand for food caused the rents of agricultural land to rise proportionately more rapidly than wages. This hit both tenants and those with little or no land. In this volatile and tense situation, agrarian capitalism became more intense. Landlords tried to increase the yield of their customary estates and to destroy the system of customary tenure. Entry fines and rents were increased, and customary tenants bought out or evicted, in order to make way for fixed-term leases. Much of the peasantry lost status, and became little different from poorly paid wage labourers. Economic growth could not provide sufficient employment for the rising numbers of poor; while economic change lessened labour security, for example through guild membership and, instead, ensured that casual labour became more common.

The growing number of paupers and vagrants greatly concerned successive governments, although more for law and order reasons than due to concern about the poor. Poverty also pressed on the neighbourliness within the parish community that was important to social cohesion, and to the maintenance of order. A number of Acts of Parliament from 1495 sought to control the problem. Compulsory poor rates were introduced in 1572, and in 1598 the relief of poverty was made the responsibility of individual parishes, a reflection of the local nature of education, health and welfare provision and the maintenance of basic law and order.

Poor relief sought to distinguish between the deserving – children, the elderly and the ill – and the undeserving poor: able-bodied men. This model, which was a religious as much as a social construct, was established before the Tudor period when there was far less of a shortage of work. The able-bodied unemployed were regarded as lazy or greedy, and were treated harshly as rogues and vagabonds. However, from the mid-sixteenth century, there was formal recognition of the able-bodied worker unable to find work, i.e. the labouring poor.

Whether or not people were in work, economic change and the impact of market pressures on prices and wages led to anxiety. For much of the population, there was scant prospect of advancement. Instead, economic pressure led to widespread malnutrition among the poor and to some starvation. Most folktales centred on peasant poverty and, in many, the desire for an unending source of food played a major part. Malnutrition stunted growth, hit energy levels, and reduced resistance to ill-health. Poor diet particularly encouraged colon parasitic infection, hepatitis and salmonella. The poor were also colder than contemporaries and more commonly in the dark. They were more harshly treated by the law.

The poverty of the majority was counterpointed by the growing comfort that characterized the wealthy, with their finer, often sumptuous, clothes, and larger and healthier dwellings. The tax assessments of the better off were low and, as landlords, they benefited from rising demand for food; so also did big farmers, leading to yeoman affluence. Building reflected affluence, as with the insertion of chimney stacks in many houses. The world of 'things' also increased and was increasingly combined with the spreading money economy. There were far fewer objects than in the modern house, in large part because of the combination of low average incomes and the absence of mass production, but more objects survived than from the previous century, and other evidence, such as probate inventories, legal records and literary references, also suggest a marked trend in this direction. More material consumption was denounced by moralists and also seen as a cause of rising crime, an alleged trend that fuelled concern about rogues and vagabonds.

The world of things had important cultural consequences. The increase in the number of musical instruments, such as lutes, reflected the interest in making music in genteel society. The availability of books, the first of which printed in England was published by William Caxton in 1474, helped to encourage rising literacy. Printing had important religious and political dimensions, especially with the publication of the Bible in English, and also made literature readily available. Public patronage was important in the growth of the theatre, which was the name given to the first purpose-built public playhouse in England, which was opened in London in 1576. This was a vernacular culture. Shakespeare wrote in English, not Latin, while the publication of the Bible in English helped to validate both the use of the language and books.

The paramount importance of London gave England a lead in the formation of a national language compared to many parts of the Continent. However, as the London dialect was based on East Anglian and was only established in consequence of the massive migration from East Anglia into London during the fourteenth and fifteenth centuries, it was therefore a fairly young standard in the sixteenth century. Furthermore, as printing continued much of the medieval dialectalism, the standardization of the language emerged only during the seventeenth and eighteenth centuries.

Although education had played a major role already in late medieval cities without any connection to printing, its importance as a means to approach and use the world of print encouraged a greater emphasis both on education and on the role of learning in education. Yet this was also socially divisive, for access to learning, for example in the grammar schools founded in the period, developed in terms of existing social structures and practices. Most people could neither read nor afford books, most men, and, even more, women, lacked formal education, and the inability of the poor to express themselves was accentuated.

This was the social politics against which the dramas of Tudor England, especially the Protestant Reformation, were to be played out. The bulk of the population were not of course consulted, but this absence of consultation was more notable than it had been ever since the Norman Conquest because change was not simply a matter of monarchs and aristocratic factions competing for the spoils of power and privilege, but, in the case of the Reformation, also a deep-seated and divisive change in the nation's ideology and culture. The extent of this discontinuity has been largely overlooked in the history of the nation for, from the reign of Elizabeth, the Reformation was seen as the national destiny and Protestantism as central to national identity. This analysis was less disruptive when the vast majority of the population was Protestant and when England was in conflict with Catholic powers, as she was for much of the period from the 1530s until the Entente Cordiale with France of 1904. At the time, however, the impact of the Reformation was brutal.

Henry VIII (1509–47) was responsible for the initial breach with Rome. A larger-than-life character with six wives, he has overshadowed his father, Henry VII (1485–1509). Yet the latter's achievements were crucial. Henry VII established the Tudor dynasty, brought an end to civil war, recreated both royal authority and the practice of firm government, and made England a more important power. This reassertion of royal power was more than a matter of the destruction of the Yorkists or a simple reaction against the protracted disorder of the Wars of the Roses, important as they both were. Far from relying simply upon 'new men' and making a clean sweep of the past, as was at one time suggested, Henry VII appreciated the need to work with the nobles and win their support. This was an uneasy process. Some nobles were kept accountable with bonds, enforced payments that were forfeit if their behaviour was unacceptable. The private armed forces of nobles were limited by statute.

Although the Tudor hold on power was fragile and Henry's use of his authority could be arbitrary and avaricious, there was no successful rebellion, and Henry defeated the Cornish rising of 1497. Law and order were enhanced, government effectiveness and finances improved, and there was no political crisis when Henry died.

In his early years as king, Henry VIII (1509–47) took a prominent role in the highly competitive international relations of the period, particularly war with France. Henry campaigned in person in 1513, winning the battle of the Spurs, a minor clash. Money for war was raised by Henry's leading minister, Thomas Wolsey, the able and greedy son of an Ipswich butcher who became Archbishop of York, Lord Chancellor (with a life patent of the office), and a cardinal. Financial demands lessened the popularity of Henry's policies. In 1525, however, the attempt to levy an 'Amicable Grant' led to serious riots and the abandonment of the tax, an indication of the limits of government power. Wolsey was also loathed by the nobles who saw him as an upstart monopolizing power.

Henry's authority was undermined by uncertainty about the succession to the throne. His wife, Catherine of Aragon, had borne five children, but only a daughter, Mary, survived. In England rule by a woman was legal, but the succession and then marriage of any female ruler was bound to be a vexed issue in a society that assumed male dominance. Henry was trying to annul his marriage even before he fell in love with Anne Boleyn. He claimed that the Pope lacked the power to dispense with the biblical injunction against marrying a brother's widow, as Henry had done. His sister Margaret had successfully gained a divorce from her second husband in 1525. Catherine, however, was also the aunt of the Emperor Charles V, the most powerful ruler in Italy, and the Pope proved unyielding.

Wolsey's failure to obtain an annulment led to his fall in 1529: his life patent was no benefit. The angry Henry went on to reject papal jurisdiction over the English Church. The Act of Restraint of Appeals (to Rome) of 1533 was the first claim of imperial status for the realm. England was proclaimed jurisdictionally self-sufficient and the sovereignty of law made in Parliament was established by Henry. By the Act of Supremacy of 1534, Henry became the 'Supreme Head' of the English Church, which was still Catholic in doctrine. The previous year, an English court had granted an annulment of Henry's marriage. He went on to marry Anne Boleyn and to have a daughter, Elizabeth, later Elizabeth I. The Act of Succession of 1534 bastardized Mary and put the children of Henry's marriage to Anne first in the succession.

Opposition was treated harshly. Sir Thomas More resigned as Chancellor in 1532, was imprisoned for refusing to swear the oaths demanded under the Act of Succession and, after a manipulated trial, was beheaded for treason in 1535. The Treason Act of 1534 extended treason to the denial of royal supremacy.

Henry's breach with Papal authority increasingly interacted with the Protestant Reformation which had begun with Martin Luther's challenge to the papacy in Germany in 1517. At this point, Catholicism was the sole permitted form of worship. A tiny Jewish minority had been expelled by Edward I in 1290. Relatively few people followed the Lollard heresy.

Hostility to the wealth and claims of the clergy was widespread, but far from new, and it did not preclude extensive popular devotion, including much church building and renovation, active support for local shrines and saints, and a continued and important role for monasteries, priories, nunneries and chantries in the spiritual, charitable and educational role of many communities. Religious vitality was also shown in local culture. Mystery plays developed in the century prior to the Reformation. Traditional religious practices remained strong, and there were few Protestants in England until Henry VIII's breach with Rome weakened traditional authority and encouraged Protestantism.

Henry himself was doctrinally conservative, and in 1521 had earned the title 'Defender of the Faith' from Pope Leo X for writing a book against Luther. In the 1530s, the growing influence of Protestantism in circles close to Henry had an effect on policy, but Henry did not wish to see any abandonment of the Catholic faith. The Church in his reign is better described as Henrician than Protestant. Catholics later considered Henry to be a schismatic rather than a heretic.

The official English Bible and the dissolution of the monasteries were the major developments of the 1530s. The first complete translation of the Bible to be printed in English, that by Miles Coverdale, was dedicated to Henry in 1535. Henry argued that the 'word of God' supported the idea of royal supremacy, and this encouraged the translation of the Bible. An official English Bible was produced in 1537, and every parish church was instructed to purchase a copy in 1538. This was a marked extension of the authority of print and a testimony to the effectiveness of the publishing industry.

A more brutal sign of royal power was provided by a widespread campaign of destructiveness. The great pilgrimage shrines were destroyed from 1535, producing much loot. Monasticism, one of the most prominent symbols of the old ecclesiastical order, an important aspect of the international character of the Church, and one that still enjoyed much popular support, was destroyed in 1536–40. Some less successful monasteries and priories had been suppressed in the 1520s, but the process begun by the 1536 Act dissolving the smaller monasteries was comprehensive. Monks and nuns were driven out, buildings looted, and estates sold. The latter brought wealth both to the crown and to those whom Henry favoured. This was the biggest transfer of wealth in England since the Norman Conquest.

The destruction of the monasteries was also a major break with the past, a shattering of popular devotion and institutional continuity that helped make it harder to think of an unchanging religious system. It was exacerbated by the attack on established practices, especially relics which were denounced as fraudulent, and the dissolution of chantry chapels in 1545 and 1547. The Berkshire commissioners closing the chantries referred to them as 'purgatory trasshe'. Henry's reluctance to support theological or liturgical change helped limit the progress of Protestantism, but he had shattered traditional patterns of faith. The belief in the efficacy of prayers for the souls of the dead in purgatory was fundamental to monasticism as well as to chantries. Its disappearance, or at least its discouragement, represented a major discontinuance in emotional and religious links between generations. The ending of masses for the dead destroyed the community of the living and the dead. Furthermore, the loss of the monasteries hit poor and medical relief. Protestant-influenced patterns of charitable giving were to develop, but there was disruption to the life of many.

For a society that had little sense of change as a positive development, the ending of monasticism and the destruction of the monasteries were very disturbing. They led to unfounded rumours about what Henry might do next, including the report that he would tax the sacraments. The sense of disquiet climaxed in 1536 with major risings in Lincolnshire and Yorkshire, the latter known as the Pilgrimage of Grace. Neither set out to overthrow the king, but both sought to reverse unpopular religious policies, including monastic dissolution. Misleading promises of pardon and concessions led the rebels to disperse and Henry inflicted retribution. There was no change in policy.

Instead, Henry was more affected by court faction, the difficulty of securing the succession, and his own changing passions. Anne Boleyn's failure to produce a son endangered her position, and she was brought down by factional hostility. After her execution on the trumped-up charge of adultery in 1536, Henry, however, made no attempt to reconcile himself with the Papacy. He married the innocuous Jane Seymour, but she died in 1537, after giving birth to the future Edward VI. Thereafter, there were several years of abrupt shifts. In 1539, Henry supported the reaffirmation of key Catholic doctrines in the Act of Six Articles, although he did not reverse the steps already taken by Thomas Cranmer, Archbishop of Canterbury 1533–55, and in 1540 he married the unattractive Anne of Cleves, only to reject her speedily and get rid of the marriage's supporter, Thomas Cromwell, a backer of moves towards Protestantism. Henry then married

Catherine Howard, a member of the powerful conservative faction headed by the Duke of Norfolk, but in 1542 she was executed for adultery, a charge more founded than when it was brought against Anne Boleyn. 'Divorced, beheaded, died; divorced, beheaded, survived.' The children's list of Henry VIII's wives leaves us with Catherine Parr, a Protestant widow who helped Henry find some peace in his last years. At the end of his reign, although remaining faithful to many aspects of Catholicism, Henry disgraced the Howards. The succession was left to Edward VI, and power to Jane Seymour's brother, Edward, who became Protector and Duke of Somerset. The legacy however was troublesome. Expensive wars with France and Scotland in the 1540s had exhausted royal resources and pressed hard on the economy and on society, although without causing a political crisis.

Henry kept his grip on the domestic situation, helped by his clear right to the throne, his unwillingness to turn too obviously to either religious option, and the selective use of terror, for example the execution of the Duke of Buckingham in 1521 and the Marquess of Exeter in 1539. He retained control of the government, as well as of the aristocracy through their attendance at court, through the court itself travelling, through shared participation in military activities and the hunt, and through patronage. These were more important than institutional state building, although the use of Parliament and its statutes to legislate the Reformation was significant for the current and future role of Parliament. Nevertheless, the idea that there was a revolution in government in the 1530s is questionable: Henry's preference for direct control remained the dominant theme throughout his reign.

The situation was less favourable under his successors. The Tudor state had relied hitherto on adult male rulers, the last minority had been that of Edward V in 1483, and the last attempt by a woman to reign that by Queen Matilda from 1135. Edward VI (1547–53) did not face comparable problems, but politics at the centre and control of the localities were both greatly complicated by religious disputes. They made it harder to ensure co-operation and consensus.

During Edward's reign, England was opened to the influence of Protestantism from the Continent, and there was a surge of state-supported and purposeful Protestant activity. Edward is generally seen as an enthusiastic Protestant, but this has been disputed and it has been argued that the drive to Protestantism came primarily from his ministers. The ambitious Protector Somerset allied with Cranmer consolidated Protestant worship in 1549, with the Act of Uniformity and the Book of Common Prayer. Due to Edward's minority, religious change took an institutional character different to that under Henry. The Council assumed the Royal Supremacy, and the Uniformity Acts of 1549 and 1552 provided a statutory institutional character to the Supremacy.

Hostility to religious change played a major role in the widespread uprisings in the South-West in 1549. The local gentry failed to suppress the risings and professional troops from outside the region had to do so. The rising that year in Norfolk was very different. It focused not on religious changes, but on opposition to landlords, especially their enclosure of common lands and their high rents, and to oppressive local governments. Led by Robert Kett, the rebels seized Norwich, but were crushed by professional troops at Dussindale. There was no comparison to the severity of the rebellions in 1381, 1450 and 1497. Nevertheless, the risings in 1549 indicated the extent to which developments in the 1530s–60s encouraged a degree of hostile popular response that menaced the political system and thus required the development of a new language and practice of apparent consultation within the political nation.

The risings of 1549 destabilized Somerset's government, and raised the stakes in the factionalized politics of the period. His aristocratic opponents blamed the risings on Somerset's opposition to enclosures and he was overthrown as Protector by the Council in 1549, and executed in 1552. The crucial new figure was John Dudley, Earl of Warwick, who became Lord President of the Council 1550–3, and Duke of Northumberland in 1551. A member of Henry VIII's service nobility, he was representative of general aristocratic views on economic regulation and social policy, in being uninterested in either. Concern about the possibility of fresh popular risings ensured aristocratic support for Northumberland, but his religious policy angered many peers. The Second Prayer Book of 1552 was more clearly Protestant than the first, and Catholic doctrine and practice were extirpated. Religious paintings were whitewashed, rood screens, stained glass and statues destroyed, stone altars replaced, and church vestments removed. Northumberland's position was endangered by Edward's poor health. This led the Duke to persuade the unmarried Edward to exclude his half-sisters, Mary and Elizabeth, from the succession. Instead, Lady Jane Grey, granddaughter of Henry VII through his second daughter, was declared next in line, married to Guildford Dudley, one of Northumberland's sons, and, when Edward died in July 1553, proclaimed queen.

However, Mary, in turn, proclaimed herself Queen at Norwich and began raising troops. Northumberland set out from London to defeat her, but his support crumbled away. The county elites, London, and the Council rallied to Mary, and, without a battle, Northumberland was arrested. This was a sign of the strength of the dynasty. Mary Tudor (1553–8) was a convinced Catholic determined to undo the Reformation. She persuaded Parliament to repeal Edward's religious legislation and her father's Act of Supremacy. Mary restored papal authority and Catholic practice, although a papal dispensation permitted the retention of the former Church lands by those who now held them. Their return would have alienated the powerful, and Mary appreciated the need to avoid doing so.

To secure a Catholic succession, Mary determined to marry her younger first cousin, Philip II of Spain. This plan helped provoke a series of anti-Spanish risings, of which the most serious began in Kent and was led by Sir Thomas Wyatt. However, unlike the risings in 1381 and 1450, London stayed firm. Wyatt was defeated, and Mary showed her father's firmness in disposing of potential rivals. Lady Jane Grey, her husband and her father were all executed. Mary's half-sister, Elizabeth, had been implicated, but Mary preferred to detain her.

Mary then married Philip and pressed on with the re-Catholicization of churches and services. There was also a political reaction with the restoration to favour of older aristocratic families whom Henry VIII had turned against; but Mary maintained the role of Parliament. Re-Catholicization was supported by the punishment of heretics: nearly 300 Protestants were burnt at the stake, including leaders such as

Cranmer. Many others fled. One, John Foxe, published in 1563 his *Acts and Monuments of the Church*, popularly known as the *Book of Martyrs*. This oft-reprinted martyrology was extremely influential in propagating an image of Catholic cruelty and Protestant bravery that was to sustain a strong anti-Catholic tradition. It has been seen as a basic text of Protestant Englishness. The reign of the sickly Mary was brief and she never had her hoped-for heir. War was declared on France in 1557, but it proved costly and unsuccessful. In January 1558 the French took Calais, the last English possession in France.

Mary was succeeded by Elizabeth I (1558–1603). The dying Queen maintained the order of succession although she greatly disliked Elizabeth. The latter's lengthy reign allowed for the consolidation of a relatively conservative Protestant church settlement, and, to a great extent, contrasted with the chaos of the preceding two reigns. She had to recover the monarchy from the weakness shown in those reigns. Personality was important. Like her grandfather, Henry VII, Elizabeth was a skilful manipulator. She sought to retain her independence: there was no equivalent to Somerset, Northumberland or Philip II. Religion was the crucial issue at the outset of the reign, and a challenge to stability such that Henry VII had not had to face. Elizabeth sought to avoid extremes. She was, nevertheless, a Protestant. Mary's ministers and favourites were mostly dismissed, and the political situation led Elizabeth in a more Protestant direction.

However, the Protestant settlement she introduced was more conservative than that of Northumberland. Elizabeth also sought to prevent further change and this led to disputes with the more radical Protestants, the Puritans. These disputes reflected the absence of a unified Elizabethan Protestant tradition, or a consensus. Nevertheless, despite Elizabeth's caution, there was no turning back to Catholicism, those who had lived in an unchallenged world of Catholicism died, and an increasing percentage of the population had been educated in a Protestant Christianity. This was also true of the clergy. With time, a better-educated and more committed Protestant parochial clergy developed.

Reformation entailed Protestantization as well as official English control and redefinition of the Church. Protestantism fostered individualism and greater self-reliance in some respects, but there was also a strong emphasis on the corporate relationship of England with God, a relationship that looked towards pressure for the Reformation of Manners. In addition, motives of charity were directed from masses for souls to bequests to the poor (which provided a sense of community). Traditional Catholic ways of looking at the world, which had enjoyed considerable popularity prior to the Reformation, faded out or were brought to a close. This was a major breach in the continuity of English history.

It was at the level of the national government that the crucial political decisions were made about which faith was to be the established one and how its worship was to be organized. Contemporary attitudes to ecclesiastical government and notions of toleration ensured that decisions, once made, had to be implemented throughout the state and with the assistance of the 'secular' government, in so far as such a distinction can be drawn. Distinctive religious arrangements became an expression and definition of national identity. At Elizabeth's coronation, the Epistle and the Gospel were read in Latin and then again in English. From 1603, English was used in place of Latin in the coronation.

Elizabeth became the most experienced politician in her kingdom, anxious to preserve the royal prerogative, but knowing when to yield without appearing weak. She had favourites, but did not give them power, and never married. Elizabeth was generally successful in coping with, indeed exploiting, divisions among her advisers. Like her father, she used the court to symbolize and control the exercise of authority. Furthermore, she reached beyond the Court and sought to improve relations with the gentry rather than going through the intermediary of aristocrats seeking to preserve regional power bases. The continued importance of informal channels of authority in a political and governmental system in which bureaucracy only played a limited role ensured that Elizabeth's role and skill were important.

Elizabeth faced a number of challenges. They focused on the interrelated issues of the religious settlement, the succession to the throne, and international power politics. Elizabeth's Protestant settlement aroused Catholic concern and this at a time of what has been termed the Counter Reformation: a major effort to drive back Protestantism. Clerics who refused to accept Elizabeth's settlement established seminaries on the Continent, most prominently Douai, to train missionaries to reconvert England. This led to government action against Catholics, especially priests who frequently had to hide in secret compartments: priest-holes. The situation became volatile in 1568 when the Catholic Mary, Queen of Scots, fled to England after unsuccessfully resisting domestic opponents. Grand-daughter of Henry VII through the marriage of his elder daughter Margaret to

James V, Mary was next in line in the English succession and her presence acted as a focus for discontent in England. Mary was imprisoned, but in 1569 efforts were made to free her. After a court conspiracy had been thwarted, the Northern Rising broke out. It was to be the last provincial rising in Tudor England. Although the Rising also affected the North-West through the involvement of the Dacres of Naworth, it centred in the North-East. Led by the Earls of Northumberland and Westmorland, whose local positions were endangered by a lack of royal favour, this rising was more threatening than earlier episodes, because there was a clear monarchical alternative to Elizabeth. However, the threat from the earls was lessened by the absence of foreign military support, and by their inability to reach and release Mary.

After the failure of the rising, royal power was strengthened in the North-East. This represented a major change in the political geography of England. Thereafter, there was not a serious 'Northern' problem (from within Northern England, as opposed to Scotland) for the security of governments based in Southern England, as there had been for much of the time going back to Northumbrian opposition to the expansion of the Old English house of Wessex in the tenth century. This change was to be consolidated in 1603 with the personal union of England and Scotland when Mary's son, James VI of Scotland, a Protestant, became James I of England. The failure of the Northern Rising was one of the major stages in the political unification of England, for it marked the end of any viable prospect of regional autonomy centred on a different political and/or religious agenda. Even in 1569, the rebellion had been intended to ensure a change in the policy of the central government. Thereafter, politics centred far more on national attempts to influence the centre, rather than local efforts to defy it, a situation different to that over much of the Continent.

The Northern Rising was followed by an escalation in tension between Elizabeth's government and Catholic Europe. In 1570, the Pope excommunicated and deposed Elizabeth. This encouraged a number of unsuccessful conspiracies designed to replace Elizabeth by Mary, especially the Ridolfi (1571–2), Throckmorton (1582), and Babington (1586) plots. The government responded firmly. Catholics were purged as Lords Lieutenant and as Justices of the Peace, and often arrested and fined. Elizabeth was reluctant to try her relative Mary, but the interception of her letters revealed that she had agreed to Elizabeth's assassination in the Babington Plot. As a result, Mary was convicted of treason, a questionable charge as she owed Elizabeth no allegiance. She was beheaded at Fotheringay Castle in 1587.

By then Elizabeth was at war with the leading Catholic ruler, Philip II. English raids on Spanish trade, particularly by Sir Francis Drake, and English military support for Dutch Protestant rebels against Philip, led to the outbreak of war in 1585. The most famous episode in this conflict, the first major 'modern' struggle to focus on the defence of England against a Continental foe, was the Spanish Armada of 1588. This was an attempt to send a large fleet up the Channel in order to cover an invasion from the Spanish Netherlands (modern Belgium) by the Spanish Army of Flanders under the Duke of Parma. As the fleet moved up the Channel it was harried by English warships. Although they had a high rate of fire, the English were able to inflict only limited damage. The Spaniards reached Calais, only to find that Parma's transport vessels would not sail until the English and Dutch squadrons had been defeated. Instead, the Spanish formation was disrupted by an English night attack using fireships, and the English fleet then inflicted considerable damage in a running battle off Gravelines. A strong south-westerly wind drove the Armada into the North Sea, and, with no clear tactical objective after Parma's failed embarkation, the fleet sought to return home via the hazardous north-about route around the British Isles. However, a succession of violent and unseasonal storms drove many ships onto the rocky shorelines of Scotland and Ireland.

The defeat of the Armada offered a powerful boost to English patriotism. Providence was seen at work, and the result was an apparent providential sanction to English Protestantism which was to be confirmed in 1688 by the 'Protestant Wind' that helped William of Orange when he invaded in order to remove the Catholic James II. The Armada thus gave specific force to a more general identification of England and the English with Protestantism. Such a notion of divine purpose had been impossible under the sway of the Papacy with its claims to universality, but the Reformation had totally altered the situation. Earlier, as a result of Lollardy, translation of the Bible into English had been associated with heresy, and at the beginning of the sixteenth century the language was still considered too 'rude' and 'barbarous' for the sacred text. In contrast, thanks to the Reformation, English became the language of God's word. In addition, the Church of England, the new State Church, was distinctive among Protestant Churches in government, liturgy and doctrine.

Furthermore, the very process of creating a State Church was a powerful and auspicious exercise of governmental authority. It represented a new definition of the state. The monarch was now head of the Church, but the Church was also representative of a chosen people with a sense of divine mandate. Protestant England was seen as God's New Israel. Foxe's *Book of Martyrs* provided an account of England as a kingdom that had been in the forefront of the advance towards Christian truth. After an order of convocation of 1571, cathedral churches acquired copies of Foxe's book, and many parish churches chose to do likewise. For those who could not read, Foxe's book still made a great impact through its woodcut illustrations. England's struggle with Spain further helped conflate a sense of national independence with anti-Catholicism, although, in fact, most English Catholics remained loyal, and this was recognized by the government after 1588.

Nevertheless, the requirement to be Protestant in order to be properly English was an important aspect of the process by which definitions of Englishness became narrower in this period. Other important aspects included the experience of foreign rule under Philip, and the standardization of language through London-based printing.

The Armada symbolizes Elizabeth's war with Spain for posterity and has been seen as the central event of the reign, but there was of course much else, and it inevitably contributes to a less heroic portrayal of both war and reign. War continued until 1604, and alongside successes, such as Drake's attack on the Spanish port of Corunna in 1589 and the defeat of the Spanish invasion force in Ireland at Kinsale in 1601, there were also failures. Furthermore, the Spanish navy and empire proved far more resilient than had been hoped and than was to be recalled by posterity. Fresh armadas were mounted in 1596 and 1597, although they were dispersed by storms. Convoy systems and improved coastal fortifications saw off English attacks in the Caribbean.

However, the voyages of Hawkins, Drake and others contributed not only to greater English knowledge of the outside world, but also to a sense of England as having a maritime destiny. This was encouraged by the writings of the geographer Richard Hakluyt (c. 1552–1616). His *Principal Navigations, Voiages, and Discoveries of the English Nation made by Sea or over land to the most remote and farthest distant quarters of the earth* appeared in 1589 and, as a longer work, in 1598–1600. Hakluyt's work served an equivalent function to that of Foxe. As many English voyages infringed the colonial claims of Spain and Portugal (which from 1580 to 1640 was ruled by the kings of Spain), this maritime destiny was fused with the anti-Catholic nationalism of confrontation with Spain. Profit as well as power was at stake. Commercial opportunities were actively pursued, whether shipping slaves from West Africa or spices from the East Indies (modern Indonesia), or privateering. Attempts to found settlements overseas began, although no lasting ones were established under Elizabeth. Transoceanic voyages sparked curiosity about the outside world. In Shakespeare's *King Henry VIII* (1613) a London porter wonders why there is so much noise: '. . . have we some strange Indian with the great tool come to court, the women so besiege us?' Foreign trade focused on London, the population of which grew greatly during the century: from about 120,000 in 1550 to about 200,000 in 1600.

Instead of easy victory over Spain, there was a long, hard and costly struggle that helped to make Elizabeth's rule more difficult. The nature of the English state hindered the successful pursuit of military operations. The marvellous representation of the commission of array at work in Shakespeare's *Henry IV part I*, involving Bullcalf, Mouldy, etc., was not a depiction of a well-oiled administration. Lacking a developed war machine to compare, for example, with that of the Turks, Elizabeth had to contract with adventurers and mercenaries in order to raise and sustain forces. Aside from serious administrative problems, including corruption, this ensured that the government had only limited control over operations.

Instead of a risky attempt to reform governmental structures in order to make financing and fighting the war easier, Elizabeth resorted to expedients that squandered goodwill and kept the war effort hand to mouth. Demands for additional taxation and attempts to raise funds by unpopular expedients, particularly forced loans, ship money, and the sale of monopolies to manufacture or sell certain goods, led to bitter criticism in the Parliaments of 1597 and 1601.

Parliament could define and articulate a sense of national interests different to that of the royal government. Henry VIII's use of Parliament to legitimate his dynastic and constitutional objectives had increased its frequency and role. Despite Henry's wishes, and largely due to the minority of Edward VI, parliamentary management became a more important issue. This was an aspect of a shift in the politics of the country away from a focus on relations between crown and aristocracy and, instead, towards relations between crown and gentry. At the centre, although the royal court remained the major focus of politics, this led to a greater role for Parliament and a stress on ideas of representation, and in the localities to the growing importance of the gentry as

Justices of the Peace. The rise of a more numerous and independent gentry with a sense and obligation of public duty, was linked to the failure of the peerage to be the prime beneficiary of the socio-political changes of the period. The creation of stronger links with this gentry was fundamental to the achievement of the Elizabethan period. It contrasted markedly with the earlier situation where politics was far more arranged in terms of aristocratic clientage systems.

The use of the gentry as the basis of local government ensured that state policy bore the imprint of local power, and the system worked reasonably well, although it was not readily responsive to changing demands from the monarch. The gentry proved less disruptive in national politics than many aristocrats had been in the fifteenth century.

Possibly as a result, there was nothing to match the crisis atmosphere of mid-century, either in domestic politics, the religious situation, social disorder, the succession, or Anglo-Scottish relations. Social strains, exacerbated by a sequence of disastrous harvests in 1596–8, led to a national poor law, not a major rebellion. The 1601 rebellion by the Earl of Essex – an attempt to take over the government – failed totally and did not lead to major disturbances. Irish opposition to the extension of English rule was overcome, although it entailed a much larger military effort than that against Spain. Elizabeth's wish to impose uniformity on dissident clergy in the Church led to discontent, but nothing worse. Puritan MPs failed in their 1587 attempt to legislate for a Presbyterian church settlement. The increasing widespread politicization that was a feature of sixteenth-century England did not present insuperable problems. Instead, it contributed to a stronger national consciousness.

Elizabeth's reign did not end on a triumphant note. There were problems aplenty, the government had a stop-gap feel to it, and Elizabeth was less adept and tolerant in her last years than she had been earlier in the reign. Yet there was no civil war comparable to that in France, and the Stuart succession was inaugurated in 1603 without a civil war. These were achievements, and would have been seen in this light by contemporaries. Shakespeare's *Henry VI – Richard III* plays, popular with Elizabethans, warned of horrors of civil war. In *Henry VI Part III* the audience sees a son who has killed his father in battle, 'O piteous spectacle! O bloody times! / Whilst lions war and battle for their dens, / Poor harmless lambs abide their enmity.'

NINE

STUART AND INTERREGNUM ENGLAND 1603–1714

James I's reign (1603–25) is frequently judged in terms of what came after – the collapse of Stuart authority under his son Charles I. Contemporaries often compared James unfavourably with his predecessor, Elizabeth. He and his reign seemed less glorious and successful, but this was not the full picture, and modern scholarly criticism of Elizabeth's latter years throws new light on James's achievements. James's reign also contrasted with contemporary crises in France and the Austrian Habsburg dominions. He kept England out of the destructive Thirty Years War (1618–48) on the Continent and, instead, preferred to act as a peacemaker, although without success. The major effort to overthrow James, the Gunpowder Plot of 1605, was unsuccessful, but was not followed by any governmental attempt to extirpate Catholicism. Instead, however, the anniversary of the plot became part of a national calendar, just as the accession of Elizabeth I on 17 November had made that day an occasion for celebration with church bells rung annually. James's reign also saw the high point of the English theatrical stage and the establishment of permanent colonies in North America – Virginia in 1607 and Plymouth in New England in 1620. Scottish colonies were 'planted' in subjugated Ulster.

The dynastic union with Scotland that followed the accession of James VI of Scotland as James I of England was successful in that James succeeded peaceably and there was no uprising in either England or Scotland aimed at rejecting the settlement, but this success in part stemmed from the limited change that was introduced. James's hopes of a measure of administrative, economic and legal union were not realized, not least because of English suspicion and hostility. Although James was able to adopt the new style, 'King of Great Britain' and a new flag, the Union Jack, the combination of the flags of St George and St Andrew, England did not find its identity compromised. Because he ruled in both kingdoms, James was able to pacify the Anglo-Scottish borders.

England had a degree of national consciousness that contrasted with the Continental stress on regionalism. This owed something to England's compactness, certainly compared with France. Thus, Parliament was a national body whereas in France the nearest equivalent, the Estates General, had less impact (and was not summoned between 1614 and 1789) than the regional Estates. Yet, this contrast requires some qualification. There was no equivalent on the British scale to the degree of unity within England, with the exception of Wales which was incorporated into the Westminster Parliament, the shrieval system and the English legal system with the Acts of Union of 1536–43. Ireland retained its separate Parliament until the Act of Union of 1800. Even within England there was variety. The Council of Wales and the Marches, originally established under Edward IV, was strengthened under Henry VIII and exercised control there until the Civil War and then again during the Stuart restoration. The Council of the North fulfilled the same function, although that of the West was short-lived. Chester, Durham and Lancaster were Palatinates, and Cornwall a semi-autonomous Duchy, although all bar Durham were in royal hands. Furthermore, although tolls were still levied on goods brought to urban markets, there were no internal tariffs, nor any significant differences in the law and its administration within England. A unitary state, England could not be divided to suit the views of a ruler as Lear did at the outset of Shakespeare's play (c. 1605).

James himself was perceptive, thoughtful and conciliatory, as well as complex and self-indulgent. His conciliatory character and appreciation of the constraints of his position helped limit religious tensions. He was no warrior king, and preferred to pursue controversy in print, for example in favour of the divine right of kings and against smoking and witches. He had several different self-images, including an authoritarian Constantinian image which had little time for opposition. Presenting himself as moderate, James castigated opponents as extremists. However, the bisexual and spend-thrift king presided over a corrupt and sleazy court which did little to foster the prestige of James or the monarchy or to win support for his policies. Although this prevailing image may be overdone, it reflects a less than happy situation.

This contributed to serious problems in parliamentary sessions, such that, with the exception of the acrimonious, and short, Addled Parliament of 1614, James ruled without Parliament between 1610 and 1621. Disputes focused on the cost of government, the organization of the Church, James's favourites, especially George Villiers, whom he made Duke of Buckingham, and foreign policy. More of the population, however, was far more affected by socio-economic pressures that reflected the rise in population and the pressure on resources in the rural economy.

The bad harvests of the 1590s and, to a lesser extent, 1600s led to rural disturbances, especially the Midlands rising of 1607. More generally, enclosure of common land by landlords led to bitterness and riots. Without romanticizing earlier rural society, there appears to have been a decline in paternalism and deference.

Yet it is striking that government was placed under pressure not by the poor but by the social elite, first in Scotland in 1637 and then in England and Wales in 1642. During the Civil War (1642–6) the strains of rural society led, especially in 1645, to a movement known as the Clubmen that sought to defend the interests of local communities, particularly from depredations by the troops of both sides. However, in general, this popular dimension made very little impact on the politics of the century.

Charles I (1625–49) lacked his father's intelligence, flexibility and corrupt cynicism. As a result, he was unable to overcome the problems that stemmed from his partisan and divisive policies. It is inappropriate to accept the hagiography of Charles that later apologists were to provide, although vilification is also misplaced. Charles lacked common sense, and his belief in order and in the dignity of kingship that, in part, stemmed from a dangerous combination of insecurity and self-confidence, led him to take an unsympathetic attitude to disagreement. After encountering severe problems with Parliament over his financial expedients, particularly the forced loan of 1626, and facing criticism in the Petition of Right of 1628, Charles dispensed with it in 1629 and launched his 'Personal Rule'. The early years of his reign showed that Charles was not interested in pursuing consensus. His high-handedness revealed character flaws as well as policy misjudgements. Yet, alongside Charles's inability to appreciate the legitimate concerns of his parliamentary opponents, there was also a failure of perspective on the part of many of the latter.

Personal rule was not to be a period of quiescent government, although, like the comparable period in James II's reign, foreign policy was cautious and limited. The unsuccessful wars with France (1626–9) and Spain (1624–30) were followed by a diplomacy of non-intervention while much of Europe continued convulsed by the Thirty Years War. Instead, there was a focus on trying to alter the domestic situation. The toleration of Catholics at court, where the Catholic French Queen, Henrietta Maria, was a prominent figure, was very unpopular, as was the Arminian tendency within the Church of England associated with William Laud, whom Charles made Archbishop of Canterbury in 1633. This Arminianism drew on ideas that were advanced from the late Elizabethan period, for example by Lancelot Andrewes. Laud sought to enforce uniformity. He was unwilling to permit Puritan clerics to comply occasionally with official standards, and insisted that parish churches should match the more regulated practice of cathedrals. This authoritarianism compounded the offensive nature of Laudian ceremonial and doctrine, especially a stress on the sacraments and on practices that emphasized the cleric, not the congregation. This was seen as crypto-Catholic by many; but Laudianism also led towards what was later termed Anglicanism.

Alongside change in the Church, there was also pressure on established assumptions from royal views and initiatives in financial and other matters. Charles's novel financial demands, particularly the extension of Ship Money to inland areas in 1635, were unpopular. Monopolies remained a grievance, and Charles inspired anger by his harsh treatment of critics. Prerogative courts under royal control, particularly Star Chamber and High Commission, gave out savage penalties; although not as savage as Elizabeth's.

Nevertheless, there was no rebellion and, despite Charles's poor political management and his isolation from many of those with local influence, there was no sign that his regime would collapse. For example, most people did not follow John Hampden in refusing to pay Ship Money. Instead of problems in England, Charles's inability to retain control of Scotland, which stemmed in large part from his determination to push through a stronger episcopacy, provoked the crisis that was to bring civil war to England. This raises the question of how far the history of England would have been different had there been no personal union with Scotland. James and Charles could have done much more to strengthen the union: each went only once to Scotland after 1603. This was particularly disastrous with Charles, who was effectively a stranger there, hence, in part, his bungling of the religious issue.

The outbreak of conflict in Scotland in 1639 led Charles to turn to Parliament in England in order to raise funds. The rapidly dissolved Short Parliament of 1640 proved obstreperous, but necessity forced Charles to summon in November what became the Long Parliament. This proved to be a focus for the discontent and fears that had built up during Charles's 'Personal Rule'. A breakdown of confidence in Charles made it difficult to deal with disputes over politics and religion. The Long Parliament turned on Charles's ministers and policies. Prerogative courts were abolished, the feared Earl of Strafford attainted and executed, and a

Triennial Act provided for Parliaments every three years. When, however, Parliament pressed on to demand changes in Church government, including the removal of bishops, and to seek to control the army needed to deal with a Catholic rebellion in Ireland, which broke out in October 1641, Charles determined to resist. On 4 January 1642, he entered Parliament in order to seize the 'Five Members', his leading opponents, but they had already fled by boat to the City of London, a centre of hostility to the king, especially after radicals won control of the Common Council. As both sides prepared for war, Charles left London in order to rally support. If the Irish Rebellion again raises the question of how far the British Isles affected the history of England, it is nevertheless clear that disagreements and suspicion over Church government in England were already acute. Furthermore, Charles was already distrusted, and rightly so.

England split. Each side had support in every region and social group. Parliamentary support was strongest in the most economically advanced regions – in the South, the East, and the large towns – but in each of these regions there were also many Royalists, and the relationship between socio-economic groups and religious and political beliefs were complex. The latter were important. Charles received much support as the focus for strong feelings of honour, loyalty and duty. There was also widespread disquiet about possible changes to Church government. In contrast, Puritans were his firm opponents. As a consequence of the role of religious and political beliefs, much rivalry was within, rather than between, social and economic groups.

Fighting in England started in July 1642, and Charles raised his standard at Nottingham the following month.

Initial moves quickly defined zones of control. In the first major battle of the war – Edgehill on 23 October – Charles narrowly defeated the main Parliamentary army under the Earl of Essex, but he failed to follow this up by driving decisively on London. When he did advance, Charles was checked at Turnham Green on 13 November. Failing to press home an advantage in what were difficult circumstances, Charles retreated to establish his headquarters at Oxford, his best chance of winning the war lost.

In 1643 the Royalists enjoyed considerable success. They overran most of West England, storming Bristol on 26 July, but their sieges of Gloucester and Hull both failed, and the principal battle near the crucial strategic axis of the Thames – at Newbury on 20 September – was inconclusive. In sum, the Royalists had many successes in 1643, but did not challenge the Parliamentary heartland.

In January 1644, the Scottish Covenanters invaded Northern England on the side of Parliament. Their joint siege of York led on 2 July to one of the two decisive battles of the war, when a Royalist relief army was defeated on nearby Marston Moor. The success of the Parliamentary cavalry under Oliver Cromwell played a major role in the battle. The North had been lost for Charles. Elsewhere, the Royalists were more successful in holding their own, but their cause was showing major signs of strain, with pressure on their morale and finances. War-weariness was also growing on the Parliamentary side and, as a consequence, radical religious sects were important in maintaining the dynamic of the war-effort.

In the second decisive battle of the war – Naseby on 14 June – the newly organized Parliamentary army, the New Model Army, defeated Charles, thanks in large part to the superior discipline of the Parliamentary cavalry. Thereafter Royalist bases fell and isolated Royalist forces were defeated. On 5 May 1646 Charles gave himself up to the Scots army in England, and the remaining Royalist strongholds rapidly surrendered.

Parliamentary victory was due in part to the support of the wealthiest parts of England and Scotland, especially London, and to the folly of Charles, but chance also played a key role, and the Parliamentarians were fortunate to be able to win before war-weariness sapped their effort. The Royalist army was impressive, and it took a long time for the Parliamentarians to create a winning team. The formation of the New Model was important. Its equipment and fighting style were essentially similar to those of the Royalists, but the New Model was better disciplined and supported by a more effective infrastructure and supply system. Promotion was by merit and Cromwell, the commander of the cavalry, chose officers and men imbued with the same religious fervour as his own. The army became a force for political and religious radicalism.

Having won, the victors fell out. Parliament, the army leadership and the Scots clashed over Church government, negotiations with Charles and army pay arrears, and these disputes exacerbated each other. The army was opposed to the creation of a Presbyterian establishment to replace that of the Church of England. Instead there was considerable support for a degree of religious pluralism, with toleration for independent sects.

This volatile situation led in 1648 to the Second Civil War. The Scots invaded on behalf of Charles, who had agreed to recognize Scots Presbyterianism, and there were a number of supporting Royalist risings. All were swiftly crushed. Cromwell defeated the Scots at Preston. The army followed up its victory by purging Parliament in Pride's Purge of 6 December 1648 in order to stop it negotiating with Charles. He was then tried for treason against the people. The army leaders were determined to punish Charles as a 'man of blood' who had killed the Lord's people. Thanks to religious zeal, the army had not been intimidated about confronting their anointed king. Charles refused to plead, claiming that subjects had no right to try the king and that he stood for the liberties of the people. On 30 January 1649, Charles was beheaded in Whitehall. This entrenched the ideological position of the new regime. Compromise with the Royalists was now highly unlikely.

For the first, and only, time England became a republic. Aside from executing the king and fighting his son, Charles II, the new regime also turned against the symbols of monarchy. The iconography of a new republican England was offered. This entailed replacing images of the monarchy and symbols of the legitimacy provided by dynastic continuity with those focusing on the nation. For example, Charles I's Great Seal, which had shown him, was destroyed and replaced by a new version depicting Parliament in session with a map of England, Ireland and Wales. Similarly royal emblems were replaced by the paired shields of England and Ireland. The House of Lords and the Established Church were also abolished. Parishes were allowed to determine their own form of worship.

The new regime faced a number of challenges. The Levellers, a radical group with much support in the army, pressed for major social and political changes, but their mutiny in the army in May 1649 was crushed by Cromwell. Having dashed radical hopes, Cromwell in 1649–52 conquered Ireland and Scotland, defeated an invasion by Charles II at Worcester (1651), and captured such Royalist outliers as the Isle of Man and the Channel Islands.

This was a military regime that pressed hard on England. The country had been badly damaged by the Civil Wars and yet there was still no peace. Instead, the 'Rump Parliament' left after Pride's Purge became involved in an expensive war with the Dutch (1652–4) that brought victories, but no decisive success. Furthermore, the Rump was bitterly divided and unable to agree on a religious settlement.

Once Ireland and Scotland had been conquered, army leaders sought control as well as responsibility. In April 1653 a frustrated Cromwell closed the Rump. He tried a radical nominated Parliament, named Barebone's Parliament after one of its members, Praise-God Barebone, but that proved a failure, and at the end of the year the disillusioned Cromwell became Lord Protector. In 1657, he became Protector with a ceremony that included much of the ceremonial of English monarchy: a coronation oath and enthronement. Cromwell also received the power to nominate his successor, although the Protectorate was not made hereditary in the sense of automatically passing to his son. Although he did not take the title of king and stressed that he was 'ready to serve not as king but as a constable', Cromwell lived in royal palaces with a court. Cromwell's coins displayed him with royal regalia. In 1657, he created a new Upper House.

Nevertheless, Cromwell's was a military regime, shot through with an intolerant sense of divine purpose. In 1655, largely in response to the Royalist Penruddock's Rising and the danger from Royalist conspiracies, authority in the localities was entrusted to Major Generals, instructed to preserve security, raise a decimation tax from former Royalists, and create a godly and efficient kingdom. This was an unpopular step. The Major Generals might have a role akin to that of Tudor Lords Lieutenant, but their social background was different. They were instructed to keep control over the Justices of the Peace and to take control of the militia, but they lacked the local social weight to lend traditional strength to their instructions. This followed the pattern set by the Rump of alienating and trying to circumvent the established gentry elites. There was also a major role for the army at the centre. Over 100 MPs were prevented from taking their seats in the second Cromwellian Parliament of 1656 because of the role of the military leaders.

Reliance on the Major Generals made it harder to demilitarize the regime and was unpopular not only with Royalists but also with many republicans. This unpopularity led in 1657 to the abandonment of the policy. The army, however, remained important. The Parliamentarian cause that had been so badly fractured by 1649 was ever more divided. At the same time, the regime seemed repressive because its oppressive Puritanism attacked popular rituals seen as superstitious or profane, such as Christmas and dancing round the maypole. In 1650 a parliamentary ordinance introduced the death penalty for adultery. Compulsory godliness, however, was unpopular as well as ineffective. The Puritan Cultural Revolution failed. There was widespread anxiety about the overthrow of order, not only in politics but also in religion, society and the household. Aside from relations within the family, there was also writing by women such as Margaret Fell in which a distinctly female note was heard. More generally, in the 1640s and 1650s, female petitioners claimed the right to comment on political issues.

The regime was more successful abroad. The navy was built up and English power was projected in the Baltic, the Mediterranean and further afield. Jamaica was captured in a war with Spain that began in 1655. In 1658 Cromwell's forces helped the French defeat the Spaniards at the Battle of the Dunes and were rewarded by being allowed to keep Dunkirk when it was captured, (Charles II was to sell it to France.) However, this bellicose policy was costly and made the burden of government more onerous.

Cromwell died on 3 September 1658. His successor as Protector, his son Richard, was weak, unable to command authority, and, crucially, lacked the support of the army. Richard was deposed in May 1659. The end of the Protectorate accentuated political divisions. The restored Rump Parliament, which sought to end military rule, was opposed by the army which itself was bitterly divided. The crisis led to surprisingly little violence, but was resolved by a show of force. The army commander in Scotland, George Monck, marched south, occupied London, and restored both order and a moderate Parliament. The Long Parliament was recalled, revoking Pride's Purge, and it in turn arranged new elections for a Convention based on the pre-war franchise. On 8 May 1660, the latter voted to restore Charles II.

Charles II (1660–85) possessed the skills his father so obviously lacked. Approachable and charming, Charles was flexible and pragmatic. George, Marquess of Halifax, one of his ministers, later wrote of Charles 'this Prince might more properly be said to have gifts than virtues, such as affability, easiness of living, inclinations to give and to forgive; qualities that flowed from his nature. . . . One great objection made to him was the concealing himself, and disguising his thoughts.' Charles sought to get his way, but lacked the intolerance and arrogance of his first cousin, Louis XIV of France.

The restoration of the Stuart monarchy was popular, but this did not solve the problems of government. The situation was not turned back to that before the crisis of the 1640s. The prerogative taxation and jurisdictional institutions of the 1630s, such as Ship Money and Star Chamber, were not restored. The 'Cavalier Parliament' of 1661 decided that all legislation that had received the royal assent from Charles I should stay in play. This meant that the legislation of 1641 against the methods of the Personal Rule remained in force, although not most of the subsequent legislation. All who had not actually signed Charles I's death warrant were pardoned, and there was no thorough purge of Interregnum officeholders, although most of the regicides who had signed the death warrant were executed, distrusted individuals were removed, and most land that had been confiscated from Royalists was returned. The ad hoc union with Scotland introduced under Cromwell was repealed.

Charles II had to rely on parliamentary taxation because he had little Crown land and was also granted the customs and excise on the basis of an inflated estimate of its true income. As a consequence, he had to respond to parliamentary views. He was only able to afford a small army. The Cavalier Parliament pushed Charles into a more rigid religious settlement than he would have preferred. In response to the Interregnum, the Act of Uniformity of 1662 led to the ejection of Presbyterian clergy from their parishes, while later developments led to the Test Acts of 1673 and 1678 which excluded Dissenters from office and Catholics from office and Parliament. This intolerance was a reaction to the breakdown of order in the 1640s and 1650s. Monarchy, Parliament, the Church of England and the position of the social elite were now all seen as mutually reinforcing. This was to prove an elusive harmony, but, in the meanwhile, there were brutal reminders of the vulnerability of human society. Between seventy and a hundred thousand people died in England in 1665 during the Great Plague, the last major outbreak of bubonic plague in Britain. The following year, the Great Fire of London destroyed about two-thirds of the city.

Political challenges were less calamitous, but still serious for the government's reputation and stability. War against the Dutch in 1665–7 and 1672–4 brought only limited success (although the captured New Amsterdam became New York), and in 1667 the humiliation of a Dutch raid on the English fleet in the Medway. War interacted with the religious and constitutional future of the country. By the Secret Treaty of Dover of May 1670, Charles promised Louis XIV that he would declare war on the Dutch, convert to Catholicism, and eventually restore the religion to England. In exchange, Charles got a pension from Louis which freed him from reliance on Parliament. Rumours about these secret clauses soon leaked out, and suspicion about Charles's intentions bedevilled the remainder of his reign, testing the relationship between Crown and socio-political elite. In 1672 Charles issued a Declaration of Indulgence in which he claimed the prerogative right to vary the parliamentary settlement of religious affairs. He suspended the enforcement of the laws against worship by Dissenters and permitted Catholics to worship in their own homes. Such moves fanned fears about Charles, as did the stop on payments out of the Exchequer in 1672 and the joint attack with Louis XIV on the Dutch the same year, and, more generally, Charles's favour for Catholics at court.

Worries about Charles increasingly overlapped with concern about the succession which became more acute than such concerns since the mid-sixteenth century. An active womanizer, Charles had no children by his wife, and this left his Catholic brother James, a Catholic convert, as his heir.

The paranoid political culture of the period led in 1678 to the Popish Plot. An adventurer, Titus Oates, claimed that there was a Catholic plot to assassinate Charles and replace him by James. The murder of Sir Edmund Godfrey, the London magistrate who took the evidence, and the discovery of suspicious letters in the possession of James's former private secretary, Edward Coleman, inflamed suspicions. The revelation by political rivals that Charles's leading minister, Lord Treasurer Danby, had been negotiating with Louis XIV fanned the flames. Danby fell, and the long-serving Cavalier Parliament was dissolved in January 1679. The alliance of Crown and Cavalier-Anglicanism had totally collapsed.

In a political atmosphere made frenetic by rumour and hard-fought elections, the Popish Plot became the Exclusion Crisis. This was an attempt to use Parliament to exclude James from the succession and to weaken Charles's government. Its leading advocate, Anthony, Earl of Shaftesbury, created what has been seen as the first English political party – the Whigs – while their loyalist opponents, who denied that Parliament had the right to alter the succession, were termed Tories. Both terms were initially applied as terms of abuse. Party activity developed in a highly charged atmosphere as politicization became more pronounced. This was especially so in London. Thus, the press, which had been developing from the 1620s and, particularly, the early 1640s, took very partisan positions.

Exclusion suffered, however, from a reluctance to risk civil war, and from the ability of Charles to retain control of Scotland and Ireland. As so often, England was inherently stable. Particular circumstances of politics and government were also important. Charles's right to summon and dissolve Parliament, which he adroitly employed in his dissolutions of January and March 1681, and his strength in the House of Lords denied Exclusion a constitutional passage. The example of the 1640s and 1650s was a powerful disincentive to any resort to violence.

The Whig failure to secure Exclusion was followed by a reaction that was helped by Charles's ability to dispense with Parliament thanks to peace, a rise in customs revenues, and a subsidy from Louis XIV. Whig office-holders were purged, while the Whig leadership was compromised by the Rye House Plot, an unsuccessful conspiracy of 1683 to assassinate Charles and James. Charles relied on the support of the Tories, and had the wholehearted backing of the Church of England. This regime enjoyed considerable support and was not reliant on force. Furthermore, despite uncertainty and opposition, Charles II's reign was more stable than the previous quarter-century. This was important not only for recovery from the mid-century conflicts but also for economic growth and development. Nevertheless, the purge of Whig office-holders, like previous purges from the early 1640s on, helped to keep local politics partisan and left a strong legacy of bitterness.

Foreign trade rose during Charles's reign. Compared to the following century, economic growth was modest and the stagnant, at times falling, population was a considerable damper on demand, but, in the seventeenth century, there was development in both agricultural and industrial production. It was not, however, without its costs and opponents. In 1654, John Evelyn visited East Anglia, recording: 'we viewed the fens of Lincolnshire, now much inclosed and drained with infinite expense, and by many sluices, cuts, mounds, and ingenious mills, and the like inventions; at which the city and country about it consisting of a poor and very lazy sort of people, were much displeased'. In practice, such change was frequently disruptive. For example, the traditional economy of the fenlanders was hit hard.

Charles died in 1685, to be succeeded by his brother, James II (1685–8). James inherited his father's worst characteristics: inflexibility and dogmatism. However, he was left a strong position by Charles, thanks to the reaction against Exclusion, the crippling of the Whigs, and the support of the Tories. James's position was further strengthened by the unsuccessful attempt made to overthrow him in 1685. One of Charles's illegitimate sons, James, Duke of Monmouth, mounted from his exile in the United Provinces (modern Netherlands) the first landing of an invasion force in England since the fifteenth century. Claiming that his parents had really been married, Monmouth was proclaimed king at Taunton and on 6 July attempted on nearby Sedgemoor a night attack on the recently advanced royal army. Surprise, however, was lost, the poorly organized rebel army was defeated, and Monmouth was soon after captured and executed.

Monmouth's defeat encouraged James to press on with unpopular policies. He increased the size of the army, despite parliamentary disquiet and its particular anxiety over the appointment of Catholic officers. Tension over the issue increased in 1685 because Louis XIV revoked the Edict of Nantes and, with it, the rights of French Protestants. This led to a flood of Huguenot refugees into London with tales of Catholic intolerance.

Unprepared to take criticism and unable to understand different views, James prorogued Parliament in November 1685 and, with less constraint, moved towards the Catholicizing of government, both central and local. Full religious and civil equality for Catholics was an unpopular goal, and the steps necessary to prepare for it were widely seen as unacceptable: the insistent use of prerogative action, especially the extension of the claim to dispense with the law, the build-up of a large army with many Catholic officers, and preparations for a packed Parliament. Catholics and Dissenters were installed as members of the corporations of parliamentary boroughs, and Catholics as Lords Lieutenant, while there were extensive purges of Justices of the Peace. All this went much further than Charles II in 1681–5, and hit hard at the relationship between Crown and elite. For example, in Hull the mayor and aldermen were dismissed.

The situation became more threatening in 1688. By his first marriage, James had had two daughters (Mary and Anne), both Protestants married to Protestants, while, as yet, he had had no surviving child by his second marriage, to the Catholic Mary of Modena, in 1673. The birth on 10 June 1688 of a Prince of Wales was a major shock. Despite reports that the baby was smuggled into the bedchamber in a warming pan, there is no doubt that the child was Mary's, although many preferred to think otherwise. Nineteen days later, Archbishop Sancroft of Canterbury and six bishops were acquitted on charges of sedition, for refusing to read James's order that the Declaration of Indulgence of 1687 granting all Christians full equality of religious practice be read from all pulpits. James's basis of support was narrow, but there was no rebellion. His position collapsed only as a result of a challenge from without.

The acquittal of the bishops was followed by an invitation from seven politicians to James's elder son-in-law, William III of Orange, to intervene in order to protect Protestantism and traditional liberties. William, in fact, had already decided to invade. In an escalating international crisis, he wished to keep England out of the French camp and, instead, to ensure that English resources were at his disposal. Nevertheless, the invitation from conspirators subsequently described as 'the immortal seven', was important to William as he wished to arrive as a liberator, not a conqueror.

William's first invasion attempt – in mid-October 1688 – was defeated by storms at sea, but, on his second attempt, after an unopposed passage, William landed at Brixham in Devon on 5 November. William was outnumbered on land by James, but the latter was hit by indecision, ill-health and a crisis of confidence that in part arose from dissension and conspiracy among the officers. Instead of fighting William, James abandoned his army. His position was also affected by a number of provincial uprisings, although alongside towns seized for William, such as Derby, Nottingham and York, were others, such as Chester and Newcastle, that successfully resisted. William refused to stop his advance in order to permit negotiations, and James fled London. Captured and returned to the capital, James was encouraged to flee a second time, so that William could claim that he had deserted the country.

This was a coup, not a revolution. William was determined to be ruler, and, far from being willing to concede that his wife, Mary, should be monarch, William insisted on a joint monarchy. Parliament declared that James had abdicated, rather than the more radical notion that he had been deposed. Parliament debarred Catholics from the succession, ending the rights of James's infant son, and Anne's rights in the succession were subordinated to those of William. Nevertheless, there were restrictions on royal power. The financial settlement left William with an ordinary revenue that was too small for his peacetime needs, obliging him to turn to Parliament for support. A standing army was prohibited unless permitted by Parliament.

What was to be termed by its supporters the Glorious Revolution was to play a central role in the Whiggish, heroic, self-congratulatory account of English development. It was clearly important in the development of an effective parliamentary monarchy in which the constitutional role of Parliament served as the anchor of co-operation between Crown and socio-political elite. Yet a less benign account is also possible, and not only from the perspective of the exiled James and his Jacobite supporters or of Scotland and Ireland in each of which the Williamite position was established only after considerable conflict. There were also grave problems in England. The instability of the ministries of the period 1689–1721 suggests that the political environment necessary for an effective parliamentary monarchy had in some ways been hindered by the events of 1688–9. A parliamentary monarchy could not simply be legislated into existence. It required the development of conventions and patterns of political behaviour that would permit a constructive resolution of contrary opinions. This took time and was not helped by the burdens of the lengthy war that followed the Glorious Revolution. William's seizure of power did not assist this process of resolution for other reasons: alongside praise for him as a Protestant and providential blessing, there was criticism of him as a usurper. These views were marginalized, not because of their inherent absurdity, or necessary incompatibility with English national character, but because the circumstances of William's reign (1689–1702) permitted him a political and polemical victory over his opponents. As a result, the Protestant and Whiggish vision associated with the victors eventually came to seem natural to the English.

If in 1688 England was successfully invaded, by 1763 Britain was the strongest power in the world. By 1688, England had seized no major territories from France or Spain; but by 1763 the situation was very different. The conflicts of the period (1689–97, 1702–13, 1739–48, 1756–63) were important not only in the expansion of the British empire, but also in the country's internal development. In the Nine Years War (1689–97), William III stemmed the French advance in the Low Countries and defeated James II's supporters in Scotland and Ireland.

The cost of the war forced William to accept the discipline of parliamentary monarchy. Elections became more frequent. The Triennial Act of 1694 ensured regular meetings of the Westminster Parliament and, by limiting their life-span to a maximum of three years, required regular elections. There were ten elections between 1695 and 1715, and this helped to encourage a sense of volatility. The war also led to a regularization of public finances that introduced principles of openness and parliamentary responsibility. The funded national debt, guaranteed by Parliament and based on the Bank of England, which was founded in 1694, enabled the government to borrow large sums of money at a low rate of interest. After the conflict was over, William was forced to accept an unwelcome degree of demobilization and strong criticism of his advisers and policies. The latter reflected not only the more prominent role of Parliament but also the greater freedom of the press: the Licensing Act had lapsed in 1695 and, thereafter, there was no system of pre-publication censorship.

Attempts to settle Anglo–French differences, which included Louis XIV's recognition of James II's son as King of England, broke down and in the War of the Spanish Succession, in which England was involved between 1702 and 1713, troops under John Churchill, 1st Duke of Marlborough, drove the French from Germany and the Low Countries, but other forces were less successful in Spain. Marlborough won major victories at Blenheim (1704), Ramillies (1706), and Oudenaarde (1708), but was less successful at Malplaquet (1709). The war ended with the Peace of Utrecht (1713), which brought French recognition of their failure to dominate Western Europe. Furthermore, wartime gains, such as Gibraltar, Minorca and Nova Scotia, were formally ceded to Britain.

The war also saw major change within Britain, especially the parliamentary Union of England and Scotland in 1707. This was the culmination of a process that had been apparent in 1650–2, 1660 and 1689–91: England and Scotland were no longer to go different ways. The Scots lost their Parliament in Edinburgh, but gained representation in Westminster. The distinctiveness of the Scottish legal system and established Church – Presbyterian since 1690 – were maintained. The implications for England appeared less important, not least because it was the more populous and wealthier of the two states. The new British political system was dominated by England. Politicians in London had to consider how best to 'manage' Scotland. There was no equivalence for Scotland. The influence on English history that Scotland had wielded between 1637 and 1647 was no more.

However tenuously, a link can be drawn between the willingness to conceive of new political structures and governmental arrangements, and increased interest in taking an active role in first understanding the world and then seeking to profit from this understanding. The medieval Church had originally set its face against any systematic 'scientific' enquiry, on the grounds that man was only intended to know the mind of God as interpreted by itself. Early Protestants, similarly, although rejecting the role of the Church, believed that all necessary knowledge was to be found in the scriptures. In the early seventeenth century, however, Francis Bacon (1561–1626) popularized the idea that God actually intended man to recover that mastery over nature which he had lost at the fall: it was (along with the Protestant Reformation) part of the preparation for the second coming of Christ.

Thus, scientific enquiry not only became legitimate, but almost a religious duty to the devout Protestant. This idea became immensely influential among the English and Dutch intelligentsia of the mid- and later seventeenth century, and had a major long-term impact in preparing the way for the so-called Scientific Revolution. The leading figure in this revolution, Isaac Newton (1642–1727), made fundamental advances in astronomy, mathematics and physics. His work contributed powerfully to a developing ideology of scientific advance.

TEN

THE EIGHTEENTH CENTURY 1714–1815

Union with Scotland and, more generally, the Revolution Settlement which followed the Glorious Revolution, were put to the test between 1714 and 1716. William III's sister-in-law and successor, Queen Anne (1702–14), had numerous children but none survived childhood. By the Act of Settlement of 1701, the house of Hanover, descendants of James I through his daughter, were promised the succession, and this led to George, Elector of Hanover, becoming George I in 1714. This was not immediately contested, but discontent rapidly developed in both England and Scotland. George replaced Anne's Tory ministers by a Whig ascendancy that left the Tories no option in government service. This reflected George's distrust of the Tories, whom he saw as sympathetic to Jacobitism – the cause of the exiled Stuarts – and also the difficulty of operating a mixed Whig–Tory ministry, although he also saw the danger of being a prisoner of a Whig majority.

The Jacobite rising of 1715–16 was the most serious response. Although it centred on Scotland, there was also a rising in North-East England in 1715. This led to an advance on Preston where the Jacobites were defeated, as the Scots had been in 1648. Thereafter, Jacobitism remained a threat, but not one that was central to political life. Indeed, until the next Jacobite rising in 1745, divisions among the Whigs took precedence. They focused on competition for ministerial office as well as on differences over foreign policy. The most powerful Whig in this period was Robert Walpole, a Norfolk gentleman landowner. Although he led those Whigs who were in opposition between 1717 and 1720, thereafter he was in office until his fall and retirement in 1742. Between 1720 and 1722, Walpole benefited from the fall-out of the South Sea Bubble, a major financial scandal that compromised leading ministerial figures, and also from the unexpected deaths of his two leading Whig opponents, Stanhope and Sunderland. He swiftly rose to dominate politics.

Walpole was invaluable to George I (1714–27) and George II (1727–60) as government manager and principal spokesman in the House of Commons, and as a skilful manager of the state's finances. He also played a major role in the successful elections of 1722, 1727 and 1734. Aside from his policies, Walpole was adept in parliamentary management and in his control of government patronage. He helped to provide valuable continuity and experience to the combination of limited monarchy with parliamentary sovereignty. While Walpole maintained a Whig monopoly of power, he took more care than his predecessors not to support policies that would alienate Tory opinion. In particular, his refusal to extend the rights of Dissenters contributed to a lessening of religious tension. As Dissent came to be seen as less of a threat, so it became easier to lessen differences between Whigs and Tory clerics.

The Walpolean system had its defeats, most publicly the failure of the Excise Scheme of 1733, a plan to reorganize indirect taxation, but it lasted until 1742, the longest period of stable one-party rule in a system of regular parliamentary scrutiny. Then, Walpole succumbed to a combination of hostility from the reversionary interest – the active opposition of Frederick, Prince of Wales – and a sense that he was somehow losing his grip. Against Walpole's wishes, Britain had gone to war with Spain in 1739 – the War of Jenkins' Ear – and he was blamed for the failure to win hoped-for victories.

Walpole's fall led to a period of political instability as politicians vied for control, but, from 1746, Walpole's protégé, Henry Pelham, 1st Lord of the Treasury since 1743, was in a position to pursue Walpolean policies: fiscal restraint, unenterprising legislation, preserving a Whig monopoly of power and the status quo in the Church, and seeking peace. If this political system maintained social inequality, that was very much what those with power expected. This was a society that took inegalitarianism for granted, although there was a certain amount of social criticism. In his *The History of the Life of the late Mr Jonathan Wild the Great* (1743), Henry Fielding offered a satirical indictment of false greatness: 'the Plowman, the Shepherd, the Weaver, the Builder and the Soldier, work not for themselves but others; they are contented with a poor pittance (the Labourer's Hire) and permit us the GREAT to enjoy the Fruits of their Labours'. The blatant corruption of the political system led to considerable criticism. In John Gay's *The Beggar's Opera* (1728), Walpole was referred to as if a crook with a series of aliases: 'Robin of Bagshot, alias Gorgon, alias Bluff Bob, alias Carbuncle, alias Bob Booty . . .'.

The religious establishment could similarly be probed both for effectiveness and for failure, some of it self-serving. Yet, alongside pluralism, non-residence, appointments due to patronage, and a very unequal system of payment of clerics, there was conscientiousness and the provision of regular services in most parishes. Methodism developed in the 1730s, but this, and other, aspects of religious enthusiasm reflected not so much a failure of the Church of England as the contradictions inherent in a national body that had to serve all as well as enthusiasts. In addition, there was an international dimension to Protestant evangelicalism, so that it is not explicable solely in English terms.

The year 1746 also saw the final crushing of Jacobitism. In 1745, Bonnie Prince Charlie – Charles Edward Stuart, the elder grandson of James II – had successfully raised much of Scotland for the Stuarts. In November 1745 he invaded England. The Jacobites did not only want a Stuart Scotland, not least because a Hanoverian England would not allow the existence of a Jacobite Scotland. Carlisle fell after a short siege, and Charles Edward then advanced unopposed through Lancaster, Preston and Manchester, reaching Derby on 4 December. Opposing forces had been outmanoeuvred. However, this was very much an invasion. The Highland chiefs were discouraged by a lack of English support (as well as by the absence of a promised French landing in Southern England). They forced Bonnie Prince Charlie to turn back from Derby on 6 December.

This may well have been a defining moment in English history. Had the Jacobites advanced they might have won, ensuring that the new state created in 1688–9 and 1707, with its Protestant character and limited government, would have been altered. Although Jacobites called for a restoration of liberties, and a balanced constitution, Jacobite victory might have led to a Catholic, conservative, autocratic and pro-French England/Britain, or, in turn, such a state might have provoked a violent reaction akin to that of the French Revolution.

Instead, Charles Edward was eventually heavily defeated by William, Duke of Cumberland, the second son of George II, at Culloden near Inverness on 16 April 1746. The Whig Ascendancy was not to be overcome from outside. Thanks to this victory, as well as to a growing economy, an expanding population, and a powerful world empire, there was a strong feeling of national confidence and superiority. This replaced seventeenth-century anxiety and a marked sense of inferiority *vis-à-vis* Louis XIV's France. Whig confidence broadened in mid-century into the cultural moulding of the notion and reality of a united and powerful country. It was no coincidence that 'Rule Britannia' was composed in 1740. Cultural nationalism and xenophobia were other aspects of growing assertiveness. In part, this was a continuation of earlier anti-Popery and, in part, involved a hostile response to cosmopolitan influences. Thus, John Gay's English-language ballad-operas, such as *The Beggar's Opera* (1728), were a response to Italian opera. In addition to the new cult of Shakespeare, the Royal Academy, founded in 1768, and its long-serving first president, Sir Joshua Reynolds, advanced the dignity of British art.

Britishness was one response to the need to create a political culture to accompany the new state formed in 1707 by the Act of Union. Sympathetic Scots made a major contribution. Yet Britishness was also in many respects a product of English triumphalism and, in part, a vehicle for it. Conceptions of Englishness, not least of the notion of a chosen Protestant nation, and of a law-abiding society, were translated into Britishness. There was a sense of superiority over Scotland, Wales, Ireland and the rest of the world. Although, in the period 1714–45, many people thought England was being ruined by the rising national debt and becoming corrupt and weak under the Hanoverians, mid-century victories helped to produce a self-confidence in England's destiny. The English dimension of Britishness is one that for long received insufficient attention, but was highlighted by Scottish and Welsh separatists in the twentieth century. They, however, emphasized the extent to which the creation of Britain rested in large part on military conquest, and underplayed the vitality of England as a model. In part, the skill of the concept of Britishness rested on its ability to draw on assessments of Englishness but not to associate them too closely with England. Alongside Britishness, there were still vigorous senses of local, provincial and national identities.

Englishness/Britishness was contrasted with Continental Europe. It was argued that the English were free, and this contributed to a public myth of uniqueness. The Common Law was seen as a particularly English creation, was contrasted with legal precepts and practice in, above all, France, and enjoyed marked attention. Liberty and property, and freedom under the law were cried up as distinctly English. Foreign commentators observed a lack of deference to the King and to aristocrats in elections and in the life of counties, even though the reality was that, as the century progressed, wealthy aristocrats grew richer and controlled more and more boroughs. The Whigs in power grew complacent and intellectually bankrupt. They forgot the demand made by the 1st Earl of Shaftesbury and the Exclusion Whigs for a freeholder franchise in all boroughs.

The defeat of Jacobitism was one stage in a struggle with France that led to fighting in 1743–8 and 1754–63 (although war was only declared in 1744 and 1756). This ended with the Thirteen colonies on the Eastern seaboard of North America, and the British possessions in India secure, with Canada and the French bases in West Africa and the West Indies captured, and with the Royal Navy unchallengeable at sea. Key victories included three in 1759, the 'year of victories', James Wolfe's outside Québec and the naval victories of Lagos and Quiberon Bay. Two years earlier, the East India Company was established as the most powerful power in Bengal when Robert Clive defeated the Nawab of Bengal at Plassey.

Imperial conquest did not conform to the mores of the early twenty-first century and there is profound ambivalence, not to say amnesia towards Britain's imperial past. At the time, however, victories and conquests abroad were deplored by few. Britain was ruled not by Quakers, but by a political elite determined to pursue national interests and destiny across the oceans of the world, and this resonated with the aspirations of the wider political public. Truly a world that is lost, but one that cannot be disentangled from the history of the period.

It was not only Britain's global position that was changing. There was also a series of developments in the economy and society that contributed to the move towards what has been subsequently termed the Industrial Revolution. Neither economy nor society was static, and for centuries the pressures of an increasingly insistent market economy had encouraged change, a process facilitated by the availability of investment income and the absence of internal tariffs. The amount of coal shipped from the Tyne rose to 400,000 tons by 1625 and to well over 600,000 in 1730–1, much of it going to London. Coal represented a major development as a fuel source. It gave a more predictable heat than timber. Coal was the main fuel in sugar refining, brewing, glass-making, salt-boiling and brick-making by 1700. The ability to create and apply power was increased with the steam engine. The first one was demonstrated by Thomes Savery in 1698, and improved by Thomas Newcomen, with his Atmospheric Engine of 1712. This pumped water out of coal mines and Cornish tin mines.

The initial value of the steam engine was specific to particular locations. Population trends were far more widespread in their impact. After population growth from 1500, the English population fell between 1660 and 1690, probably, in part, due to enteric fevers and gastric diseases, but, thereafter, the population began to pick up. The population for England and Wales probably rose from 5.18 million in 1695 to 5.51 in 1711 and 5.59 in 1731 and, despite a serious demographic crisis in 1741–2, 6.20 in 1751. Thereafter, it rushed ahead, to 8.61 million in 1801.

Average age at first marriage fell from the 1730s to the 1830s, particularly from the 1730s to the 1770s. Infant mortality rates fell in the second half of the eighteenth century, maternal rates throughout the century, and adult rates particularly in the first half of the century. Marital fertility among women aged thirty-five and over rose from mid-century. The rise in marital fertility was probably the consequence of a fall in stillbirths, and this can be seen as evidence of rising living standards.

The rising population affected both rural and urban England. In the countryside, where the bulk of the population lived until the mid-nineteenth century, rising demand for food-stuffs benefited landlords and tenant farmers, not the landless poor. Agricultural wages remained below fifteenth-century levels in real terms. The position of the rural poor was further hit by enclosure. About a quarter of England's agricultural land was directly affected by enclosure through Acts of Parliament, of which there were 5,265 for England alone in 1750–1850. Much of the Midlands in particular was enclosed during the century. Enclosure made it easier to control the land, through leases. Rents and land values rose to the profit of landowners. Enclosure also made it easier to control people as many yeoman farmers became labourers. Enclosing landowners created wide disruption of traditional rights and expectations, common lands and routes. The propertyless lost out badly, especially with the loss of communal grazing rights. This was not a rural society of simple deference and order, but one in which aristocratic hegemony was seen as selfish by many, as custom was displaced by harsh statutory enactments. Landed society celebrated its position and spent its money on splendid stately homes and on surrounding grounds which increasingly changed from geometric patterns towards a naturalistic parkland style that was developed by 'Capability Brown'. This was to become part of the visual character of Englishness, a counterpoint to the hedgerows of the enclosed worked landscape. Both reflected the power relationships of the period.

Some of the rural population migrated to the towns, helping to counter the impact of the higher death rates there. The percentage of the population living in towns, defined as settlements with more than about 2,000 people, rose from about 17 in 1700 to about 27.5 in 1800. The most important by far was London. In 1700, it had more than half a million people and in 1800 more than a million, making London by then the most populous European city and over ten times larger than the second city in England. As a result, London established notions of urban life. Through its central role in the world of print, London shaped news, opinion and fashion. It was the centre of finance and government, law and trade. The West End of London established the 'classical' style of Georgian town-building. London was disproportionately important to the character of England, in so far as such a concept can be used. It helped promote the interaction of bourgeois/middle-class and aristocratic thinking and values, and also helped secure the influence of commercial considerations upon national policy. Furthermore, London helped to mould a national economic space, although it is clear that specialization for the London market was accompanied by the persistence of more local economic patterns.

London was the Britain/England visited by most foreigners who praised its constitution and society and held them up as a model. Institutions and practices such as trial by jury, a free press, Parliamentary government and religious toleration were widely praised, although their problems and limitations could be overlooked.

The extent to which London offered different prospects to those of landed society was captured by George Lillo in his play *The London Merchant* (1731). This deliberately focused on ordinary people. 'A London apprentice ruined is our theme' declared the prologue. In the dedicatory preface to the printed version, Lillo claimed that tragedy did not lose 'its dignity, by being accommodated to the circumstances of the generality of mankind. . . . Plays founded on moral tales in private life may be of admirable use'.

Other towns also expanded and played a major role. In 1700, there were only five English towns with more than

10,000 inhabitants: Norwich, Bristol, Newcastle, Exeter and York. By 1800, the number (twenty-seven) included important industrial and commercial centres in the North and Midlands, such as Manchester, Leeds, Sheffield, Sunderland, Bolton, Birmingham, Stoke and Wolverhampton. Smaller towns also expanded.

Urban economies were helped by the growing commercialization of life and by the rise of professions such as law and medicine. The infrastructure of, and for, money transformed the nature of the domestic market and of townscapes. New covered markets and shops were opened, as were banks and insurance offices. In a world of 'things', where increasing numbers could afford to purchase objects and services of utility and pleasure, towns played a central function as providers of services as much as of commercial and industrial facilities. Theatres, assembly rooms, subscription libraries and shops all provided services to townspeople and to the nearby rural population. Parks and walks replaced old town gates and walls. This helped bring renewed cultural activity to provincial centres. The dynamic character of urban life was seen in the number of town histories published – 241 between 1701 and 1820. This was civic pride with a purpose. Town life was presented as the cutting edge of civilization. Towns were crucial to provincial culture and also to the vitality of the middling part of society, which was subsequently to be known as the middle class.

Towns were also the nodes on the transport system. This expanded greatly with the creation of turnpike trusts, authorized by Parliament to raise capital and charge travellers in order to construct turnpike roads. By 1770 there were 15,000 miles of turnpike road in England, and most of the country was within 12.5 miles of one. Although turnpike trusts reflected local initiatives, a national system was created. Travel was made faster and more predictable by the development of stagecoach services, the cross-breeding of fast Arab horses, the replacement of leather straps by steel coach springs, and the introduction of elliptical springs. The time of a journey from Manchester to London fell from three days in 1760 to 28 hours in 1788.

Speed was less important for the coal moved by the new canals developed from the 1750s. They cut the cost of transporting bulk goods. By 1790, the industrial areas of the Midlands were linked to the Trent, Mersey, Severn and Thames. This was not new technology, but the rate of canal construction reflected demand from a rapidly burgeoning economy as well as the availability of investment and a sense that change was attainable and could be directed. The last was most important to what is known as the Industrial Revolution. A belief in its possibility and profitability fired growth.

This was a case not only of more of the same, important as that was, but also of changes in the nature of the economy, society, and culture. The relative importance of industry as a source of wealth and employment rose, and England became less agricultural. Industrialization contributed powerfully to a culture of improvement, a conviction that modern achievements were superior to those of former times, and an at times heroic exultation of the new world of production, seen for example in paintings of industrial scenes such as Coalbrookdale.

Coal and steam power were increasingly important. Coal was not only a readily transportable and controllable fuel. It was also plentifully available in many areas, although not in most of

South or East England. Combined with the application of steam power to coal mining, blast furnaces, and the new rolling and slitting mills, this led to a new geography of economic activity. Industry was increasingly attracted to the coalfields, especially to the North-East, to South Lancashire and to South Staffordshire. James Watt's improvement to the steam engine made it more energy efficient and flexible. In the 1790s, developments in metallurgy made it easier to produce malleable iron. Other industries, such as textiles, also benefited greatly from technical developments which increased productivity and created a sense of ongoing improvement. In his *Inquiry into the Nature and Causes of the Wealth of Nations* (1776), Adam Smith regretted expenditure on successive wars but continued:

> though the profusion of government must, undoubtedly, have retarded the natural progress of England towards wealth and improvement, it has not been able to stop it. The annual produce of its land and labour is, undoubtedly, much greater at present than it was either at the restoration [1660] or at the revolution [1688]. The capital, therefore, annually employed in cultivating this land, and in maintaining this labour, must likewise be much greater. In the midst of all the exactions of government, this capital has been silently and gradually accumulated by the private frugality and good conduct of individuals, by their universal, continual, and uninterrupted effort to better their own condition. It is this effort, protected by law and allowed by liberty to exert itself in the manner that is most advantageous, which has maintained the progress of England towards opulence and improvement in almost all former times, and which, it is to be hoped, will do so in all future times.

This assessment of economic progress as dependent on freedom, the rule of law and limited government was to be very important to the English conception of national history and development. It failed to give much attention to the social problems arising from economic growth.

While it is important not to exaggerate the scale of economic change, especially the number of factories, it was more extensive in Britain than elsewhere in Europe or the world. Industrialization was to make Britain's the most powerful economy in the world, but this did not prevent a series of major political failures in the last third of the eighteenth century, including the loss of the Thirteen Colonies in the War of American Independence (1775–83) and defeat at the hands of Revolutionary France in 1793–5. The first reflected widespread, although far from universal, American suspicion of the policies and intentions of George III (1760–1820), and a British failure to adapt parliamentary sovereignty to the needs and aspirations of colonists. The British government underestimated the extent of opposition and then found it difficult to conduct the war successfully.

Major American towns, such as New York and Philadelphia, could be captured, but decisive victory eluded the British, and in 1777 they lost one army at Saratoga. Furthermore, after France (in 1778) and Spain (1779) entered the war, the British were in a more vulnerable position, as these powers could contest British control of the sea. In 1781, the army in Virginia was surrounded and forced to surrender at Yorktown. This ied to a collapse of confidence in the war, the fall of Lord North's government, and a willingness to concede independence. This was done in 1783. The British also had to cede territory to France and Spain.

The loss of America raises questions about the effectiveness of British government, but it was far from easy to govern transoceanic empires in a flexible fashion. It is more instructive to note the essential political stability of Britain in the 1750s–80s. This description of England may seem surprising, as this was a period noted for constitutional disputes, especially in the 1760s, 1782–4 and 1788–9, and also for extra-parliamentary action, some of it radical, for example the Wilkesite agitation of the 1760s and the Yorkshire Association movement of the early 1780s. However, discord was compatible with a stable political system, although a degree of ambivalence towards the notion of a loyal opposition helped to blind many contemporaries to this. Ministries were stable as long as they could avoid unforeseen problems and retain royal confidence. They did not lose general elections. Lord North, Prime Minister 1770–82, won the elections of 1774 and 1780, but was brought down in March 1782 by his inability to secure a satisfactory solution to the American Revolution.

William Pitt the Younger, Prime Minister 1783–1801 and 1804–6, won the elections of 1784, 1790 and 1796, but nearly fell in 1788–9 due to George III's apparent madness, and resigned in 1801 because he could not persuade George to accept Catholic emancipation. Pitt the Younger brought an important measure of stability after the political chaos and general loss of confidence of 1782–3. He revived government finances and helped ensure a revival of British international influence. In 1787, British-encouraged Prussian intervention in the United Provinces (modern Netherlands) overthrew the pro-French Dutch government.

More generally, British government relied on co-operation with the socio-political elite, and lacked the substantial bureaucracy and well-developed bureaucratic ethos that would have been necessary had it sought to operate without such co-operation. This co-operation extended to newly prominent social and economic interests. They were incorporated into the state.

The major challenge to this system came from the French Revolution. This began in 1789, and aroused widespread interest in England. As the Revolution became more radical, this interest became more hostile to the Revolution. The French threat to Britain's Dutch ally in the winter of 1792–3, led in 1793 to the outbreak of war. Both the domestic response and the war itself caused major problems. Radicalism was encouraged by the example of France. This led both to government action and, from 1792, to a wave of loyalism in England. The government sought to suppress radical organizations. Habeas Corpus was suspended, radicals were tried for sedition, and their newspapers suffered from the rise in newspaper duty. The Treasonable Practices Act and Seditious Meetings Act of 1795 sought to prevent denunciations of the constitution and large unlicensed meetings. These measures hindered the radical societies.

Radicalism was weakened by its association with France. Parliamentary reform, which had been widely supported in the 1780s, was not pressed forward. The francophile and increasingly radical Earl of Shelburne, who had been Prime Minister in 1782–3, found that his ideas were unpopular. In 1787, he had written, 'it is the Public which decides upon measures with us'. In 1791, he praised the French National Assembly for determining that the right of making peace and war came from the nation, not the Crown, and he urged the British government to follow the example of trusting the people. In 1798, Shelburne pressed the Lords for parliamentary reform 'while it could be done gradually, and not to delay its necessity till it would burst all bounds'. Yet, the political world had become more conservative and cautious thanks to the Revolution. Reform was retarded. Signs of popular agitation were increasingly viewed with suspicion. Trade unions were hindered by the Combination Acts of 1799 and 1800.

These moves owed much to the acute problems of the war years. The cost and economic disruption of the war led to inflation, the collapse of the gold standard under which the value of paper currency was met by the Bank of England (1797), the introduction of income tax (1799), the stagnation of average real wages, and widespread hardship, particularly in the famine years of 1795–6 and 1799–1801. These problems were accentuated by the benefits that others, such as farmers, drew from the economic strains of the period. Aside from serious food rioting, there were also, in 1797, naval mutinies that owed much to anger over pay and conditions. The mutinies threatened national security.

Yet, despite this, the country did not collapse. The greater popularity of George III in the 1790s helped. He cultivated the image of being a father to all and did not inspire the negative feelings that focused on his French and Spanish counterparts. The association of radicalism with the French also helped to damn it for most people, not least because of the anarchy, terror and irreligion associated with the Revolution. Patriotism received a new boost in the lengthy struggle, which was less divisive than the War of American Independence. In response to the French Revolutionaries and their allies, nationalism was defined in a conservative fashion, and conservatism was increasingly nationalist in tone and content. War with France was justified on moral grounds. Loyalism was a genuine mass movement. The widespread volunteer movement helped raise forces to repel any planned invasion. In the 1800s, 'God Save the King' came to be called the national anthem.

The war sorely tested Britain. In July 1791, London audiences applauded the final lines of George Colman's new play *The Surrender of Calais*:

> Rear, rear our English banner high
> In token proud of victory!
> Where'er our god of battle strides
> Loud sound the trump of fame!
> Where'er the English warrior rides,
> May laurelled conquest grace his name.

This was not to be the experience of British forces when war broke out in 1793.

In 1794 the British were driven from the Austrian Netherlands (Belgium), in 1795 the French overran the United Provinces, and from 1796 Britain was threatened by invasion. Despite important naval victories, especially the Glorious First of June (1794), Cape St Vincent (1797), the Nile (1798), and Copenhagen (1801), in 1802 the government had to accept the Peace of Amiens which left Britain isolated and France dominant in Western Europe.

The abortive Irish rising of 1798 and the unsuccessful French attempt to intervene encouraged an Act of Union between Britain and Ireland in 1800; the Act came into effect on 1 January 1801. Following the 1707 Act of Union between England and Scotland, it created a single state for the entire British Isles, although it was to have only limited success in producing a lasting primary British identity. Alongside such an identity, national allegiances remained, particularly in Ireland.

Napoleon had seized power in France in 1799, and in 1803 distrust of his aggressive expansionism led to a resumption of the conflict. In the face of preparations for invasion, volunteer units manoeuvred along the South coast. In 1805, the French tried to achieve a covering naval superiority in the Channel, but their complex scheme was mishandled and thwarted by an alert British response. Cancelling his invasion plans, Napoleon turned east to attack Austria. En route from Cadiz for Italy, the Franco-Spanish fleet was intercepted off Cape Trafalgar by Horatio Nelson on 21 October 1805, and heavily defeated, with the loss of nineteen ships of the line, in the greatest of all British naval triumphs. Nelson, however, died in the moment of triumph.

Trafalgar did not prevent Napoleon from defeating Austria (1805) and Prussia (1806). French control of much of Continental Europe helped encourage a sense of British distinctiveness and superiority, but Napoleon sought to exclude Britain from European trade. This proved impossible, but indicated the threat posed by French dominance. Napoleon's attempt to impose control on Spain and Portugal provoked bitter resistance from 1808 which was aided by British troops. Initially, the British struggled to protect Portugal, but they were increasingly able to challenge the French position in Spain. By late 1813 the Duke of Wellington was leading the British army into South-West France. By then, Napoleon had been defeated in Russia

(1812) and Germany (1813). With France invaded in early 1814, Napoleon was forced to abdicate. He sought to regain power in 1815, but on 18 June was defeated at Waterloo by an Allied army under Wellington in which the British played a key role.

By then Britain was dominant through much of the transoceanic European world. Amphibious British forces captured the French overseas bases, such as Mauritius and Pondicherry, as well as many of those of France's client states, for example the Dutch bases of Cape Town and Batavia (Jakarta). Furthermore, during the Revolutionary and Napoleonic wars, Britain defeated her Indian rivals – Mysore and the Marathas – and prevented America's attempt to conquer Canada in the War of 1812. As British negotiators sat down at Vienna to help redraw the map of Europe, Britain's century was beginning.

ELEVEN

THE NINETEENTH CENTURY 1815–1914

A number of narratives can be offered for this period: the spread of empire, the growth of the economy, the changes in society, and the development of the political system. The order in which these are discussed offers an implicit prioritization, but it is far from clear how this should be defined. On the global scale, the spread of empire was most striking. Possibly the most important theme, however, because it created the resources for everything else, was the development of the economy, although this development, in turn, reflected changes and conditions in a variety of spheres. Empire created markets, and political and social circumstances contributed to growth.

Although changes in the eighteenth century already discussed were important, the scale of development in the nineteenth century was unprecedented and it was then that the industrial revolution affected the whole country. Britain set the pace in technology, and the ideology and thrill of modernization, not least with the dramatic development of the railway in which Britain led the world. The development of the locomotive provided the technology for the rail revolution, and industrialization supplied the necessary demand, capital and skills. George Stephenson opened the Hetton Railway in 1822, the Stockton and Darlington Railway following in 1825. In 1829 Stephenson's locomotive *Rocket* won the Liverpool and Manchester Railway's locomotive trials.

Trains were the icon of the new age. They cut journey times for both passengers and freight, created new links, and had a powerful psychological impact. 'Space' had been conquered. New sounds and sights contributed to a powerful sense of change. Railway stations, such as Isambard Kingdom Brunel's Paddington, were designed as masterpieces of iron and glass. Trains were also celebrated in art.

The train had many effects throughout politics, society and the economy. Gladstone used the railways to campaign nationally in the 1870s and 1880s, while news and fashions sped round the country. Time within Britain was standardized, because railways needed standard time for their timetables. The economy was affected, whether by opening up urban markets for liquid milk, speeding Burton-upon-Trent beer around the country, or encouraging the iron industry. The belief in the beneficial impact of the train was captured in Charles Dickens' *The Uncommercial Traveller*. The traveller was pressed by the landlord of the Dolphin's Head to sign a petition for a branch line: 'I bound myself to the modest statement that universal traffic, happiness, prosperity, and civilization, together with unbounded national triumph in competition with the foreigner, would infallibly flow from the Branch.' In his story 'Our School', however, the train was less benign. Revisiting the scene of his education, he found the memory violated: 'A great trunk-line had swallowed the playground, sliced away the schoolroom, and pared off the corner of the house.'

The railway was not the sole way in which communications improved. Steamships transformed coastal and long-distance trade. The telegram was the Victorian equivalent of the internet in speeding up the transmission of messages. More generally, the economy became dramatically different to that in the rest of Europe. The production of coal and iron was greater than that in any other country. Economic growth was helped by the benefits of readily available capital, an increasingly productive agricultural sector, and the burgeoning markets of a growing home and colonial population.

There were qualitative as well as quantitative changes. As factories became more important, so the necessary investment required for the most efficient implementation of particular processes rose, and this further encouraged a concentration and specialization of activity. Factory production became more pronounced as mechanization gathered pace.

Not all parts of the country benefited equally. Although the spread of the rail system introduced new routes, the situation was broadly similar to that in the late eighteenth century, with a concentration on the coalfields. Areas without coal, such as East Anglia and the South-West, suffered de-industrialization or did not develop industries, although other factors were also important. The relative economic and demographic importance of the key industrial zones, the North and the Midlands, rose as that of the South and East fell.

Economic change produced social pressure. Post-war depression and demobilization exacerbated the situation from 1815. Population growth led to under- and un-employment. Dominated by the landed interest, Parliament in 1815 passed the Corn Law Act, which prohibited the import of grain unless the price of British grain reached 80 shillings a quarter. The original measure was replaced by a sliding scale in 1828. The Corn Law kept the price of food artificially high, leading to food riots among hungry agricultural labourers who suffered from a long-term fall in wages, as well as from unemployment and under-employment. Some attacked agricultural machinery, especially threshing machines, or resorted to arson, animal maiming and intimidation by anonymous letters. Robert Sharp, a Yorkshire village schoolmaster, complained in his diary: 'I have seen long and said often that the rage for enclosing open fields and commons was one great cause of the ruin or poverty of the rural population. . . . Crowds of labourers, who now as a boon ask for employment and cannot have it, but at such a rate that hunger is always in their train'. New industrial technology was blamed for unemployment, and this led Luddites and others to destroy machines. The influential radical journalist William Cobbett (*c.* 1763–1835), wrote from Derby in 1829:

> The situation of the greater part of the operative manufacturers, in this county, in Nottinghamshire, and in Leicestershire, is said to be truly deplorable. There are supposed to be thirty thousand stocking-frames; and the wages of the weavers have declined to such a point, as to leave the poor creatures scarcely the means of bare existence . . . one of the consequences . . . is the unsaleableness of the coarser parts of butcher's meat . . . their dress, their looks, their movements, and the sound of their voices, correspond with their debasement with regard to their food. Potatoes appear to be the best of their diet. Some live upon boiled cabbage and salt . . . And this is ENGLAND!

This volatile situation was very different to that in England prior to the French Revolution. It led to repressive legislation, most prominently the Six Acts of 1819 which were a response to the Peterloo Massacre of that year. In this, a panic charge by mounted yeomanry on a reform crowd in Manchester led to eleven deaths and many injuries. The episode inspired widespread revulsion and was called Peterloo as an ironic reflection on Waterloo. The radical poet Percy Bysshe Shelley (1792–1822) depicted it in *The Mask of Anarchy* as:

> . . . Trampling to a mire of blood
> the adoring multitude

and called for a popular rising: 'Ye are many – they are few.' Most radicals, however, rejected the use of force as dangerous and counter-productive. A small group of extremists plotted in 1820 to murder the entire cabinet and establish a republican government, but they were arrested in Cato Street.

The king, George IV, scarcely helped the popularity of the establishment. Prince Regent in 1811–20, while his father was incapacitated by porphyria, and king in 1820–30, George was a self-absorbed, though spreading, voluptuary. At the outset of his reign, he tried to divorce his wife, Caroline, and to remove her royal status. Her cause was taken up by public opinion, and the government felt that it had to abandon its campaign against her, although she was successfully denied a coronation. George could offer neither leadership nor charisma. He was proof that British government was no longer dependent on the calibre of the monarch. *The Times* remarked in 1830, 'Never was there a human being less respected than this late king . . . what eye weeps for him?'

Increasing pressure for political change in the early 1830s focused on demands for a reform of Parliament in order to make it more representative. This was not a matter of democracy in the sense of a universal male suffrage, still less a universal adult suffrage, but rather the notion of interests, the idea that Parliament should be representative of the wealth and weight of the community, and, specifically, the belief that there was an important 'middle class' that deserved greater political importance. Reform was pushed hard by the Whigs under Lord Grey, who gained power in 1830. The Tories resisted, especially in the House of Lords, but gave way when William IV (1830–7) reluctantly agreed to make sufficient new peers to create a majority for change in order to bring a resolution to the political crisis.

The subsequent First Reform Act of 1832 was the first major change to the franchise and political geography of England since the short-lived Interregnum constitutions of the 1650s. A notionally uniform borough franchise, based on households rated at £10 annually, was established. The distribution of seats was also reorganized to reward growing towns, such as Birmingham, Bradford and Manchester, and counties, at the expense of 'rotten boroughs', seats with a limited electorate that were open to corruption. The over-representation of the South-West was reduced. Voting qualifications still differed between boroughs and counties, the size of electorate still varied greatly by seat, and women still lacked the vote, but about one-fifth of all English adult males could vote after 1832, an increase of approximately 50 per cent.

Grey was to complain in 1837 that the Reform Act had made 'the democracy of the towns paramount to all the other interests of the state', which was not what he had intended. The following year, William Wordsworth (1770–1850), one of the greatest of the Romantic poets and initially a radical and a supporter of the French Revolution, revealed, in his *Protest Against the Ballot*, the extent of the conversion to conservatism that was to help him gain a Civil List pension in 1842 and to become Poet Laureate in 1843. It began:

> Forth rushed, from Envy spring and self-conceit,
> A Power misnamed the SPIRIT of REFORM,
> And through the astonished Island swept in storm,
> Threatening to lay all Orders at her feet
> That crossed her way.

Wordsworth continued by urging St George to stop the introduction of the ballot as it threatened to spawn a 'pest' worse than the dragon he had slain. Not one of Wordsworth's masterpieces, the poem underlines the hostility and fear that reform aroused in many circles. Others, however, were dissatisfied with the limited extent of reform, and felt that the premiership of the inactive Whig Lord Melbourne (1834, 1835–41) was overly passive. Melbourne indeed had little interest in proceeding much further towards reform after the passage of the Municipal Corporations Act of 1835, although that act encouraged the party politicization of corporations.

This reluctance to endorse further reform led in the late 1830s to a working-class protest movement, known as Chartism, that called for universal adult male suffrage, a secret ballot and annual elections. The Six Points of the People's Charter (1838) also included equal constituencies, the abolition of property qualifications for MPs, and their payment, the last two designed to ensure that the social elite lost their control of the representative system. Chartism enjoyed particularly strong support in industrial areas. It represented a powerful rejection of the ethos of the governing orders.

Parliament, however, resisted Chartist mass-petitions (1839, 1842, 1848), and there was no collapse of the political system – England did not share in the disorders of 1848, the year of revolutions on the Continent. The Chartist movement declined rapidly as a result of its failure in 1848. Growing prosperity was also important – mass support for Chartism was apparent only in times of recession. Although the 1850s were not substantially more favourable for many workers, they were less desperate than the 1840s. The repeal of the Corn Laws in 1846 was also important in allowing the propertied classes to come together in 1848 to prevent revolution from below. Earlier, the Anti Corn Law League, founded in 1838, had been a product of middle-class dissatisfaction with the limits of 1830s reform.

The pressure that economic circumstances placed on the bulk of the population is indicated by the decline in the height of army recruits in the second quarter of the century. More generally, the strains of industrialization in the early nineteenth century caused much social and political tension. Unlike cotton textiles, many other industries were slow to experience technological transformation, with the result that general living standards only rose noticeably from mid-century. The unstable credit structure exacerbated slumps. The Factory Acts regulating conditions of employment in the textile industry still left work there both long and arduous. The 1833 Act established a factory inspectorate to oversee its enforcement, a major step, and prevented the employment of children under 9; but 9–10-year-olds could still work 9-hour days, and 11–17 year olds 12 hours. The 1844 Act cut that of under-13s to 6½ hours and of all women to 12; those of 1847 and 1850 reduced the hours of women and under-18s to 10 hours. Nevertheless, working conditions remained harsh, especially for those paid on a low piece-rate basis, such as many of the workers in tailoring. This led to criticism, for example Thomas Hood's poem 'The Song of the Shirt' (1843) and Charles Kingsley's novel *Alton Locke: Tailor and Poet* (1850), the latter a call for Christian Socialism, but not radical activism, as well as for sanitary reform.

If the bulk of the working population faced difficult and unpredictable circumstances, the situation was even worse for those who were more 'marginal' to the economy. Henry Stuart, who reported on East Anglian poor relief in 1834, found three main groups of inmates in the parish workhouses, often 'abodes of misery, depravity and filth': the old and infirm, orphaned and illegitimate children, and unmarried pregnant women, the last a group that was generally treated harshly, far more so than the men responsible. The Poor Law Amendment Act (1834) introduced national guidelines, but the workhouse system that it created was not generous to its inmates. The abolition of out-relief for the poor led to a harsh institutionalization. In Wimborne workhouse, beds had to be shared, meat was only provided once a week, there were no vegetables, other than potatoes, until 1849, men and women were segregated, and unmarried mothers had to wear distinctive clothes. In the mid- and late 1830s, there were numerous attacks on workhouses.

Social assumptions and conventions pressed harder on women than on men. This was true of property rights and social mores, for example attitudes to adultery. Women, not men, were blamed for the spread of venereal disease. Under the Contagious Diseases Acts (1864, 1866, 1869), passed because of concern about the health of the armed forces, women suspected of being prostitutes, not men who also might have spread disease, were subjected to physical examination and detention, if infected, in garrison towns and ports. After an extended campaign, in which women acquired, in the Ladies National Association, experience of acting as political leaders, the Acts were repealed in 1886.

Charity could temper hardship, but it often entailed deference, if not subordination, for its recipients. For example, Andrew Reed's charity established in 1813 for the education of orphans led to the foundation of schools at first Clapton and then Watford. (Girls and boys were, as was usual, educated separately.) Subscribers to the charity were awarded votes and widows had to lobby them to gain entry for their offspring.

> Hell is a city much like London
> A populous and a smoky city;

Shelley's statement in *Peter Bell the Third* (1819) seemed increasingly appropriate. Fast-expanding towns became crowded and polluted, a breeding ground for disease as well as crime and other social problems. Mortality rates remained high, though, thanks in part to vaccination, smallpox declined. Infant mortality rates rose in the first half of the century. Cholera, a bacterial infection largely transmitted by water affected by the excreta of victims, struck first in 1831. By 1866 about 140,000 people had died of cholera. Disease struck most at the poor living in urban squalor, but also threatened the rich. The Prince of Wales nearly died of typhoid, another water-borne infection, in 1871. Dysentery, diarrhoea and enteric fever were significant problems and frequently fatal. The death or illness of breadwinners wrecked family economies, producing or exacerbating poverty and related social problems. They also encouraged fatalism.

Neither these social problems, nor political discontents, led, however, to revolution in 1848. There was no equivalent in England to the attempted insurrection by the Young Ireland nationalist movement. Instead, 1848 saw the Public Health Act which created a General Board of Health and an administrative structure to improve sanitation, especially water supply. The new Act enabled the creation of local Boards of Health. The one that was constituted in Leicester in 1849 was instrumental in the creation of a sewer system and in tackling other aspects of the urban environment, such as slaughter-houses and smoke pollution.

The contrast with the violent nature of political development on the Continent led to a measure of complacency. Having suffered from defeat and colonial rebellion from the early 1790s, Britain's colonial and maritime rivals were to be absorbed in domestic strife and Continental power politics over the following four decades. This helped Britain to pursue an isolationist policy. Meanwhile, as reform legislation was passed within Britain, so, at the same time, British imperial power spread throughout the world, and the two processes were fused, as, first, self-government, and, later, dominion status, were granted to the 'white colonies'. New Zealand achieved self-government in 1852, Newfoundland, New South Wales, Victoria, Tasmania and South Australia in 1855, Queensland in 1859; the dominion of Canada was created in 1867.

It is scarcely surprising that an optimistic conception of British history was the dominant account in academic and popular circles. A progressive move towards liberty was discerned, a seamless web that stretched back to Magna Carta in 1215 and the constitutional struggles of the barons in medieval England and forward to the nineteenth-century extensions of the franchise. These were seen as arising naturally from the country's development. A sense of English manifest destiny, that was not lessened by the wider British dimension, encouraged sympathetic interest in the Anglo-Saxons. This theme was not new. The notion of an Anglo-Saxon liberty and constitutionalism that had been brought under the Norman yoke had been discussed in the seventeenth and eighteenth centuries. It was repeated in the nineteenth century, and taken further both in academic controversy and in public resonance, not least with the celebration of King Alfred.

The Whig interpretation of history was central to the English public myth. It offered a comforting and glorious account that seemed appropriate for a state that ruled much of the globe, that was exporting its constitutional arrangements to other parts of the world and that could watch the convulsions on the Continent as evidence of the political backwardness of its societies and the superiority of Britain. The leading British role in the abolition of the slave trade and the emancipation of the slaves also led to self-righteousness and a degree of moral complacency, not least about the position of the poor in Britain. The transportation of convicts to Australia did not stop until 1868. In addition, the nineteenth century was very much a period of Evangelicalism, which was by no means confined to the middle class, and this further encouraged a sense of national distinctiveness and mission.

There was confidence in the present, faith in the future. In 1857 William Bell Scott stated 'that the latest is best . . . not to believe in the nineteenth century, one might as well disbelieve that a child grows into a man . . . without that Faith in Time what anchor have we in any secular speculation'. His painting *The Nineteenth Century, Iron and Coal* (1861), was set in Newcastle and sought to capture, as he stated, 'everything of the common labour life and applied science of the day'. It depicted a heroic scene of human activity and energy: workers at Robert Stephenson's engineering works, one of the largest manufacturers of railway engines in the world, an Armstrong gun, the steam of modern communications, telegraph wires.

The England of Queen Victoria (1837–1901) had a sense of national uniqueness, nationalistic self-confidence and a xenophobic contempt for foreigners, especially if not Protestant. Nationalism (expressed generally in terms of Britishness) played a major role in the contemporary sense of distance from the Continent. This owed much to a rejection of foreigners and foreignness, and the loss of the cosmopolitanism that had characterized much of the eighteenth-century elite. Other factors also played a role, including the development of a sense of national identity, politically, economically, culturally, and ethnically, in the Continental states of the period. The reign of Victoria was the age of the reassertion of France under first Napoleon III and then the Third Republic, as well as of the unification of Germany (1871) and Italy (1870). Political reform on the Continent indeed ensured that by 1865 some European states had more extensive franchises than those of Britain.

Whether they had a 'democratic' facet or not, Continental states increasingly seemed better able to challenge British interests. British governments worried about the plans and actions of their Continental counterparts. Invasion by France, by steam ships and even including through a planned Channel tunnel, was feared in 1844, 1847–8, 1851–2 and 1859–60, while Russian moves in the Balkans led Britain to go to war with her: the Crimean War (1854–6). This was the last war that Britain fought with a European power until the First World War broke out in 1914, an unprecedented length of time.

The war was characterized by administrative incompetence, heavy losses in manpower and a series of military misjudgements, most famously the Charge of the Light Brigade into the face of Russian artillery at Balaclava in 1854, an action that was as outmoded and unsuccessful as the attempt to defend rotten boroughs in 1832. An imperial power that could conquer much of the world lacked the military strength, crucially a large European army, to compete effectively in European power politics. Nevertheless, the war also indicated Britain's continued ability to project her power around the world, naval attacks being mounted on Russian coasts as far as Kamchatka, and, in this, she was assisted by technological advances. The warships sent to the Baltic in 1854 were all fitted with steam engines, and also benefited from Brunel's work on gun-carriages.

Britain was still clearly the leading imperial power at the end of the century. She ruled a quarter of the world's population and a fifth of the land surface. Between 1860 and 1914, Britain also owned approximately one-third of the world's shipping tonnage and by 1898 about 60 per cent of the telegraph cables, a crucial aspect of imperial government and defence planning. Between 1890 and 1914, she launched about two-thirds of the world's ships and carried about half of its marine trade. In *Cargoes*, John Masefield (1878–1967) was able to present the three ages of marine trade through a 'Quinquireme of Nineveh', a 'Stately Spanish galleon' and, lastly, a 'Dirty British coaster' carrying a cargo of British exports. In his novel *Great Expectations* (1860–1), Charles Dickens describes Pip's journey down the Thames and its

> tiers of shipping. Here, were the Leith, Aberdeen, and Glasgow steamers, loading and unloading goods . . . here, were colliers by the score and score . . . here . . . was tomorrow's steamer for Rotterdam . . . and here tomorrow's for Hamburg . . . again among the tiers of shipping . . . hammers going in ship-builders' yards. . . .

Investment abroad ensured that overseas income as a percentage of UK gross domestic product rose from 2 in 1872 to 7 in 1913, the sum invested being far more than for any other European country: in 1914, 43 per cent of the world's foreign investment was British and Britain was the sole state in Europe selling more outside the Continent than in European markets. The inflow of interest helped to maintain a strong balance of payments and thus to keep up the exchange rate of the pound.

These were also years of still spreading territorial control, although much of empire was acquired as a result of what Disraeli called 'prancing proconsuls', rather than of policy set in London. Britain gained the most important share of the two leading colonial carve-ups of the period, the scramble for Africa and the seizure of hitherto unclaimed island groups. She became the leading power in Southern and East Africa;

successfully invading Egypt in 1882, defeating the Mahdists of Sudan at Omdurman (1898), a battle in which the young Winston Churchill served, gained what were to become British Somaliland, Kenya, Uganda, Zambia, Malawi and Zimbabwe, and eventually defeated the Afrikaner republics of Southern Africa, the Orange Free State and Transvaal, in the Boer War of 1899–1902. The war proved far more difficult than had been anticipated, and highlighted the multiplicity of problems facing Britain at the turn of the century, but the ability of the state to spend £250 million and deploy 400,000 troops was a testimony to the strength of both its economic and imperial systems, while the unchallenged control and retention of the South African ports allowed Britain to bring her strength to bear. On the other hand, many contemporaries were deeply worried by Britain's performance and the war was followed by a budgetary crisis.

British strength also spread throughout the oceans of the world. Between 1850 and 1914 her list of island possessions was enlarged by the Andaman, Nicobar, Gilbert and Ellice, Kuria Muria, South Orkney, South Shetland and Cook islands, Malden, Starbuck, Caroline, Pitcairn, Christmas, Phoenix, Washington, Fanning and Jarvis islands, Fiji, Rotuna, the Solomons, Tonga, Socotra, and South Georgia. British naval power was supported by the most wide-ranging and largest number of bases in the world, a testimony to the global reach of the British state. In 1898 these included Wellington, Fiji, Sydney, Melbourne, Adelaide, Albany, Cape York (Australia), Labuan (North Borneo), Singapore, Hong Kong, Weihaiwei (China), Calcutta, Bombay, Trincomalee, Colombo, the Seychelles, Mauritius, Zanzibar, Mombasa, Aden, Cape Town, St Helena, Ascension, Lagos, Malta, Gibraltar, Halifax (Nova

Scotia), Bermuda, Jamaica, Antigua, St Lucia, Trinidad, the Falklands and Esquimalt (British Columbia). The peacetime army grew in size to 195,000 men in 1898, and this force was supported by a substantial body of native troops in the Indian army, the basis for a powerful expansion of British power in Southern Asia in the Victorian period. Sind was conquered in 1843, Baluchistan and Kashmir became British vassals in 1843 and 1846 respectively, the Punjab was annexed in 1849, and by 1886 all Burma had followed. The Indian Mutiny of 1857–8 was a severe shock, and the Afghan tribes resisted several invasions successfully, but, in co-operation with the landlords and native princes, the British governed India with considerable success.

Britain's global impact was not only a matter of imperial rule. British explorers, particularly James Bruce, David Livingstone, Mungo Park and John Speke, explored much of Africa. Others explored Australia and Canada, while the Royal Navy charted the oceans of the world.

Yet the process of late Victorian expansion took place in a context of European competition that was far more serious and gave rise to more concern than the position in 1815–70, worrying as that had been at times. The British economy remained very strong, and new industries, such as engineering and automobiles, developed. The pace of scientific advance and technological change was unremitting, and British scientists led in a number of fields. Michael Faraday (1791–1867), the son of a Surrey blacksmith, discovered electromagnetic induction in 1831, making the continuous generation of electricity a possibility. The development of commercial generators later in the century led to the growing use of electricity. New distribution and retail methods, particularly the foundation of department and chain stores, helped to create national products.

The international context, however, was less comforting. This was due to the greater economic strength of the major Continental powers, particularly Germany, their determination to make colonial gains in pursuit of their own place in the sun, and the relative decline in British power. These factors combined and interacted to produce a strong sense of disquiet in British governmental circles.

The growth of German economic power posed the starkest contrast with the situation earlier in the century. The annual average output of coal and lignite in million metric tons in 1870–4 was 123 for Britain, 41 for Germany; by 1910–14 the figures were 274 to 247. For pig-iron the annual figures changed from 7.9 and 2.7 in 1880 to 10.2 and 14.8 in 1910; for steel from 3.6 and 2.2 (1890) to 6.5 and 13.7 (1910). The number of kilometres of railway rose in Britain from 2,411 (1840) to 28,846 (1880) and 38,114 (1914); in Germany the comparable figures were 469, 33,838 and 63,378. In 1900 the German population was 56.4 million, that of Britain, excluding Ireland, 37, and including it, 41.5. In the Edwardian period, Britain's second most important export market, after India, was Germany.

The tremendous growth in German power posed a challenge to Britain, in whose governing circles there had been widespread support for German unification and a failure to appreciate its possible consequences. France and Russia were also developing as major economic powers, while American strength was ever more apparent in the New World and, increasingly, the Pacific. Given the importance of imperial considerations in governmental, political, and popular thinking, it is not surprising that British relations with and concern about the Continental powers registered not in disputes arising from European issues, but from differences and clashes centring on distant, but no longer obscure, points on the globe, ranging from confrontation with France at Fashoda in the forests of the Upper Nile in 1898, to the islands of the Western Pacific. French and German expansion in Africa led Britain to take countermeasures, in West Africa, the occupation of the interior of the Gambia in 1887–8, the declaration of the protectorate of Sierra Leone in 1896, the establishment of the protectorates of Northern and Southern Nigeria in 1900, and the annexation of the Gold Coast in 1901. German moves in East Africa led to the establishment of British power in Uganda in the 1890s. Suspicion of Russian designs on the Ottoman (Turkish) Empire and French schemes in North Africa led the British to move into Egypt; concern about French ambitions led to the conquest of Mandalay (1885) and the annexation of Upper Burma; while Russia's advance across Asia led to attempts to strengthen and move forward the 'North-West Frontier' of British India and the development of British influence in southern Persia.

Specific clashes of colonial influence interacted with a more general sense of imperial insecurity. In 1884 there was concern about British naval weakness and the increase in the French navy; in 1889 public pressure and the need to give credibility to Mediterranean policies obliged the government to pass the Naval Defence Act, which sought a two-power standard, superiority over the next two largest naval powers combined. Expenditure of £21,500,000 over five years was authorized. The importance of naval dominance was taken for granted. In the preface to his *History of the Foreign Policy of Great Britain*

(1895), Captain Montagu Burrows RN, Professor of Modern History at Oxford, wrote of 'this fortress-isle of Britain, safely intrenched [*sic*] by stormy seas, confronting the broadest face of the Continent, and, later on, almost surrounding it with her fleets, was and was not, a part of Europe according as she willed'. The myth of national self-sufficiency peaked in these years. Naval strength was a prerequisite of such an ideal.

By the turn of the century, it was Germany, with its great economic strength and its search for a place in the sun, that was the principal threat, replacing or diminishing earlier anxieties about France and Russia. British resources and political will were tested in a major naval race between the two powers, in which the British launched HMS *Dreadnought*, the first of a new class of battleships, in 1906. A projected German invasion was central to *The Riddle of the Sands* (1903), the novel by Erskine Childers that was first planned by him in 1897, a year in which the Germans were indeed discussing such a project. Military discussions with France following the Anglo-French entente of 1904 were to play a major role in leading Britain towards the First World War.

The state that was taking part in this growing confrontation with imperial Germany was different to that of the early years of Victoria's reign. England had become more urban and more industrial. Its population was more literate and educated and was linked by modern communications and a national press. Changes in the press were symptomatic of the modernization of the country. One of the many ways in which Victorian London was at the centre of English life and that of the empire was that of the provision of the news. Through its press, which lay claim to the title of the 'fourth estate' of the realm, London created the image and idiom of empire and shaped its opinions. Aside from this political function, the press also played a central economic, social and cultural role, setting and spreading fashions, whether of company statements or through theatrical criticism. In what was increasingly a commercial society, the press played a pivotal role, inspiring emulation, setting the tone, fulfilling crucial needs for an anonymous mass-readership.

The press was itself affected by change, by the energizing and disturbing forces of commercialization and new technology. It was to be legal reform and technological development that freed the Victorian press for major expansion. Newspapers had become expensive in the eighteenth century, in large part due to successive rises in Stamp Duty. In the mid-nineteenth century these so-called 'taxes on knowledge' were abolished: the Advertisement Duties in 1853, the Newspaper Stamp Duty in 1855 and the Paper Duties in 1861. This opened up the possibility of a cheap press and that opportunity was exploited by means of a technology centred on new printing presses and the continuous rolls or 'webs' of paper that fed them. A steam press was first used by *The Times* in 1814. Web rotary presses were introduced in England from the late 1860s. Mechanical typesetting was introduced towards the end of the century.

New technology was expensive, but the mass readership opened up by the lower prices that could be charged after the repeal of the newspaper taxes justified the cost. The consequence was more titles and lower prices. The number of daily morning papers published in London rose from 8 in 1856 to 21 in 1900, and of evenings from 7 to 11, while there was also a tremendous expansion in the suburban press. The repeal of stamp duty permitted the appearance of penny dailies. The *Daily Telegraph*, launched in 1855, led the way and by 1888 had a circulation of 300,000. The penny press was in turn squeezed by the halfpenny press, the first halfpenny evening paper, the *Echo*, appearing in 1868, while halfpenny morning papers became important in the 1890s with the *Morning Leader* (1892) and the *Daily Mail* (1896), which was to become extremely successful with its bold and simple style. It testified to the dynamic combination of entrepreneurial capitalism and the market created by the expanding urban working class.

The *Echo* peaked at a circulation of 200,000 in 1870. The papers that best served popular tastes were the Sunday papers, *Lloyd's Weekly News*, the *News of the World* and *Reynolds's Newspaper*. *Lloyd's*, the first English paper with a circulation of over 100,000, was selling over 600,000 by 1879, over 900,000 by 1893 and in 1896 rose to over a million. The Sunday papers relied on shock and titillation, drawing extensively on police court reporting.

In comparison an eighteenth-century London newspaper was considered a great success if it sold 10,000 copies a week (most influential papers then were weeklies), and 2,000 weekly was a reasonable sale. Thus an enormous expansion had taken place, one that matched the vitality of an imperial capital, swollen by immigration and increasingly influential as an opinion-setter within the country, not least because of the communications revolution produced by the railway and better roads. The development of the railways allowed London newspapers to increase their dominance of the national newspaper scene. Thanks to them these papers could arrive on provincial doorsteps within hours of publication. Railways also led to the massive development of commuting in London.

The press gave Charles Dickens (1812–70) early employment. His subsequent novels reflected many of the concerns of mid-Victorian society. Dickens himself was a supporter of reform in fields such as capital punishment, housing and prostitution. Among his novels, *Bleak House* (1852–3) was an indictment of the coldness of law and Church, the delays of the former and the smugness of the self-righteous Reverend Chadband; *Little Dorrit* (1855–7) an attack on imprisonment for debt, business fraud and the deadening bureaucracy of the Circumlocution Office, his symbol for government. Dickens's friend and fellow-novelist Wilkie Collins (1824–89), was criticized by the poet Algernon Swinburne for sacrificing his talent for the sake of a mission. His novels dealt with issues such as divorce, vivisection and the impact of heredity and environment, the last a major concern to a society influenced by the evolutionary teachings of Charles Darwin and thus increasingly concerned by living standards.

Such concern led to a determination to reform, i.e. change, popular pastimes. Leisure was to be made useful: drink was to be replaced by sport. Organized sport expanded, in part a response to the clearer definition of leisure time in an industrial and urban society, to the reduction in working hours, and to the increase in average real earnings in the last quarter of the century. Professional football developed, while there was also a boom in middle-class sports, such as golf, and lawn tennis whose rules were systematized in 1874. By 1895 the *Daily News* covered racing, yachting, rowing, lacrosse, football, hockey, angling, billiards, athletics, cycling and chess. Less respectable traditional sports and pastimes, such as cockfighting, ratting and morris-dancing, lost popularity or were suppressed.

Reform was the leading divisive issue, reform of the protectionist system and reform of the franchise. Robert Peel's repeal of the Corn Laws (1846) was designed to encourage free trade and thus help exports as well as to ensure sufficient food supplies for the towns, but, because it ended agricultural protectionism, repeal split the Tories. This was followed by the repeal of the Navigation Acts (1849) by the Whig/Liberal government under Lord John Russell. Free-trade became a central theme of British policy. Reform was linked to the growth of middle-class culture and consciousness in the great Northern cities such as Newcastle and Leeds. The civic gospel was expressed architecturally in their great Town Halls: Manchester's was opened in 1877. Their newspapers played a major role in orchestrating opinion in favour of reform. The Anti-Corn-Law League was a symbol of middle-class aggression, while the mismanagement of the Crimean War helped to boost middle-class values of efficiency in politics at the expense of the aristocracy. This was linked to the movement of Whiggism to Liberalism in the 1840s, 1850s and 1860s, as, in acquiring middle-class support, the Whigs became a party fitted for the reformist middle class. Reform was central to their appeal. The appeal of politics was referred to in Wilkie Collins's *The Moonstone* (1868):

> The guests present being all English, it is needless to say that, as soon as the wholesome check exercised by the presence of the ladies was removed, the conversation turned on politics as a necessary result. In respect to this all-absorbing national topic, I happen to be one of the most un-English Englishmen living.

More active local government was an important source and instrument of reform with, for example, the public health movement from the 1840s, the laying out of public parks, especially after the Recreation Grounds Act (1859) and the Public Health Act (1875), and the building of libraries for workers, though much was funded by charity or public subscription. A professional police force replaced the yeomanry and the sometimes incompetent constables, and provided a much more effective check on working-class immorality. The police were a powerful weapon of middle-class cultural dominance. Peel's Metropolitan Police Act (1829) created a uniformed and paid force for London, and was a response to the problems of keeping order and maintaining the law in the rapidly expanding cities. The old magistracy system was no longer adequate. This process was extended by acts of 1835 and 1839, and the County and Borough Police Act (1856), in part a product of major riots in Lancashire towns such as Wigan in 1852–3, made the formation of paid forces obligatory. The new police largely replaced individuals as prosecutors in cases of criminal justice in England and Wales. The Hanoverian legal code was transformed. In the 1830s–50s the death penalty was abolished for most crimes. The last hulk (prison ship) was closed in 1858. Instead, prisons were built and reformatory regimes developed.

Knowledge about prison conditions and other such social issues was spread by the 'Condition of England' movement, which was linked to the cult of novels that was so strong from the 1840s on. Leading novelists, such as Elizabeth Gaskell in *Mary Barton* (1848) and Charlotte Brontë in *Shirley* (1849), focused on social problems. There was a great expansion of reading, and the expanding middle-class also patronized a major upsurge in art, poetry, and the performance and production of music. Cities such as Birmingham, Liverpool, Manchester and Newcastle started large art collections, musical institutions such as the Halle Orchestra in Manchester (1857), and educational bodies. Civic universities were created. Mason Science College, which eventually became part of the University of Birmingham established in 1900, was founded in 1880 by Sir Josiah Martin, a self-educated manufacturer of split-rings and steel pen-nibs. He spent part of his fortune on local orphans as well as on his new foundation which was designed to be especially useful for local industries.

Men such as Martin set the tone of much of urban Victorian England. Their views and wealth were a tremendous stimulus to the process of Improvement, civic and moral, that was so central to the movement for reform. Furthermore, much of this process of improvement focused on Northern and Midland cities. It was these that benefited from industrialization, rather than the market towns that were the centres of rural England. The latter lost relative importance even before the agricultural problems that became more acute in the 1870s. As a consequence, the pattern of urban growth and provincial culture was very different to what it had been in the eighteenth century. In addition, the towns that were growing rapidly did not seek to act as social magnets for the surrounding gentry, but rather to develop specifically urban attitudes and interests. The urbanization of England was a matter not only of people living in towns and cities, but also of a political and cultural process that ensured that the rural interest was far less important than in France or Germany. This had important consequences for the country's politics. There was to be no rural political party in the age of the mass franchise, either one of landlords or later of peasants. The Conservatives might have developed in that direction, but, instead, they made a major effort to win the support of suburban opinion.

Middle-class interests increasingly set the legislative agenda. The Second Reform Act, passed by a minority Tory government (1867), nearly doubled the existing electorate and, by offering household suffrage, gave the right to vote to about 60 per cent of adult males in boroughs. The Earl of Derby, Conservative Prime Minister in 1852, 1858–9 and 1866–8, described the measure as 'a great experiment and "taking a leap in the dark"'.

The Liberal victory in the following general election (1868) led to the first government of William Gladstone (1868–74). He pushed through a whole series of reforms, including the disestablishment of the Irish Church, and the introduction of open competition in the Civil Service (1870) and of the secret ballot (1872). The 1870 Education Act divided the country into school districts and required a certain level of educational provision, though its provisions were resisted. In Ealing, for example, tenacious efforts by the Church of England to protect voluntary education and resist the introduction of public Board Schools, ignoring the implications of rapid population growth, left 500 children unschooled twenty-five years after the Act. The end of long-established distinctions, variations and privileges played a major role in the reform process. The Endowed Schools Commission established in that year redistributed endowments and reformed governing bodies. The Church of England underwent a similar change.

Gladstone was a formidable and multi-faceted individual, a classical scholar and theological controversialist, a hewer of trees and a rescuer of prostitutes. A Tory Treasury minister in the 1830s, he became the leading Liberal politician of the age, committed to reform at home and a moral stance abroad. His political skills bridged the worlds of Parliament and of public meetings, for, under his leadership, Liberalism became a movement enjoying mass support. Gladstone's strong Christian faith was important to his political life. It affected his foreign as well as his domestic policy. However, he was to find international and Irish problems intractable and his attempt 'to pacify Ireland' by providing home rule (an Irish Parliament responsible for internal affairs) did not produce a lasting solution.

The Tories or, as they were now called, Conservatives, came to power in 1874 under Benjamin Disraeli (1804–81), an opportunist and skilful political tactician who was also an acute thinker, able to create, around the themes of national identity and pride, and social cohesion, an alternative political culture and focus of popular support, to Liberal moral certainty. Disraeli sought to preserve what he saw as the traditional strengths of the country. He was keen to maintain the landed order and was a warm, although not uncritical, supporter of Victoria. Disraeli also backed social reform, although less energetically than his Liberal opponents and than was subsequently to be claimed. Legislation on factories (1874), Public Health, Artisans' Dwellings, and Pure Food and Drugs Acts (1875) systematized and extended the regulation of important aspects of public health and social welfare. The Factory Act (1874) limited work hours for women and children in the textile industry. The Prison Act (1877) established state control. These were, however, less important for Disraeli and owed less to his personal attention than his active foreign policy which involved the purchase of shares in the Suez Canal (1875), the creation of the title of Empress of India for Victoria (1876), the acquisition of Cyprus (1878), and wars with the Afghans and Zulus.

Economic difficulties and political problems, skilfully exploited by Gladstone in his electioneering Midlothian campaigns (1879–80), led to Conservative defeat in the 1880 election. Imperial and Irish problems, however, affected Gladstone's second government (1880–5), with the First Boer War (1880–1) in South Africa, the occupation of Egypt (1882–3), the massacre of Colonel Gordon and his force at Khartoum (1885), the Coercion Act, designed to restore order in Ireland (1881), and the murder of Lord Frederick Cavendish, the Chief Secretary for Ireland, in Phoenix Park, Dublin, by the Invincibles, an Irish secret society (1882).

It proved easier to introduce and implement reform in England than in Ireland. In 1884, the Third Reform Act extended to the counties the household franchise granted to the boroughs in 1867, so that over two-thirds of the adult males in the counties received the vote. Mass democracy was coming nearer. The changing political world was captured in Anthony Trollope's novel *The Duke's Children* (1879–80). The constituents of the fictional Silverbridge were now less under the control of the Liberal Duke of Omnium, although the influence of the family still played a role:

> They had loyally returned the Duke himself while he was a commoner, but they had returned him as being part and parcel of the Omnium appendages. That was all over now . . . they . . . thought that a Conservative would suit them best.

That being so, and as they had been told that the Duke's son was a Conservative, they fancied that by electing him they would be pleasing everybody. But, in truth, by so doing they would by no means please the Duke.

The Duke wanted to maintain the family's Liberalism, but his heir, Lord Silverbridge, had his 'own ideas. We've got to protect our position as well as we can against the Radicals and Communists'. 'I cannot admit that at all, Silverbridge. There is no great political party in this country anxious either for Communism or for revolution.' Silverbridge, however, saw politics in terms of class not 'the public . . . The people will look after themselves, and we must look after ourselves'.

The process of reform, both political and social, continued with the Redistribution of Seats Act (1885), the Local Government Act (1888), creating directly elected county councils and county boroughs, and the Workmen's Compensation Act (1897), obliging employers to provide compensation for industrial accidents. A welfare state was developing. State intervention in education helped in the decline of illiteracy.

The political situation was, however, complicated by the longstanding malaise over the Irish question. Fenian terrorism in Ireland, England and Canada led to casualties, and there was both pressure for land reform and agitation for home rule for Ireland (the creation of an Irish parliament). Liberal proposals for home rule were defeated in 1886 and 1893 at Westminster, where they helped to divide politicians. Conservatives led the resistance, but the defeat of the First Home Rule Bill in 1886 was due to the defection of 'Liberal Unionists' from Gladstone's third government.

The political hegemony of the Liberals was destroyed that year as the Conservatives, under Robert, 3rd Marquess of Salisbury, won the general election. Though the Liberals won the 1892 election, the Conservatives dominated the period 1886–1905. Salisbury (Prime Minister 1885–6, 1886–92, 1895–1902) and his successor and nephew, Arthur Balfour (1902–5), followed a cautious policy on domestic reform. Salisbury, a Marquess and owner of Hatfield House, one of the palaces the English domesticate as 'stately homes', derived most of his disposable income from urban property, including London slums. He brought the Conservatives considerable success, but his government came to seem tired in the early 1900s. The Boer War proved far more difficult and costly than he had anticipated, and Salisbury also failed to keep the step ahead of the game that is so important to political success (albeit frequently risky). Thus, Salisbury cannot escape responsibility for the divisions over protectionism that were to affect the government from 1903, nor for the failure to maintain sufficient middle-class support to avoid a sweeping electoral defeat in 1906.

Politics itself was increasingly affected by class issues and alignments, not least as a consequence of the developing problem of labour relations. There was growing pressure for more radical political and social policies. Joseph Chamberlain's 'Unauthorized' Liberal Programme of 1885 called for land reform, and was followed, in 1891, by the Newcastle programme which also called for the reform or abolition of the House of Lords. The social order could be harsh as well as inegalitarian. That year, Tom Masters, a thirteen-year-old Northamptonshire farm labourer, was whipped by his employer for insolence.

Pressures from within the Liberal party were soon supplemented by the creation of more explicitly working-class movements, both political and industrial. The development of trade unions reflected the growing industrialization and unification of the economy, the growth of larger concerns employing more people, and, by the end of the century, a new, more adversarial and combative working-class consciousness. The Trade Unions Congress (TUC), a federation of trade unions, began in 1868, unionism spread from the skilled craft section to semi- and un-skilled workers, and there were major strikes in the London gasworks and docks in 1888–9. Keir Hardie, Secretary of the Scottish Miners' Federation, founded the Scottish Labour Party (1888) and the Independent Labour Party (1893). The latter pressed for an eight-hour day and 'collective ownership of means of production, distribution and exchange'. Six years later, the TUC advocated an independent working-class political organization, which led, in 1900, to the formation of the Labour Representation Committee, the basis of the Labour Party.

These developments contributed to a situation of sustained doubt, if not a crisis of confidence, in late Victorian society. This society did not seem beneficent to the growing numbers who were becoming both emancipated and politicized; while many commentators were concerned about the relative weakness of Britain, economically and politically, compared to the leading Continental states. British industries no longer benefited from cheaper raw materials, energy and labour. Foreign competition was responsible for closures: in 1901, for example, the Tudhoe ironworks which employed 1,500 men was shut down. There was less confidence that British institutions and practices were best. In the 1890s and early 1900s, there was much interest in the German educational system, and much envy of its 'practical' orientation. Salisbury was not alone in being pessimistic on the future of the empire. These varied strands of disquiet were to lead to fresh pressure for reform and new political divisions in the period up to the First World War.

The British could take pride in the spread of empire and the triumphalism of Queen Victoria's Gold and Diamond Jubilees in 1887 and 1897, but the divisions of the first half of the century that had diminished or disappeared in its prosperous third quarter were re-emerging, taking on new forms and being accentuated by new sources of tension. Economic change brought significant levels of social disruption. In Cornwall, for example, serious falls in the prices of copper and tin in the late 1860s and 1870s, in part due to growing world competition, led to a decline in the number of mines and heavy emigration. The Cornish diaspora amounted to about 210,000 in 1891, about 42 per cent of all the Cornish-born population. About 45 per cent of these were living in England and Wales, but the rest were spread over much of the world.

More generally, emigration was frequently a comment on a loss of hope about personal circumstances in England and the product of a strong belief that life, or, at least, opportunities were better abroad. Nineteenth-century emigration was far greater in scale than that in previous centuries. It helped ensure that the English language and English culture continued to play a major global role once the tide of British power receded in the twentieth century. Large numbers emigrated to the USA, Canada, Australia, New Zealand and

South Africa. Far fewer emigrated to tropical colonies in Africa, South Asia or the West Indies. English emigration was but part of a wider movement of emigrants both from throughout the British Isles and from Europe as a whole. As English emigrants tended not to form recognizable and often self-conscious ethnic communities, their role has been unduly minimized. In proportional terms they were indeed less important than emigrants from Ireland, many of whom moved to England: the Irish-born population of England and Wales rose from 1.8 per cent to 3 per cent of the total population between 1841 and 1861. Nevertheless, the migrant ship was also very much part of the history of the English in the nineteenth century.

The loss of people was matched by one of cultivated land. Land reclamation of all types declined rapidly with the onset of the agricultural depression of the 1870s. (With the exception of the First World War, this depression continued virtually unabated until the outbreak of the Second World War.) The Fens were particularly badly affected by this process because drainage schemes and pumping stations were very expensive to maintain. Many farmers were unable or unwilling to pay the rates to the Catchment Boards responsible for the drainage. As a result not only did reclamation practically cease but large areas of the Fens which had once been cultivated were allowed to revert to pasture land or used for turf-cutting for household fuel. In other areas of heavier soils, such as those in the Midlands and Essex, vast tracts of land were allowed to revert to rough grazing or even left derelict.

The transformation of the countryside from a place of work was important to changing notions of rural England. The existence of an extensive food-producing empire and Britain's mastery of the seas created an imperial food order which rendered England's rural areas economically marginal. The wealth of empire also contributed to a high point for a landed elite, as many of the more successful entrepreneurs purchased their own estates as a means of gaining social respectability and to indulge in the enjoyment of country sports such as hunting and shooting. Imports helped cut food prices, which increased the value of the urban working-class wage. However, agricultural wages were generally low, and rural poverty in counties such as Dorset was a serious problem, although it was generally under-rated in comparison with urban conditions.

The appeal of an image of country life was combined with concern about the character and impact of urban society, and thus the 'state of the nation'. Infant mortality rates were high: in the North-Eastern mining communities half the total deaths occurred in the range 0–5 years, and a high proportion in 5–15. Many families lived in only one room. Gastro-intestinal disorders linked to inadequate water and sewerage systems were responsible for very high infant mortality rates in a number of cities, such as Bradford. Poor urban sanitation, housing and nutrition were blamed for the physical weakness of much of the population. The army found this a serious problem at the time of the Boer War and the First World War, the Metropolitan Police thought their London recruits physically weak, and defeats at the hands of the visiting New Zealand All Blacks rugby team in 1905 led to discussion about a supposed physical and moral decline arising from the country's urban and industrial nature. There was concern about what was termed the 'residuum' and, in particular, that birth rates among this group were higher than those among the middle-classes. Eugenicist ideas enjoyed considerable impact in the 1900s. There was also anxiety about the apparent extent of atheism among the urban working classes, and in February 1886 disturbances after a meeting of the unemployed in Trafalgar Square led to pressure for action over unemployment.

The concern for social welfare that was such an obvious feature of late-Victorian values played a role in the amelioration and control of living conditions, especially the decline of epidemic disease. The supply of clean water was improved or begun and, thanks to Sir Joseph Bazalgette, London at last acquired a sewerage system appropriate for the capital of a modern empire. Typhus virtually disappeared by the 1890s, typhoid was brought under partial control, and death rates from tuberculosis and scarlet fever declined. Improved diet, thanks, in part, to a significant fall in food prices, played an important role in the decline in mortality rates, while medical advances, not least the replacement of the 'miasma' theory of disease by that of 'germs', helped, although mortality contrasts between registration districts persisted. There was a noticeable, though not invariable, relationship between life expectancy and population density: crowded cities, such as Liverpool, having very much higher mortality rates. The only infection seriously to affect adults by 1900 was tuberculosis, although the childhood killers were still rampant. The decline in infectious diseases began before medicine had the expertise to influence their morbidity and mortality directly.

Public health problems, however, also existed in small towns and rural areas. Reports on the situation in Bruton in

Somerset in the 1870s and 1880s graphically described insufficient and defective toilet arrangements, inadequate sewerage disposal and a lack of clean water. A reluctance to spend money ensured, however, that, as in mid-century London, plans to improve the situation were delayed and, though the sewerage system was finally improved, Bruton did not construct a water supply system in the Victorian period.

Social welfare was linked to a growing institutionalization of society that led to the construction of schools, workhouses and asylums. The Wiltshire asylum was opened in Devizes in 1851, replacing private madhouses run for profit. By 1914 a basic national network of infant and child welfare centres had been created. Health-visiting was expanding. Educational authorities had been made responsible for the medical inspection of schoolchildren. Far from unconstrained capitalism, this was increasingly a regulated society. Social welfare, however, was not designed to provide comfortable living standards. Alfred Doolittle, the fictional London dustman in George Bernard Shaw's play *Pygmalion* (1914), remarked: 'We're all intimidated. Intimidated, maam: that's what we are. What is there for me if I chuck it but the workhouse in my old age? I have to dye my hair already to keep my job as a dustman.'

Although social welfare attracted widespread political support, there were differences as to how it should be funded. Furthermore, there were serious policy differences, reflecting fundamental disagreements over Ireland, trade union relations and the nature of the political system. Ireland was the most threatening issue, for the determination of the Ulster Protestants to resist home rule led to a serious crisis in 1914, with signs of serious disquiet among part of the army in

Ireland: the 'Curragh Mutiny'. After the two general elections of 1910, the Liberals were dependent on the support of Irish MPs in order to stay in power. Furthermore, the removal of the veto power of the House of Lords in 1911 made Irish Home Rule at last seem a viable prospect. However, Ireland proved an issue that tested willingness to accept the verdict of parliamentary politics. It also indicated a potential lawlessness that was not characteristic of English politics in this period, other than for marginal groups, such as radical suffragettes. The formation of the Ulster Unionist Council (1905) and the Ulster Volunteer Force (1913) revealed the unwillingness of the Ulster Protestants to subordinate their sense of identity to Irish nationalism and to accept home rule. They were assisted by the Conservatives, from 1912 the 'Conservative and Unionist Party', who did their best to resist the Home Rule Bill introduced in 1912.

The Conservatives meanwhile had suffered successive defeats (1906 and twice in 1910) at the hands of the Liberals, who were backed by the new Labour party. Victors in the landslide 1906 election, the Liberals governed until a coalition government was formed in 1915. They, particularly the dynamic Welsh radical, David Lloyd George, were determined to undermine the power and possessions of the old landed elite, and keen to woo Labour and the trade unions. In 1906 the Liberals passed a Trade Disputes Act that gave unions immunity from actions for damages as a result of strike action, and thus rejected the attempts of the courts, through the Taff Vale case (1901), to bring the unions within the law. The Mines Regulations Act (1908) limited the number of hours that miners could spend underground. Lloyd George, Chancellor of the Exchequer (1908–15), wished to move the Liberals to the left, and he pushed through a 'People's Budget', introducing new taxes for the wealthy. The opposition of the Conservative-dominated House of Lords to this led to the Parliament Act (1911), which removed their right to veto Commons legislation. The Lords only passed this as a result of the danger that otherwise the king would create enough peers to force through the legislation, the threat employed in 1832 to push through the First Reform Act. The net result was an underlining of the degree to which the sovereignty of Parliament meant the power of the House of Commons.

That year, Lloyd George had also defused the first general railway strike. He was committed to government intervention as also to the state provision of solutions to problems of social welfare, such as the creation of a system to ensure proper care for the elderly. Rising prices put pressure on living standards in the 1900s and early 1910s. There were a number of major strikes in 1910–12, as well as the continued growth of the Labour Party and of trade union membership, and a vociferous suffragette movement (demanding the vote for women). The militant tactics of the Women's Social and Political Union were designed to force public attention. Labour officially endorsed women's suffrage in 1913. The situation seemed increasingly volatile. Labour won twenty-nine seats in the general election of 1906 and forty in that of 1910, although it was not until 1922 that it emerged as the second largest party. In 1914, moreover, the Liberal Party displayed few signs of decline at the hands of Labour. 'New Liberalism' was seen by Liberals as an alternative as much to Socialism as to the Conservatives, despite the fact that it provided an ideological underpinning to the Lib–Lab 'progressive alliance', prior to 1914. Indeed, the Liberal attempt to thread a middle way between capital and labour in this period became characteristic of the twentieth-century state.

In 1914, over 75 per cent of the working class was, as in the Black Country, prepared to vote Liberal or Conservative, rather then Labour. Ethnic, religious, regional and occupational division were as important as class issues. The coal miners were one group of workers that was increasingly important. Their numbers in Britain had risen from over 315,000 in 1865 to 1.13 million in 1914.

The local political geography of the country was very varied; so also was its social character. William Davies, author of *The Autobiography of a Super-tramp* (1908), recorded of his period hawking laces in Swindon:

> The success with which I met in this town astonished me, owing, I believe, to its being a working man's town, and not filled with half-pay officers and would-be aristocrats that cannot afford, but still feel it their duty, to live in fine villas in the locality of a royal residence. The poor, sympathetic people seemed to understand a man's wants. Business was often transacted without the utterance of words.

England, on the eve of world war, was still in many respects an hierarchical society. Victoria's grandson, George V (1910–36), summoned 'My loyal subjects' to war in 1914. Hereditary monarchy was still important, and society was obviously scarcely egalitarian. Third-class passengers were not allowed on Great Western Railway expresses until 1882. Despite criticism from writers such as Dinah Mulock, in her *John Halifax, Gentleman* (1857), and radicals, the aristocracy had survived as major players in political and social life until the very end of the nineteenth century, in part thanks to investing in urban property and industry and sometimes marrying rich women, and by assimilating new members from the *nouveaux riches*, but thereafter they suffered major blows. Disraeli had predicted in 1880 that 'the politics of this country will probably for the next few years consist in an assault upon the constitutional position of the landed interest', in both government and property. This was delayed by the Conservative revival under Salisbury, but the whole drift of social, economic and political development was against the landed order. Death duties were introduced in 1894. Greatly-expanded institutions with a meritocratic ethos – the civil service, the professions, the universities, the public schools and the army – were all very significant in the creation of a new social and cultural Establishment to replace the aristocracy in the late nineteenth century. Education and skills, rather than pedigree, were emphasized, and this helped lead to the reform of the public schools and the expansion of the university sector. The armed forces played a much less dominant role in England than in the leading Continental states, where they served as a base for continued aristocratic, or at least landed, influence. In England the old landowning political elite had its dominance of the electoral process challenged in 1832 and, thereafter, a steadily decreasing percentage of MPs came from it. Mr Merdle, the great 'popular financier on an extensive scale' in Dickens's *Little Dorrit*, was 'a new power in the country . . . able to buy up the whole House of Commons'. The Liberal Herbert Asquith, a barrister, was in 1908 the first prime minister not to have his own country house, though he was to end up with one and an earldom. The outlawing of the duel was part of a process whereby traditional aristocratic rules of honour and codes of conduct were subordinated to the laws of a state that favoured what George Bernard Shaw termed 'middle-class morality'.

Successive extensions of the franchise had not brought the vote to women, though they were socially less dependent than is generally assumed and than their legal situation might suggest. Furthermore, in local government, women had become both electors and elected representatives. In the latter role, they tended to be involved specifically in local government welfare services. Women were also very prominent in philanthropy, where they tended to be the agents by whom middle-class notions of 'respectability' were transmitted (not without conflict) into the working-class areas of towns and cities.

The political, religious, intellectual and educational authority of the Church of England had been challenged and knowledge had been secularized, but the Church still played a major role in a society which was still very much Christian in its precepts. Issues of ritualism and establishment were major political concerns. There were numerous clergymen. Christian notions of charity and responsibility played a bigger role in nineteenth-century social welfare than ideas of state-driven automatic provision, although these became important from the 1900s. Albeit that in 1857 Parliament expanded the possibilities for separation from a spouse, which, hitherto, had only been through expensive parliamentary divorce hearings or through the ecclesiastical courts, in 1872 there were only 200 divorces in England and Wales and in 1901 only 600. Although disestablished in

Ireland in 1868 and Wales in 1914–20, there was to be no disestablishment in England.

The principal challenge to the Church of England came not from atheism, but from the rise of Dissent between 1790 and 1850, though the re-emergence of 'public' Catholicism, with the re-establishment of the Catholic hierarchy in 1850 and massive Irish immigration, also caused tension. The Irish-born population of England and Wales rose to 602,000 in 1861, about 3 per cent of the total population. Their impact was increased by concentration in a few cities, such as London, where the Irish were 5 per cent of the population in 1861, and Liverpool, where the percentage was near 25. Although industrialization could encourage secularism, it also helped produce religious revival, for example in Cornwall and the Durham coalfield.

Aside from the public role of the Church of England, there was also a whole set of assumptions that encouraged a sense of English/British uniqueness. The right of the British to rule over other peoples was still taken for granted, and Darwinism, with its stress on natural selection, seemed to give new force to it. The Primrose League, a popular Conservative movement launched in 1883, enjoyed much support in the 1880s and 1890s for its defence of Crown, social system and empire. By modern standards, this was a very racialist society. Although Disraeli was baptized into the Church of England, his Jewish background was an issue both in 'polite society' and in public prejudice. Less well-connected individuals faced more blatant exclusion.

And yet there had also been major change, necessarily so as both cause and consequence of a society with a mass electorate, universal compulsory primary education, and widespread urbanization and industrialization. The scale had been massive. The 1911 census of England and Wales reported that the urban population had risen from 8.99 million in 1851 to 28.16 million in 1911, an increase from 50.2 per cent of the total population to 78.10 per cent. This was a formidable strain on the urban infrastructure and social fabric. Changes had brought widespread social dislocation, instability and fears. Deference and traditional social patterns, never as fixed as some thought, had ebbed. In place of the social and political hierarchy and the powerful established Church of a century earlier, there was considerably more fluidity, although it is important not to exaggerate the stability or deference of the older rural society. This was shown both by rural opposition to agrarian society, for example widespread arson in the first half of the century, and by more personal responses to social policing. Thomas Newcome, Rector of Shenley in Hertfordshire 1800–49 and a JP, recorded in 1822: 'Two Girls – Sunday Scholars formerly – who came before me without feeling or shame (but such little measure as I could inject it into them) to swear Bastards to Ridge parish . . . I detail the above as "Signs of the Times".'

The new and newly expanded cities and towns created new living environments in which the role and rule of the old world was far less. To many commentators, these environments were disturbing, even corrupting. Railways created new economic and social relationships, new leisure and commuting options. Their construction destroyed or damaged many of the most prominent sites of the past including Berwick and Newcastle castles and Launceston Priory, and wrecked the canal system. The geography and townscape of London was changed by the train, including underground railways, the tram, and new roads, such as

Kingsway and Northumberland Avenue, which respectively destroyed a red light district and the splendour of Northumberland House. The pace of change aroused considerable disquiet, giving rise to the foundation of conservationist movements, such as the Society for the Protection of Ancient Buildings and the National Trust.

Technology was like a freed genie, bringing ever more changes. Railway and telegraphy were succeeded by motor car and telephone, electricity and wireless. The twentieth century started with the belief that science could solve the problems of the time. Disillusionment was not to begin until after seeing the role of science in the two world wars, and, more strongly, until the environmental movement in the 1960s. The growth of the genre of 'scientific romance' testified to the seemingly inexorable advance of human potential through technology. In *The Coming Race* (1871), by Sir Edward Bulwer Lytton, one of the leading men of letters of his age and a former Conservative Secretary for the Colonies, a mining engineer encountered at the centre of the earth a people who controlled 'Vril', a kinetic energy offering limitless powers. The novel is largely forgotten, other than through Bo[vine]vril. Science fiction played a greater role in the work of H[erbert] G[eorge] Wells (1866–1946), who had studied under Charles Darwin's supporter, the comparative anatomist T.H. Huxley. Man's destiny in time and space was a central question for Wells, reflecting, in part, the intellectual expansion offered by the evolutionary theory outlined by Darwin in his *The Origin of Species* (1859), and by interest in manned flight. His first major novel *The Time Machine* (1895) was followed in the *War of the Worlds* (1898) by the account of a Martian invasion of England.

Developments were in fact less lurid, but they still changed many aspects of human experience. The first demonstration of electric lighting in Birmingham was in 1882, the Birmingham Electric Supply Ltd following seven years later. The first original, full-size British petrol motor was produced in 1895; the first commercial motor company was established at Coventry in 1896, and motor buses were introduced in about 1898. The first successful flight by the American Wright brothers in 1903 was swiftly followed by Blériot's flight across the Channel. Lord Northcliffe remarked 'England is no longer an island.' The Motor Car Act of 1903 extended the rights of the motorist, the motor bus was introduced in London in 1905 and, four years later, the national Road Board was founded to lend energy and cohesion to road construction. Motor transport led to the widespread tarring of roads from the early 1900s, a visual and environmental change. By 1914 there were 132,000 private car registrations. There were also 124,000 motor cycle registrations and 51,167 buses and taxis on the road. Cars ensured that bicycling, which had boomed following the development of the safety bicycle in 1885, descended the social and age scales. A new world of speed and personal mobility, with its own particular infrastructure, was being created. If cars were still a luxury, every such innovation contributed to a sense of change that was possibly the most important solvent of the old order.

TWELVE

TOWARDS THE PRESENT
1914–2008

War and, from 1947, the loss of empire framed the political experience of England from the outbreak of the First World War (1914) to the 1960s, but the social and economic context as well as the nature of personal experience were to be transformed totally as a result of technological innovation and application. The nineteenth century had brought major changes but the contemporary age has truly witnessed revolutionary transformation in theoretical and applied science and technology in most fields, whether transportation, the generation and distribution of power, medicine, contraception, agricultural yields, or the accumulation, accessing, storing and manipulation of information. The wealth created would make it feasible to suggest that humanity's lot on earth could be substantially improved, that society could, and thus should, provide health, welfare, education and culture. Change, however, would be so all-encompassing that fear about permanent damage to the environment would become a major issue from the 1960s, and worried voices had been raised earlier.

In this brave and troubled new world, it was possible for people to travel and transmit ideas as never before, to create and destroy in new ways, and on a scale hitherto only graspable in imaginative fiction, to synthesize and manufacture new substances, tastes and sounds, and thus create, from the fertile minds of humans, a world in which humans, their desires, needs and imagination seemed the sole frame of reference, the only scale.

For someone of over eighty at the beginning of the twenty-first century (a growing percentage of the population), it was not only the individual major technological innovations of their lifetime, whether atomic energy or contraceptive pill, television or microchip, jet engine or computer, bio-technology or artificial hip, that were of importance, in affecting, directly or indirectly, insistently or episodically, their life, but also the cumulative impact of change. Science is the freed genie. It is not possible to put it back in the bottle of past assumptions.

More generally, the past ceased to be a readily recoverable world, a source of reference, value and values for lives that changed very little, and became, instead, a world that was truly lost, a theme-park for nostalgia, regret, curiosity, or, less attractively, a sense of empowerment through alleged grievance. The numerous war memorials erected after the First World War lamented not only the all too many who had died far before their time, but also a world that had passed, although the war boosted the High Church element of the Church of England, which was prepared to pray for the dead. However, by the end of the century the Christian message could no longer provide reassurance to the vast bulk of the population and England had become one of the more secular societies in Europe. A significant flight from Christianity occurred in the 1960s, under the impact of ideologies and social changes.

Change was first a matter of displacement. Migration had always been important in English history, especially in the nineteenth century, with movement to the new industrial areas and emigration to the colonies, but in the contemporary age the pattern of the people has changed even more radically, most literally with the post-1945 creation of new towns, although their number was small compared with the numbers of new towns created in the twelfth and thirteenth centuries. The population of rural England altered as agriculture became less important and other activities far more so. In 1921–39, the number of agricultural labourers fell by a quarter, and the pace quickened after the Second World War. Horses were replaced by tractors, and local water-mills fell into disuse. Hand-milking was replaced by machines.

This assault on rural England was deplored and resisted by conservationists who drew on a strong sense that change and modernization threatened identity and values. The cult of the outdoors contributed to a commitment to the landscape that was especially strong in the inter-war period: 1918–39. This took many forms. In music, it was seen in the positive response to Elgar and Vaughan Williams, in painting to the popularity of 'authentic' rather than modernist works. The crafts movement developed from the 1900s, in large part as an affirmation of a vernacular culture that was worth defending. In fiction, there were ruralist writers, such as Henry Williamson whose works included *Tarka the Otter* (1927). In his *The Linhay on the Downs* (1938) he referred to 'the harmony of nature', a central theme in much inter-war culture.

One of the most influential disseminators of the ruralist image of England was H.V. [Henry Canova Vollam] Morton (1892–1979). Born in Birmingham and a journalist, he was one of the most popular writers of his day. His *In Search of England*, first published on 2 June 1927, had two other editions in 1927, three each in 1928, 1929 and 1930, four in 1931, and appeared in its twenty-fourth in 1937. It was the most influential of a whole genre of tour guides to parts of England that were very popular in the inter-war period. They reflected the possibilities for individual touring created by spreading ownership of cars. There were about two million by the outbreak of the Second World War in 1939.

To Morton, the countryside was integral to national life: 'The squares of London, those sacred little patches of the country-side preserved, perhaps, by the Anglo-Saxon instinct for grass and trees, hold in their restricted glades some part of the magic of spring. I suppose many a man has stood at his window above a London square in April hearing a message from the lanes of England.'

At the close of the book, the reader already taken by car to Land's End and then to the Scottish border and back to Kenilworth 'in the heart of England', is offered a rural idyll when Morton meets a vicar who provides an attractive account of timelessness:

> We are, in this little hamlet, untouched by ideas, in spite of the wireless and the charabanc. We use words long since abandoned. My parishioners believe firmly in a physical resurrection. . . . We are far from the pain of cities, the complexities. Life is reduced here to a single common denominator . . . We are rooted in something firmer than fashion. . . . the newspapers are only another kind of fairy story about the world outside.

Morton's book thus closes with an assertion of faith and a powerful account of an identity of people and place: 'I went out into the churchyard where the green stones nodded together, and I took up a handful of earth and felt it crumble and run through my fingers, thinking that as long as one

English field lies against another there is something left in the world for a man to love.' Morton saw the peasantry as 'the salt of the earth' and a kind of well of virtue and character from which the nation received constant refreshment. This view might now seem conservative, but Morton in fact was a Labour supporter, a populist, a democrat, and moderately collectivist.

In some quarters, there was also a sense of the occult power of the landscape. This was true, for example, of interest in ley lines, and could also be in novels such as Sylvia Townsend Warner's *Lolly Willowes* (1926), with its account of the Chilterns. Similar ruralist themes echoed in the second half of the century, although not continually, in the 1950s rather than the 1960s for example. However, although they helped maintain an idyll of rurality, they could not preserve the countryside. Morton's vicar indeed is pensive about the lord of the manor, 'poor now as a church mouse but rooted to the land . . . When he dies . . . I suppose they will sell to pay the death duties and then . . .'. Indeed many landowners sold up and the countryside was being rapidly built over.

Rural prosperity improved during the Second World War as domestic production was expanded to cope with the cut in food imports. After the conflict, there was no return to the pre-war situation. The 1947 Agriculture Act created a favourable climate for agricultural expansion through the provision of guaranteed prices and the concept of deficiency payments which were adopted in the 1950s. The Act paved the way for rapid agricultural expansion based on the application of science and technology. Farming was transformed from a way of life to a business-orientated activity in which financial considerations dominate.

NEW HISTORY OF ENGLAND

This remained the case, with agriculture continuing to shed workers, but the situation deteriorated anew, and a sense of malaise became especially strong in many parts of rural England in the 1990s. This malaise was both economic – a combination of low agricultural commodity prices, greater foreign competition, a strong pound, a public health crisis in beef production, falling consumption of dairy products, and the major role of supermarket chains as purchasers – and a more general sense that government and urban society no longer cared about rural society. Given the role of the countryside in sustaining traditional images of Englishness, this was particularly striking. The subordination of the traditional rural role of producing food has been shown from the 1980s when the cost of agricultural support encouraged the European Community now European Union to introduce 'set aside', initially on a voluntary basis. Farmers were paid not to grow arable crops on designated fields which were to be left fallow.

Other non-urban activities, such as forestry, mining and quarrying, have also either declined or dramatically cut their workforces. These changes have led to the depopulation of many rural regions, especially upland areas and those beyond commuting distance from towns. This decline is not a case of the destruction of age-old lifestyles, for the rural world of 1900 was in many respects no older than the major changes of the period 1500–1800, while the depopulation of some rural areas had already been a major problem in Tudor England and even more in 1350–1500. Change is and was constant, and yet, in terms of the sense of place and identity of the English population of last century, the past seemed more fixed and the scale of change therefore revolutionary. The countryside has become, for many of its inhabitants, a place of residence or retirement rather than of work, and urban attitudes have been introduced, as in complaints about the noise produced by farm animals or bellringers. The successful campaign in the 1990s and 2000s to ban hunting was very much seen in this light. In much of rural England, housing has become scarce and expensive as a result of purchase by commuters, while the problems of the rural economy have led to a large number of rural households living below the poverty line.

At the other end of the social scale, though state subsidies for agriculture from the 1940s helped farmers and land-owners, Lloyd George's tax changes and the disappearance of the vast labour force of cheap servants had already hit country house life, and many country houses were demolished or institutionalized. Over 600 were destroyed or abandoned between 1920 and 1975; many others transferred to the National Trust or became reliant on paying visitors. The dominance of much of rural England by the aristocratic estate became a thing of the past. The influence of landowners in the politics of agriculture was replaced by that of farmers.

Visually and environmentally, rural England has also changed greatly. Redundant farmsteads have fallen into ruin or been destroyed. Amalgamating fields and bulldozing hedges have led since the 1950s to the replacement, as in many parts of Cambridgeshire, Essex and Suffolk, of the earlier patchwork of small fields surrounded by dense hedges, by large expanses of arable land, bounded often by barbed-wire fences. This has had serious environmental consequences, as have changes in the use of more marginal lands. Large plantations of coniferous trees have been planted on upland moors and on the Suffolk Breckland. Marshlands have been drained and are now intensively farmed. Upland valleys, such as the North Tyne and the Durham Derwent, have been drowned for reservoirs. Others are threatened, as water use and shortage becomes a more acute problem. The condition of farmland has also become an issue. Pesticides are used extensively in agriculture, and enter the ground-water system.

More generally, the conquest of nature has become ever more comprehensive and insistent. There has been great concern about the impact on animal and plant life of intensive agricultural practices and of development. Animal habitats have been destroyed or disrupted, as lakes, ponds and marshes are drained, copses cut down, hedges grubbed up, and long grass cut. Pesticides affect animal breeding. The loss of the 'dawn chorus' is an obvious sign of the frequently insidious impact of change on natural life. Again, this relates to traditional conceptualizations of Englishness, for, as in other countries, this has, in large part, rested on an apparent or alleged relationship between people and the natural environment. This organic account of identity is fundamentally ruralist, and conservative, although not in the sense of conservatism as the creed of capitalism, indeed far from it.

For example, new technology in the shape of television helped popularize democratic images of rural and provincial England. The BBC comedy series *Last of the Summer Wine*, launched in 1973, had audiences of up to 16 million by the early 1980s. Filmed in the Yorkshire town of Holmfirth, it depicted an attractive countryside around a small Pennine town in which people could readily wander. Furthermore, this celebration of northernness and the Pennine environment was presented in terms of a comedy of character that played on another aspect of national identity, tolerance of eccentricity. Thus, in the series, the disreputable grubby, poorly dressed, ferret-keeping Compo was presented positively. Moreover, the rural world of *The Archers* has remained the most popular and longest-lasting radio 'soap'.

People have moved not only off the land, but also away from declining industrial regions. This was an aspect of the way in which increasing mobility was important to the demographic history of England. Areas that were collectively the nineteenth-century 'workshop of the world' became industrial museums and regions of social dereliction, designated as problems requiring regional assistance, as under the Special Areas Act (1934). During the slump of the 1930s, unemployment in Sunderland rose to 75 per cent of shipbuilders and half of the working population, and was associated with hardship and higher rates of ill-health. This was part of a crisis of heavy industry and mining that was not restricted to the 1930s, but that recurred savagely in the 1980s. As a consequence, much of the North and the West Midlands lost their capacity to generate new jobs faster than old ones were lost.

In addition, crowded inner-city areas lost people as slums were torn down. Instead, people moved to new developments in 'green-field' sites, in the countryside, or on the edge of older settlements. The former were new towns, the first garden city being Letchworth (1903); the latter suburban sprawl, the suburbia where a far greater percentage of the population than hitherto came to live. The expansion of suburbia in the first four decades of the twentieth century was encouraged by a lack of rural planning controls and by the agricultural depression which encouraged farmers to sell land in order to survive. The process is still continuing. The Labour government elected in 1997 compelled local authorities to release rural land for new houses.

Designed to allow the expanding middle class to realize their earning potential, to escape from the crowded and polluted conditions of the city, and to join in the expanding hobby of amateur gardening, new housing was both cause and consequence of a massive expansion of personal transportation. Commuting led to an increase in first train and later car use. In the 1920s and 1930s, the development of the London tube system allowed a major spread of the city to the north, while national private ownership of cars increased by over 1,000 per cent. By 1937, over 300,000 new cars were being registered annually. 'The sound of horns and motors', referred to in T.S. Eliot's poem *The Waste Land* (1922) was becoming more insistent. The railways had often pioneered feeder bus services, but, from the 1920s, the competition of road transport became serious for them. After a fall in car ownership during the Second World War, its rise accelerated rapidly, especially after petrol rationing ended. In terms of thousand million passenger-kilometres, private road transport shot up from 76 in 1954 to 350 in 1974, an increase from 39 to 79 per cent of the total. This gain was made at the expense of bus, coach and rail transport and also cycling. Nationalized in 1948, the railways lost money from the late 1950s, and the Beeching report of 1963 led to dramatic cuts in the network. There were 12.2 million cars in Britain in 1970, 21.9 in 1990. A motorway system was created, beginning with the M6 Preston by-pass, opened by the Prime Minister, Harold Macmillan, in December 1958. The M1 from Watford to Birmingham rapidly followed. As rural usage grew, it became necessary progressively to supplement existing roads. Every town soon required its by-pass; Exeter's was opened in 1938, Newbury's second one in 1998 after bitter struggles with anti-road protesters in 1995–6. Car exhaust emissions led to environmental pollution, while by the early 1990s 45,000 children were being hurt on the roads every year and among those aged five–fifteen two-thirds of deaths were the result of road accidents.

Greater personal mobility for the bulk, but by no means all, of the population, enabled and was a necessary consequence of lower-density housing. The spatial segregation of the population was scarcely novel, but it became more pronounced, and an obvious aspect of what was termed the 'underclass', in both town and countryside, was their relative lack of mobility. Employment patterns also changed. In place of factories or mines that had had large labour forces, most modern industrial concerns were capital intensive and employed less labour. A growing number of the rising percentage of the population who were retired left the cities to live in suburban, rural or coastal areas, such as Exmouth and Worthing. New shopping patterns developed, with the rise of the supermarket in the 1950s and the hypermarket in the 1980s. By 1992, 16 per cent of the total shopping space in Britain was made up of shopping centres, such as Brent Cross in North London, Lakeside at Thurrock in Essex, The Glades in Bromley, Kent, Meadowhall in Sheffield and the Metro Centre in Gateshead. They were moulders of taste and spheres of purchasing and leisure activity at the centre of the consumer society. Most of their customers came by car, abandoning traditional high street shopping. 'Out of town' shopping was essentially classless, unless non-owners of cars count as a class. It avoided the 'in-town' social divides of the working class using Woolworths and the middle classes using Marks and Spencer and John Lewis. Instead, anyone who could drive there blended into a new environment. Related changes in location were also of great importance in other fields, including education. In 1971, 14 per cent of junior school children were driven to school, in 1990 64 per cent, in part a response to the withdrawal of local authority aid for home–school transport.

Consumerism and technology, the two closely related, have been crucial features of the contemporary age. Their impact has been very varied. Thus, the spread, in the 1930s, of affordable cars with reliable self-starter motors, so that it was not necessary to crank up the motor by hand, led to a wave of 'smash and grab' raids, as the criminal fraternity took advantage of the new technology. Greater mobility totally changed the pattern of crime. In response, in London, the Metropolitan Police experimented with mounting ships' radios in cars and were able to develop a fleet of Wolseley cars thus equipped with which to mount an effective response. The post-Second World War world was to bring computer fraud, but also the use of sophisticated forensic techniques. Traffic offences brought middle-class individuals into contact with the police and the courts, and led to changes in attitudes towards the police.

Labour-saving devices reduced the burden of housework, easing the struggle with dirt and disease, although they also ensured that household use of water increased considerably. The declining burden of housework was linked to a major social shift of the century, the end of the servant. This, however, was also more complex, as, alongside the replacement of human labour by machines, for tasks such as washing clothes, other forms of personal care remained important or became more so. As a greater percentage of women, especially middle-class women, stayed in the labour force while married, so child care became more important as an issue. So also did care of the elderly. Old practices and systems of care by the immediate or extended family and by the community declined in effectiveness (although it is important not to exaggerate their earlier success) and, instead, it proved necessary to hire assistance, although most of this was institutional in character.

The communication of messages has also been revolutionized. Telephone ownership has risen to a high level; fax machines and mobile phones became important in the 1980s; and the growing numbers of personal and company computers facilitated the use of electronic mail. In the 1990s, electronic shopping and the distant office became realities.

The number of radio and television channels has multiplied. Radio broadcasts began in 1922; the British Broadcasting Corporation, a monopoly acting in the 'national interest' and financed by licence fees paid by radio owners, was established in 1926; and it began television services in 1936. Commercial television companies, financed by advertising, were not established until 1955. The situation was thus very different to that in the USA. The greater role of the public sector in Britain was at once product and cause of a different society. In inter-war Britain capitalism was much more regulated, as part of a semi-corporate state, than was the case in the USA, although far less so than was to follow in the 1940s, first with wartime controls and then with post-war nationalizations.

Television ownership shot up in the 1950s, the numbers of those with regular access to a set rising from 38 per cent of the population in 1955 to 75 per cent in 1959. By the early 1990s, ownership and access rates were far higher, and the larger number of regular channels had been supplemented for many by cable and satellite channels, the receiving dishes altering the appearance of many houses as television aerials had earlier done. By 1992 over a million Sky Television dishes had been sold. Over 50 per cent of households had video recorders, giving them even greater control over what they watched.

Television succeeded radio as a central determinant of the leisure time of many, a moulder of opinions and fashions, a source of conversation and controversy, an occasion of family cohesion or dispute, a major feature of the household. By 1999 the average person was watching more than 2½ hours of television daily. A force for change, a great contributor to the making of the 'consumer society' and a 'window on the world', which demands the right to enter everywhere and report anything, television has also become increasingly a reflector of popular taste. Just as radio had helped to provide common experiences: royal Christmas messages from 1932, Edward VIII's abdication speech in 1938, the war speeches of Winston Churchill, heard by millions, as those of Lloyd George could not be; so television fulfilled the same function, providing much of the nation with common visual images and messages. This really began with the coronation service for Elizabeth II in 1953, a cause of many households purchasing sets or first watching, and, thanks to television, the royals have almost become members of viewers' extended families, treated with the fascination devoted commonly to the stars of soap operas. Indeed, both the 'New Elizabethan Age', heralded in 1952, and the discontents of the 1990s and 2000s about the position and behaviour of the royal family, owe much to the 'media'; although it was a newspaper article by John Grigg (Lord Altrincham) attacking the courtiers who surrounded Elizabeth II that started criticism of the monarchy during her reign.

Television is central to much else: the advertising that is so crucial to the consumer society, and the course and conduct of election campaigns. Parliament is televised, and much of public politics has become a matter of soundbites aimed to catch the evening news bulletins. The world of the spin doctor, such as Alistair Campbell under Tony Blair, is dependent on the role of television.

The BBC's mission beyond England was indicated by specific governors for Wales and Scotland, although the BBC was slow to establish separate services for both. In contrast, the regional structure of independent television promoted both English regionalism and Scottish and Welsh autonomy. Television also contributed to the increasingly noisy nature of life, although other consumer goods were also a problem. By the late 1990s, noise was the biggest source of complaints to local authorities, more than rubbish or litter. In 1996, the Noise Act made it possible to confiscate offending hi-fi equipment.

Technological change contributed to an economic situation in which the annual output of goods rose appreciably for most of the period, while per capita (person) output, consumption and leisure similarly rose, despite a major growth in population. Even the 1930s, the period of the Slump, was, for most of those in work, a decade of rising real wages, improved housing, wider consumer choice and a better quality of life. The 1930s was a period of new and developing electrical goods, many bought on hire-purchase, of radio, television and the 'talkies'. Large numbers of cinemas were constructed: despite its relatively low population, Suffolk alone had forty in 1937. This, however, was of scant value to the unemployed, nearly three million in late 1932, and, despite a strong recovery between 1934 and 1937, still above one million until 1941. About one-third of Derbyshire's miners were out of work in 1931–3, and the 1933 Derbyshire march of the National Unemployed Workers' Movement had such slogans as 'We refuse to starve in silence. . . . We want work schemes'. Many of those who had work nevertheless faced low wages, a life of shifts and expedients, inadequate food and poor housing, but, for many others, the 1930s was a period of prosperity and this helped to account for the very substantial victory of the National Government in the 1935 election.

The same contrast was true of the recessions at the beginning of the 1980s and the 1990s. Alongside high unemployment, and social strains manifested in rising crime rates and urban riots, many of those in work had high living standards. Unemployment was seen as a price worth paying for low inflation, although the unemployed were not consulted, any more than the victims of inflation had been in the 1970s. Ownership of telephones, washing machines, dish-washers, cars and video-recorders all rose. In both recessions, however, the rising ownership of goods was, in part, met by increased imports, while industry was harmed by the high exchange-rate of sterling as the interests of producers were subordinated to those of finance, not least due to a determination to reduce inflation.

Contrasting assessments of such periods – the 1930s have been presented as both 'the devil's decade' and an age of social stability, and the reputation of the Thatcher years of 1979–90 is also very mixed – indicate not only the problems of historical evaluation, but also the relationship between such evaluation and contemporary policy debates. Thus, for example, so-called 'new right' historians emphasized a positive account of the 1930s, suggesting that this situation of growth and stability collapsed due to the Second World War and was succeeded by decades of misgovernment and excessive emphasis on social welfare. In contrast, in the late 1990s, in large part encouraged by Labour's success in the 1997 election, there was a resumption of criticism of policies and conditions in the 1930s, a restatement of the value of Britain's role in the Second World War, and a more positive account of the post-war creation of the welfare state. Instead of blaming the Attlee governments of 1945–51, there is criticism of the Conservative ministries of 1951–64 for failing to sustain reform and of those of 1979–97 for reversing it. These controversies in part reflect the politicized character of recent history, but they also capture the variety of the past.

Economic growth and changing political and social assumptions led to the development of national social security and educational provision and, from 1948, of a national health service, ensuring that the indigent and ill were offered a comprehensive safety net, while a range of services were provided free at the point of delivery to the whole of the population. Earlier measures, such as free school meals (1907), non-contributory old-age pensions (1908), labour exchanges (1909), the National Insurance Act (1911), and the establishment of the Unemployment Assistance Board (1934), were limited, but an improvement on the previous situation, and the establishment of antenatal screening in the 1920s was important. Further developments were widely supported in the three decades after the Second World War, a period when 'One-Nation Toryism' and 'Butskellism' (apparent Conservative/Labour convergence) reflected a measure of continuity between Labour (1945–51, 64–70, 74–9) and Conservative (1951–64, 70–4) governments, although it is important not to minimise differences and tensions over principles and policies between the two parties, even in the 1950s.

The creation of the welfare state, by the 1945–51 Labour governments under Clement Attlee, reflected a conviction that social progress and economic growth were compatible, and that, indeed, a major purpose of the latter was to achieve the former. More generally, stable employment and social security were seen as important goals. State regulation and welfare provision affected much of national life. Housing, for example, was regulated and then improved. Following the 1915 Rent and Mortgage Interest Restrictions (War) Act, which owed something to the Clydeside rent strikes of that year, private landlordship became less profitable, tenants' rights more secure, and renting from local authorities, 'council housing', more important.

After the First World War, there was state support for new housing and local authorities were very active. Slums were swept aside and their inhabitants moved into new housing estates, particularly after 1945. Extolled at the time, and illustrated alongside castles and cathedrals in guidebooks of the 1960s, they have subsequently been attacked as lacking in community feeling and being breeders of alienation and crime. Attacks on the quality of public-sector housing appears most appropriate for system-built housing of the 1960s, rather than for that of the 1950s. Insufficient is known about the attitudes of those rehoused in the 1950s to pass judgement on the success of the policy, although clearly the decline in waiting lists was popular and many would have welcomed the opportunity to live in properties with inside toilets.

Similarly, there has been disagreement about the social and educational consequences of the comprehensivization of education, the abandonment, in the 1950s and especially from 1965, of streaming of children by ability into different schools after examination at the age of eleven. The division between grammar and secondary-modern schools under the earlier system was criticized in the 1950s and 1960s as socially divisive, and as reinforcing and replicating the traditional white collar/blue collar divide. Grammar school entry was dominated by the middle class. Secondary moderns were regarded as offering less. The introduction of a comprehensive system was a controversial policy that touched raw nerves about social as well as educational issues. The inclusiveness offered by the comprehensive system proved illusory, not least because the experience of education offered in middle-class areas was generally different to that in 'problem schools'. Furthermore, the percentage of children in private schools rose markedly in the 1980s. These schools continue to be perceived as both cause and consequence of class distinction, although they are as much a comment on the apparent limitations of the state system. Major expansions in higher education in the 1960s and from the early 1990s dramatically increased the percentage of school-leavers continuing in full-time education, and thus eventually the graduate population, but it is not clear that the hopes inspiring this process, especially that of fulfilling the economy's requirements for skills, have been met.

Though for long regarded as one of the triumphs of social welfare policy, the National Health Service (NHS), established in 1948, was harmed from the outset by the limitations of centralized control and the measures taken in order to win the consent of interest groups, especially doctors and dentists. It subsequently suffered from the rising cost of medical treatment, a consequence of the greater potential for medical action, increasing longevity, and rising expectations of care. Private health care expanded and the state of the NHS was a major issue in the general elections of the 1990s and 2000s.

At the beginning of the twenty-first century, large numbers still died prematurely from diseases such as cancer and heart failure. The rate of infant mortality remained higher in Britain than in many other developed countries. Yet, at great cost, the NHS was able to maintain the policy of treatment free at the point of delivery, so that many of the anxieties about the availability and cost of medical treatment that the poor faced earlier in the century and that were, for example, important in the 1930s, ended. The NHS also established a much fairer geographical and social allocation of resources and skills than had existed hitherto, and there was a positive effort to develop medical education and specialized services spread across the regions rather than concentrated, as earlier, in a few centres, principally London.

Uniform health provision through the NHS played a major role in the dramatic change in the medical condition of the population that has characterized this century, though other factors, such as improved diet, were also of great importance, and neither the NHS nor the welfare state as a whole ended major social differences in health indicators and life experiences. Britain was in the forefront of medical research and development throughout the century and, as general medical knowledge increased enormously, so the ability to identify and treat disease has increased exponentially, although, as late as the inter-war period, doctors were experts at diagnosis and prognosis, but, for most conditions, could do little in the way of treatment; insulin and pernicious anaemia were exceptions. The big transformation – the 'therapeutic revolution' – only came after 1945, with antibiotics on one hand and steroids on the other, and with the pharmaceutical journey through the chemical spectrum which threw up immunosuppressive drugs, new anaesthetics, etc.

These improvements touched the lives of millions and totally altered the condition of the people and the nature of disease. There was an impact on all age groups. For example, the discovery of insulin in 1922 and its use from the mid-1920s enabled young diabetics to live. England played a major role in the understanding and treatment of mental illness. The twentieth century brought recognition of the importance of psychological and mental processes, and the diagnosis and treatment of mental illness was revolutionized. The development from the 1940s of safe and effective drugs helped in the treatment of major psychoses and depression, dramatically improving the cure rate.

Antibiotics were of enormous benefit for dealing with infections, which, of one kind or another, were a very common cause of death in the first half of the century. Tuberculosis, which killed one adult in eight at the beginning of the twentieth century, was largely conquered thanks to the use of antibiotics, as well as to better diet and the programme of mass BCG vaccination. Antibiotics also helped with other bacterial infection; urinary infections for example came to be more readily treated.

The common childhood diseases which caused high mortality and high morbidity in children in the early part of the twentieth century, such as measles, whooping cough and diphtheria, had been declining since before the First World War, but were further reduced by the post-1945 introduction of immunization programmes for the entire child population. Immunization for whooping cough came in the 1950s, and for measles in the 1960s; for mumps only after 1985; and German measles, for children other than adolescent girls, only after 1990. From the 1970s on, there was a limited introduction of population screening for the early detection and treatment of other diseases, such as breast and cervical cancer. The 1980s saw the increasing development and use of anti-viral agents for the treatment of viral infections.

Surgical treatment dramatically increased. The two world wars, especially the second, saw a major improvement in surgical techniques, with, for example, the development of plastic surgery. A major increase in anaesthetic skills, due to greater knowledge and the introduction of increasingly sophisticated drugs, meant that complex surgical operations could be performed. Once serious operations, such as appendicectomies, became routine and minor. The range of research and development now encompasses skin grafts and artificial knee joints. There were major advances in the treatment of the heart, and bypass and transplant surgery have been completely developed since the Second World War. The first successful renal transplant was carried out between identical twins in 1953, but problems of rejection bedevilled the operation for others until they were overcome in 1963. It was only after this resolution of rejection that major transplant surgery became a clinical reality.

Medical advances led to dramatic changes in the pattern of causes of death, although related developments in public health were also of great importance. Since 1945, the Clean Air Act (1956) and other environmental measures, safety at work awareness and the Health and Safety at Work Act, and growing understanding of the dangers of working in smoke-filled buildings and with asbestos, all contributed, not least to the decline of chest illnesses. The hazards of drinking to excess and, particularly, of smoking became generally appreciated and were addressed by government action, although success was less than universal. Furthermore, government was very slow to address the problem of smoking through legislation; and action was for long limited to a crack-down on advertising. Action against alcohol took place only in the context of the First World War. Despite a significant anti-alcohol lobby, government has since taken little action except in terms of drink-driving laws. Government inaction on both smoking and alcohol was widely seen as due to powerful commercial (and taxation) vested interests. Lung cancer death rates are still rising among women, and health education in this respect is known to be failing among teenagers.

This is even more true of diet. Food intake was controlled during the Second World War, with rationing organized to encourage a healthy diet. The poor benefited from more protein and vitamins, the better-off from a cut in the consumption of meat, fat, eggs and sugar. Infant mortality declined, the average age of death from natural causes increased. After rationing ended, however, it proved hard to promote sensible eating. More generally, health education is still struggling, especially among the poorer classes, specifically those whose educational aspirations and general expectations are low.

Whereas large numbers of children died in the first half of the twentieth century and infections were a major cause of death, now later-onset diseases, such as heart disease and cancers, are far more important, and infections kill people who are suffering from associated disorders and who are at the extremes of life. Average life expectancy for all age-groups persistently rose during the century, the major exception being those aged between fifteen and forty-four during the 1980s, although social differences remained; by the late 1990s those from low-income groups generally died about five years sooner than the better-off. The rise in life expectancy has led, however, to a new age structure, as a result of the increasing number of pensioners, and to the problems posed by the greater number of people over eighty-five with the increasing dependencies associated with age. This had a major impact on social welfare, especially pension provision. Currently, the cost of supporting pensioners amounts to about half the social security budget. People over the age of sixty-five are also the most frequent users of health services and much of the debate within the personal social services over recent decades has been concerned with residential or community care options for older people.

In addition, not all illnesses were in retreat. Possibly as a result of increasing car exhaust emissions, respiratory diseases, such as asthma, definitely rose, and some others may also be increasing. The massive increase in the import, treatment and burying of hazardous waste in the 1980s has led to concern about possible health implications. Diarrhoeal diseases as recorded in food-poisoning and virus-related infections have risen since 1940. Tuberculosis and malaria have made a comeback. If global warming continues, then it is likely that this trend will become more marked. In addition, medical advances created new problems. The belated realization that blood transfusion could induce new disease resulted in the 1970s in the routine screening of blood products for hepatitis B. It also took time before the hazards of HIV transmission through blood products were realized, with tragic consequences in particular for haemophiliacs.

If the age-structure of the population changed totally as a result of medical advances, so also did many aspects of people's lives. Contraceptive developments dramatically increased the ability of women to control their own fertility and played a major role in the emancipation of women, as well as in the 'sexual revolution', the change in general sexual norms, of the 1960s on. Sex and conception were separated. The situation of the approximately 20 per cent of couples who are infertile changed thanks to new techniques such as in vitro fertilization. Though AIDS developed as a new killer, antibiotics dealt with most other sexually transmitted diseases.

Pain was increasingly held at bay by more effective and selective painkillers, bringing relief to millions suffering from illnesses such as arthritis and muscular pain. Thus the condition of the people really changed. They were healthier and longer-living. Nutrition improved considerably, average height increased for both men and women, and the country was affluent and health-conscious enough to emphasize the newly perceived problem of the over-weight.

Yet the modern age was also a period when Britain's relative economic performance declined appreciably with reference to traditional and new competitors. In 1960–81, although the country participated in the general economic expansion of the 1960s, Britain's annual growth in gross domestic product was lower than that of all the other eighteen OECD countries. This followed the 'slow growth' of Britain in the 1950s. The average standard of living fell beneath that of Germany, Japan, France and Italy in the post-1960 period. A sense of decline, pervasive at times, was especially characteristic in the 1970s. The cover of the satirical journal *Private Eye* on 10 January 1975 showed the oil-rich King of Saudi Arabia, with the caption 'Britain Sold Shock. New Man at Palace'. Ironically, the discovery of oil in the North Sea shortly beforehand was to help ease Britain's balance-of-payments problem, though it did not prevent continued economic decline relative to competitors who lacked that resource.

In addition, structural changes in the economy created major problems, particularly widespread unemployment, often over two, and in some cases over three, million during the 1980s and 1990s, a decline in manufacturing industry with serious associated regional problems, and difficulties in maintaining a stable currency. There were many long-term causes for these weaknesses. England was much more successful at innovation than at commercially exploiting the advances made by its scientists. Problems also arose from low levels of investment or investment in the wrong sectors, and from an amateur tradition in management and economic policy-making. Science and technology were rapidly harnessed during the two world wars when it was imperative, but peacetime attitudes were less supportive. The failure of the development of secondary technical schools proposed in the 1944 Education Act had important implications for England's economic performance and social mobility.

England's initial success in industrialization had been predominantly a result of private enterprise, with the state taking a passive role. Free trade limited the amount of state regulation. The relatively small-scale undertakings which had developed were ill-equipped in terms of size, attitudes and policies to foster and exploit the scientific discoveries of the twentieth century. In this sense, England's early lead in industrialization may have become a handicap in the twentieth-century race for expansion.

These weaknesses interacted with aspects of the 'political economy', not least the rising power of trade unions with their generally perceived determination to put sectional interests first, the conviction of politicians that they could improve the economy, and a variety of interventionist policies that have generally not had this result. Trade union membership rose from 1½ million (1895) to 11½ million (1975). Union leaders such as Jack Jones, General Secretary of the Transport and General Workers' Union 1968–78, wielded great influence in the 1960s and 1970s. They played key roles in what was a corporatist state, Jones forging a Social Compact with the Labour government of Harold Wilson in 1974: the unions were to moderate wage demands in return for an acceptable legislative programme. Strikes for substantial wage increases, that could not be justified by the price of coal, by the National Union of Miners, some of whose leaders were motivated by political hostility, defeated the Conservative government of Edward Heath when it attempted to restrain wage inflation in 1972 and, crucially, 1974. The miners' strike of 1984–5 was only beaten by the government of the determined Margaret Thatcher (Conservative PM 1979–90) after a long struggle, and then in part because the poorly led miners were divided and the weather good; many indeed refused to strike. Thanks to television and power cuts, people became accustomed respectively to the immediacy of picket-line violence and to baths in the dark.

A 'winter of discontent' in 1978/9, in which 'secondary picketing' had played a major and disruptive role, helped Thatcher to victory in 1979. A determined opponent of consensus policies and attitudes, which she felt had ruined the country, Thatcher had little time for discussions with trade union leaders (or they with her) and passed a whole series of legislation to limit their powers, a task that Harold Wilson had failed to achieve in 1969 when the white paper 'In Place of Strife' was withdrawn due to trade union and Labour Party opposition. Under Thatcher, in the late 1980s, trade union militancy became less common; and the level of industrial action (strikes) continued to fall in the 1990s. By 1990, only 48 per cent of employees were union members and the number covered by closed shop agreements had fallen to ½ million, compared to 4½ million a decade earlier. Far more wage negotiations were at a local level.

Other aspects of the 'political economy' also created serious problems. Especially from the 1940s, government economic management was inconsistent. There was a lack of continuity in economic policy, for example over regional aid. The steel industry was nationalized in 1949 and 1967, and privatized in 1953 and then again after 1979, alongside gas, electricity, telephones, water, the railways and much else, as the Conservatives under Thatcher, and then in 1990–7 John Major, strove to diminish the role of the state, and also to help finance government expenditure without raising taxation. Throughout the century, economic growth did not match political expectations, leading to disagreement over expenditure priorities, and the major rise in government expenditure and employment since 1914 increased the importance of these disputes. The national budget was unable to sustain the assumptions and demands of politicians on behalf of, for example, social welfare and defence. The devaluation of the pound by 30.5 per cent in 1949 was, for example, followed by public expenditure cuts, leading to the introduction of prescription charges and resignations by left-wing Labour ministers.

Alongside the often unsuccessful management of the economy by politicians, such as the overvalued rate at which the pound returned to the gold standard in 1925, and the delay in devaluing sterling until 1967 by the government of Harold Wilson, Labour Prime Minister (1964–70, 74–6), there was also, at times, a serious neglect of aspects of the economy, symbolized by the remark of Sir Alec Douglas-Home, who renounced his earldom to become Conservative Prime Minister (1963–4), that his grasp of economics was of the 'matchstick variety'. All post-1945 premiers, with the possible exception of James Callaghan (Labour 1976–9), spent too much time on foreign policy and found it difficult to abandon the habit of seeing Britain as a major international player. These were politicians who cared more about Cape Town than Consett or Baghdad than Birmingham, and poor economic management was in part to blame for high rates of inflation, which rose to an average of 15.8 per cent in 1972–5, and for the subsequent need to turn to the International Monetary Fund for assistance (1976). The last reflected the post-war failure of the British system, at least as it was operated in the mid-1970s.

An overall rate of economic growth was scant consolation to those with diminished experiences and disappointed expectations. And yet, a striking feature of the domestic and international problems that England encountered is that they did not lead to a radicalization of politics. The First World War helped focus the already powerful role of political and social pressures in fragmenting, and yet also transmitting, Victorian liberalism, which had been the dominant secular ideology of the nineteenth century. The British Communist Party was formed in 1920, there was a General Strike in 1926, and the 1930s saw the formation by Sir Oswald Mosley of the New Party, which subsequently evolved into the British Union of Fascists (BUF). Some writers of the period expressed the fear that sinister conspiracies lay behind political and industrial problems. This was the theme of Sapper's (Lieutenant-Colonel H.C. McNeile) *Bulldog Drummond* (1921). John Buchan (1875–1940), a Scottish writer who served in Intelligence during the First World War before becoming an MP and Governor-General of Canada, discerned in *The Three Hostages* (1924) 'wreckers on the grand scale, merchants of pessimism, giving society another kick downhill whenever it had a chance of finding its balance, and then pocketing their profits . . . they used the fanatics . . . whose key was a wild hatred of something or other, or a reasoned belief in anarchy'. In *The Big Four* (1927) of the detective writer Agatha Christie (1890–1976), the best-selling British author of the century, 'The world-wide unrest, the labour troubles that beset every nation, and the revolutions that break out in some . . . there is a force behind the scenes which aims at nothing less than the disintegration of civilization . . . Lenin and Trotsky were mere puppets'. Technology was at the service of this force 'a concentration of wireless energy far beyond anything so far attempted, and capable of focusing a beam of great intensity upon some given spot . . . atomic energy', so that the Big Four could become 'the dictators of the world'. Such sinister threats facing Britain were to be a staple of spy thrillers, as in the novels of Ian Fleming (1908–64), beginning with *Casino Royale* (1953). Adventure stories, many of which testified to the imaginative potency of the new technology, they also revealed a sense of the nation under threat, an imaginative extension of the challenges facing the country.

Yet radicalism was to make little impact in Britain and the continuity of parliamentary government was not overthrown. Instead, liberalism (though not the influence of the Liberal Party) was diffused among all the major parties, thus sustaining a liberal consensus, although different groups emphasized different aspects of the liberal message. The General Strike was defeated by the firmness of the Baldwin government and the resulting lack of nerve of the Trade Union leadership, and the membership of the BUF did not exceed 50,000. The economic upturn of 1934 and Baldwin's sensible management of politics stemmed rising support for Mosley. Despite their subsequent reputation, far more Cambridge undergraduates of the 1930s were interested in sport than in Communist activism. The limited extent of radicalism was even more true after the Second World War. Nazi activities discredited the extreme right, while the policies and eventual failure of the Soviet Union struck successive blows at the credibility of the far left.

The Labour Party drifted to the left in the 1970s and was affected by 'entryism' by far-left groups, so that there was little to choose in the 1980s between the views of some Labour MPs and Western European Communists. This, however, helped to lead to four successive Labour failures in the general elections of 1979, 1983, 1987 and 1992, the most unimpressive record of any political party since the decline of the Liberals after the First World War, and one achieved despite serious economic difficulties for Conservative governments at the beginning of the 1980s and before the 1992 election. The attempt to create a collectivist society by means of state action, a new-model society planned in accordance with socialist principles, was rejected by the electorate, and in the late 1980s by the Labour Party under the leadership of Neil Kinnock (1983–92). Kinnock's successors, John Smith (1992–4) and Tony Blair (1994–2007), moved Labour away from the left, helping it to win major electoral victories in 1997, 2001 and 2005. Similarly, successive public opinion polls in the 1980s and early 1990s revealed limited support for much of the agenda of the 'New Right', and clear support for the welfare state, especially the National Health Service. The recessions of the early 1980s and 1990s did not lead to a revival of left-wing radicalism, and the circulation of the Communist daily newspaper, the *Morning Star*, fell below 10,000.

The relationship between the absence of a successful challenge to the political system, or at least a major trans-formation of it, and the lack of sustained defeat abroad is unclear. Germany, Japan, France, Italy and Austria-Hungary all suffered serious defeat in the First and/or Second World Wars, leading to a political and institutional transformation which was as important for the subsequent success of most of those societies as the rebuilding of economic systems on which attention is usually focused. No such process took place in Britain. Indeed, in several respects, the essential features of the political system are still those of 1914, a hereditary monarchy, albeit one that adopted the British name of Windsor in 1917, a bicameral Parliament, with the House of Commons being the more powerful and only elected chamber, national political parties, albeit with recognizably different regional and social bases of support, and a centralized British state without regional assemblies, although from 1999 with devolved assemblies and executives for Scotland, Wales and Northern Ireland. Britain remains in some respects an elective dictatorship. The social system is still markedly inegalitarian, and the political system, the civil service, the armed forces, the professions, the banking system, large companies and the universities are dispro-portionately dominated by those whose background cannot be described as working-class; which is not surprising as the working class, however defined, has shrunk rapidly. Instead, it is the middle class that has expanded and taken over. The Conservatives stressed the modest origins and difficult upbringing of John Major, and that his successor William Hague had attended a comprehensive school, but these circumstances were not true of the bulk of their Cabinet or parliamentary colleagues. Blair's government and that of Gordon Brown are very much middle-class in their composition and aspirations.

And yet, there have also been major changes, which can be summarized under the headings of Ireland, Empire, Europe and democratization. War tore the guts out of the empire, weakening it in resources and morale. The first major loss was Ireland. Half a million men of Irish descent volunteered to fight for George V in 1914; fewer than 2,000 rose in the Easter Rising of 1916 in Dublin, an unsuccessful attempt to create an Independent Irish Republic; but the 1918 general election was largely won in Ireland by Sinn Fein, Nationalists under Eamonn de Valera, who refused to attend Westminster and demanded independence. British refusal led to a brutal war in 1919–21 between the British authorities and republican Irish, followed by partition and effective independence for the new Irish Free State. Vestigial British authority was extinguished by the Republic of Ireland Act (1948). Much of Ulster became Northern Ireland, which remained part of the United Kingdom represented at Westminster, was self-governed and became very much a Protestant state, its Catholic minority suffering a measure of discrimination, as indeed did Protestants in the south. In Northern Ireland, this sectarian division led to violence in the 1960s, leading to the intervention of troops (1969) and the suspension of the regional government (1972).

The loss of Ireland revealed the weakness of the empire when confronted by a powerful nationalist movement. The First World War (1914–18), in which Britain had played a major role on the victorious side, mobilizing her resources of people and wealth as never before, was, however, followed by the extension of the empire to its greatest extent. The war began with pistol shots in Sarajevo, the assassination by Serbian terrorists of Archduke Franz Ferdinand, the heir to the Austro-Hungarian empire, and pitted a large coalition, in which Britain, France, Russia until 1917, and, from 1917, the USA were the major powers, against Germany, Austria-Hungary, Bulgaria and Turkey. The German invasion of Belgium, as a means to outflank French forces, led Britain, which had guaranteed Belgian neutrality, to declare war on 4 August 1914. The German drive, first on Paris and then on the Channel ports, was thwarted, and in late 1914 both sides dug in on the Western Front. The concentration of large forces in a relatively small area, the defensive strength of trench positions, particularly thanks to the machine-gun and rapid-firing artillery, and the difficulty of making substantial gains if opposing lines were breached, ensured that, until the collapse of the German position in the last weeks of the war, the situation was essentially deadlocked. British attacks, as at Neuve-Chapelle and Loos (1915), the Somme (1916), and Arras and Passchendaele (1917), led to major losses of men with little gain of territory. Overall, one in eight of the British who served were killed.

The discontent of many soldiers with the situation led to thousands of courts martial, while shell-shock affected large numbers. The unimaginative nature of generalship, with its strategy of attrition, did not help. Douglas Haig, who was appointed to the command of the army in France in December 1915, believed that the war would be won by determined leadership, superior morale and offensive operations. He saw the British as a chosen race who would be purified by victory. The war was eventually won as a result of a combination of factors including the blocking of German offensives in 1914, 1916 and 1918, the successful and skilful Allied advance on the Western Front in 1918, the collapse of Austria-Hungary, and the exacerbation of the military, economic and domestic problems facing the Germans which destroyed their will to fight.

Though the Western Front dominated strategy and was responsible for most of their 750,000 dead, there were attempts to search out a weaker front and to strike at Germany's allies. These led to the disastrous expedition to the Dardanelles (1915), whose forceful advocate, the energetic First Lord of the Admiralty, Winston Churchill, resigned, and to failures in Iraq and at Salonika (1916), but also to Allenby's successful campaign in Palestine (1917–18). The German colonies were overrun. Though the threat from the German surface fleet was blocked at the indecisive battle of Jutland (1916), their submarines took a heavy toll of merchant shipping, but their impact was lessened by the use of convoys and the entry of the USA into the war.

The scale and duration of the struggle led to an unprecedented mobilization of national resources, including, after over two million men had volunteered to fight for king and country, the introduction of conscription (1916), and state direction of much of the economy. Conscription was a major departure, as Britain had hitherto been unusual among major European states in having none. This was seen as an aspect of Britain being a freer society. The war gave a tremendous boost to the role of the state and the machinery of government. The Cabinet Office was created in 1916. The allocation of resources by the government led to a rise in civilian living standards and an improvement in the life expectancy of those among the worst-off sections of the pre-war working class who were not conscripted. Unemployment fell and wages rose, helping offset a major rise in prices. The affluent were affected by a quadrupling in income tax, and everyone by major rises in indirect taxes, for example duties on beer and tea, and by a major extension of custom duties.

In contrast to the limited conflicts of the previous hundred years, this was total war. It saw a mobilization of images of nationhood and a sustained active patriotism not witnessed since the invasion fears of the Napoleonic period. Traditional images played a major role. New banknotes showed the king alongside a new representation of St George killing the dragon, the last a device in continuous use on British coins since 1817. The symbols of the four nations – rose, shamrock, thistle and daffodil – were only incorporated into the watermark. A new, more triumphal image of St George followed in 1917.

The Defence of the Realm Act passed in 1914 gave the government extensive emergency powers including over property and labour. It was a big step away from the Victorian liberal culture which had survived into the more interventionist 'New Liberalism' of the Edwardian period. The sway of the government was greatly extended, not least with censorship. For example, in 1918 Rose Allatini (who wrote as A.T. Fitzroy) and her publisher were prosecuted under the Act for publishing *Despised and Rejected*, a novel about a gay artistic pacifist. The publisher was fined and the books were burnt.

The defeat of the German empire meant that its place in the sun was distributed among the victors, Britain gaining League of Nation mandates for Tanganyika, part of Togo and a sliver of the Cameroons, all in Africa, and Nauru Island in the Pacific. War with Germany's ally Turkey led to the annexation of Cyprus and Egypt (1914), and the gaining of mandates over Palestine (now Israel and Palestine), Transjordan and Iraq when Turkey's empire was partitioned at the end of the war. Ardent imperialists, such as Lord Milner and Leo Amery, pressed for the strengthening of the empire, partly in the hope that this would mean that Britain need never be dragged into the Continental mire again. British influence increased in both Persia and Turkey, and British troops operating against the Communists in the Russian civil war that followed their coup in 1917 moved into the

Caucasus, Central Asia, and the White Sea region and were deployed in the Baltic and the Black Sea.

This high-tide of empire, however, was to ebb very fast, especially after post-war economic growth gave way in the early 1920s to major difficulties. The strain of the First World War, the men lost, the money spent, the exhaustion produced by constant effort, left Britain unable to sustain her international ambitions, and this was exacerbated by political division. Lloyd George had split the Liberal party when, in order to bring more decisive war leadership and further his own ambition, he had replaced Asquith as Prime Minister at the end of 1916, and he was dependent on Conservative support, a measure that strained postwar Conservative unity. Thus, despite Lloyd George's strutting the imperial stage, there was an absence of stable leadership. In 1922, there was a Conservative revolt from below, by backbenchers, junior ministers and constituency activists, leading, at a meeting of the parliamentary Conservative Party at the Carlton Club, to a decision to abandon the coalition. This led to the fall of both Lloyd George and the Conservative leader, Austen Chamberlain, who had sought continued support for the coalition. The new leader, Andrew Bonar Law, formed a totally Conservative government, and easily won the 1922 general election. Far from breaking the mould of British politics, Lloyd George was consigned to the political wilderness. When he had had power, Lloyd George had been unwilling to support electoral reform, the proportional representation that would have helped the Liberals in the 1920s, and, once out of power, could not obtain such reform.

Liberal disunity helped in the rise of Labour, which became the official opposition after the 1922 election. Its trade union alliance allowed Labour to identify itself as the natural party of the working class and thus to benefit from the extension of the franchise, and the doubling of trade union membership from 4 million in 1914 to 8 million in 1920. The 1918 Reform Act gave the vote to men over twenty-one fulfilling a 6-months residence qualification and to women over thirty, increasing the electorate from 8 to 21 million. Women did not gain electoral equality until 1928. A Redistribution Act was based on the principle of equal size of constituency electorates.

The new larger electorate was potentially volatile and winning its support posed a considerable challenge to politicians, similar to that that had confronted Disraeli and Gladstone. The complex manoeuvres of three-party politics led to minority Labour governments under Ramsay MacDonald in 1924 and 1929–31, but the first was short-lived and the second was badly affected by the world economic crisis that began in 1929. In 1931, the government split over the cuts believed necessary to balance the budget in order to restore confidence in sterling. A cut in unemployment benefit was rejected by the trade unions and the bulk of the Labour party, but MacDonald and a few supporters joined the Conservatives and some Liberals in forming a National Government which continued in power until the wartime coalition was formed in 1940. MacDonald was succeeded as Prime Minister by the Conservative leader Stanley Baldwin (1935) and he in turn by Neville Chamberlain (1937), and the government won the general elections of 1931 and 1935. Labour lost working-class voters as a result of the economic problems of 1929–31, while the National Government benefited from the economic upturn of

1934. Although as the dominant part of a coalition, the Conservatives were the governing party for much of the 1930s, as they had also been of the 1920s. The impact of the First World War, the particular political developments of the period, and the strength of conservative assumptions and beliefs ensured that the inter-war period was more conservative than what came before or after. The 'Bright Young Things', such as Evelyn Waugh, who set the tone in the 1920s and early 1930s, displayed a frivolous escapism, but there was a slight hysteria and hollowness about it, and many of them looked back to the Victorian period for a kind of permanence.

The 1920s were a period in which British governments drew in their horns. Inflation had risen to 50 per cent in 1919. The spending review known as the Geddes Axe (1922) led to cuts in education, housing and the armed forces. The homes that those 'heroes' who had survived the mud and machine-guns of the Somme and Passchendaele, and the other mass graves of humanity on the Western Front, had been promised, were not all built, as Treasury opposition thwarted some of the aspirations of the 1919 Housing Act. Abroad, intervention in Russia had been a failure and in the Middle East, revolt in Egypt (1919) and Iraq (1920–1) led to Britain granting their independence in 1922 and 1924 respectively, while British influence collapsed in Persia (1921) and the British backed down in their confrontation with Turkey (1922–3), the last a crucial factor in Lloyd George's fall. Unable to maintain Ireland or their extra-European pretensions in the 1920s, the British were also to fail to sustain the 1919 Peace of Versailles settlement in Europe and the League of Nations outside it. These failures were a consequence both of what had already been obvious in the decades prior to the First World War, the problems created by the rise of other states and Britain's global commitments, and the particular strains arising from that conflict and from subsequent developments.

And yet the empire was still very much a living reality in the inter-war period. In some respects, links developed further, a process given concrete form in the majestic buildings designed by Sir Edwin Lutyens and Sir Herbert Baker for the official quarter in New Delhi and finished in the 1930s. Economic links with the empire became closer. Imperial Airways, a company founded with government support (1924), created new routes for the empire. Weekly services began to Cape Town (1932), Brisbane (1934), and Hong Kong (1936); in contrast, thanks to the problem of flying the Atlantic, they only began with New York in 1946. It took nine days to fly to Cape Town in 1936, fourteen to Adelaide, but these were far less than sailing times. Commitment to the empire was demonstrated in a different form by the major new naval base for the defence of the Far East built at Singapore.

The empire faced serious problems in the 1930s, not least pressure from the Indian National Congress and serious disturbances in Palestine. As with Ireland in 1914, it is not clear what would have happened in India had there not been war. The Government of India Act (1935), though bitterly opposed by Conservatives such as Churchill, who saw its moves towards self-government as a step towards the abandonment of empire, was designed to ensure the British retention of the substance of power, but the provincial elections of 1937 were a success for Congress. Nevertheless, it was the Second World War (1939–45) that exhausted and undermined the empire, even as it brought the British occupation of yet more territory, Somaliland and Libya, both formerly Italian, and led Churchill to consider the annexation of the latter.

The Second World War cost fewer British lives than the First, and spared the British army from being put through the mangle of the trenches, but, in several respects, it was much more close-run for Britain. As in 1914, she went to war to resist German aggression and to fulfil the logic of her alliance politics, but in 1939–40 Hitler's Germany destroyed the British alliance system. The Eastern Front was ended within weeks as Poland was defeated (1939), Stalin's Soviet Union taking its share, while the Western Front was rolled up in a German *Blitzkrieg* that overran the Netherlands, Belgium and France (1940). Expelled from the Continent, although able by bravery and skill to save much of the army in the evacuation from Dunkirk, Britain had the valuable support of the empire and control of the sea, but the last was challenged by the potent threat of German air power and still more by German U-boats (submarines). She appeared to have lost the war, and it is not surprising that several major politicians were willing to consider a negotiated peace with Hitler. In May 1940, Viscount Halifax, the Foreign Secretary, was ready, if Hitler made one, 'to accept an offer which would save the country from avoidable disaster'.

Hesitation was ended by the replacement of Neville Chamberlain, a Prime Minister identified with the appeasement of Germany in the 1930s and with failure in war, by Churchill (1940). Convinced of the total rightness of the British cause and the utter untrustworthiness of Hitler, he was determined to fight on, however bleak the situation might be. The blunting of German airpower in the Battle of Britain led Hitler to call off Operation Sealion, his planned invasion of Britain (1940), but British successes against the Italians in North Africa that winter were followed by a victorious German offensive there and by their conquest of Yugoslavia and Greece, the latter entailing the defeat of British forces in Greece and Crete.

The loss of Crete in May 1941 was the last major defeat for an isolated Britain before the war changed completely. Hitherto its European allies had offered little as London had become a collecting house for governments in exile. The German attack on the Soviet Union (June 1941) and the Japanese attack on Britain and the United States, followed by the declaration of war on the Americans by Japan's ally Germany (December 1941), totally altered the situation. There were still to be serious blows, especially in early 1942, when Malaya and Singapore rapidly fell to a smaller but better-led Japanese force, and the Battle of the Atlantic against U-boats was not won until early 1943, but Britain was now part of an alliance system, linked to the strongest economy in the world. As Britain and her new allies successfully blunted German and Japanese offensives in late 1942, the long and stony path to victory appeared clearer. The Americans defeated the Japanese at Midway, the Soviets the Germans at Stalingrad, and the British the Germans at El Alamein in Egypt. In May 1943, the Germans surrendered in North Africa. In September 1943, the British and the Americans landed in Italy, and Italy surrendered unconditionally. The following June, Anglo-American forces landed in Normandy and in May 1945 the Germans surrendered. As with the last campaigns against Napoleon, Russian strength had played a crucial role, but the Anglo-American achievement had also been considerable, not least because they were also bearing the brunt of the war with Japan, a conflict that ended with Japanese surrender in September 1945 following the dropping of American atom bombs the previous month.

Nuclear weapons were the most spectacular application of technology to warfare, but, in both world wars, British technology, especially in metallurgy and electronics, had made major contributions to advances in weaponry, not least tanks in the First World War and radar in the Second. Moreover, wartime propaganda gave a powerful thrust to the reiteration of notions of national identity. The theme of shared struggle was very powerful. These notions were strengthened by the accessible neo-Romanticism of culture in this period, certainly in painting, writing, music and film.

The war, however, fatally weakened the empire. Britain lost prestige and resources; her Dominion allies, especially Australia, had to look to America for support; and there was a loss of confidence in the legacy of the past within Britain. The surrender of 'impregnable' Singapore to the Japanese on 15 February 1942, after a poorly conducted campaign in Malaya and the loss of the *Prince of Wales* and the *Repulse* to Japanese bombers, was either the most humiliating defeat in modern British history, or one to rank with Cornwallis's surrender at Yorktown in 1781. Cornwallis's army had marched out to the tune of 'The World Turned Upside Down', and its surrender had led directly to the loss of the American empire. That of Singapore destroyed British prestige in Asia. Combined with the need for Indian support in the war against advancing Japanese forces, it spelled the end of empire in the Indian subcontinent, the heart of the British imperial experience. In 1942, the Indian National Congress was offered independence after the war in return for support during it, an offer it spurned with the 'Quit India' movement. The Labour Party, which first and unexpectedly became a majority government in 1945, as a result of a reaction against the Conservatives as a party of privilege and pre-war division and in favour of the collectivism and social welfare offered by Labour, was committed to Indian independence. This was achieved in 1947, though at the cost of partition between India and the new Muslim state of Pakistan, and about a million deaths in Hindu–Muslim clashes.

Despite Indian independence, that of Burma (1948), and the ending of the Palestine mandate in 1948, Britain was still a major imperial power and the Labour government, particularly its Foreign Secretary, Ernest Bevin (1945–51), had high hopes of using imperial resources, especially those of Africa, to strengthen the British economy and make her a less unequal partner in the Anglo-American partnership. Bevin acted in a lordly fashion in the Middle East, but empire ran out in the sands of rising Arab nationalism and a lack of British resources. The British faced a number of imperial problems in the early 1950s, including the Malayan Emergency (a communist uprising which was tackled successfully), but it was the Suez Crisis of 1956, an attempt to destabilize the aggressive Arab nationalist regime of Gamul Abdul Nasser in Egypt, that exposed their weakness clearly. Just as echoes of the appeasement of dictators in the 1930s were initially to be voiced, misleadingly, when the Argentinians invaded the Falklands in 1982, so in 1956 the Conservative Prime Minister,

Anthony Eden (1955–7), who had resigned as Foreign Secretary in 1938 in protest at appeasement, was determined not to repeat its mistakes and accept Nasser's nationalization of the Suez Canal. Acting in concert with France and Israel, Eden sent British forces to occupy the Canal Zone. The invasion was poorly planned, but it was American opposition and its impact on sterling that was crucial to weakening British resolve and thus leading to a humiliating withdrawal. A lack of American support had been a major problem for the empire ever since the Second World War; in 1956 American anger made Britain's dependent status obvious.

The following fourteen years saw the rapid loss of most of the rest of the British empire. The British people might not have been European-minded after 1950; but neither were they imperial-minded, and, after Suez, many leading Conservatives, especially Harold Macmillan, Prime Minister 1957–63, and Iain Mcleod, whom he appointed Colonial Secretary, became deeply disillusioned with the empire and ready to dismantle it, a process that was hastened by colonial nationalist movements, though criticized by some right-wing Conservatives. Empire was proving too expensive, too troublesome, and too provocative of both the USA and the Soviet Union. By 1969 none of Africa remained under British rule, and the east of Suez defence policy had fallen victim to the impact of the devaluation of sterling in 1967. British forces withdrew from Singapore in 1971. Looked at differently, empire was abandoned by the government without any consultation of the public who may have been more imperial-minded than was appreciated.

Britain's status as a major power was no longer territorial, no longer a consequence of empire, let alone economic strength. It was, instead, precarious, and a result of its being, from 1952, one of the few atomic powers, and of its active membership, in American-led international organizations, especially NATO, the North Atlantic Treaty Organization of which it was a founder member in 1949. Britain was also a permanent member of the Security Council of the United Nations.

NATO was designed to defend Western Europe against the Soviet Union, for the defeat of Germany in the Second World War was followed by fears of Soviet plans and by a 'cold war' that lasted until the late 1980s. Already in mid-1944 planners for the Chiefs of Staff were suggesting a post-war reform of Germany and Japan so that they could play a role against a Soviet Union whose ambitions in Eastern Europe were arousing growing concern. On 14 March 1946, the British embassy in Moscow asked if the world was now 'faced with the danger of the modern equivalent of the religious wars of the sixteenth century' with Soviet communism battling against Western social democracy and American capitalism for 'domination of the world'. By January 1947 Clement Attlee, Labour Prime Minister 1945–51, had decided to develop a British nuclear bomb. The Berlin Crisis (1948) led to the stationing of American B-29 strategic bombers in Britain and British forces played a role in resisting Communist aggression in the Korean War (1950–3). They were the second largest United Nations contingent after the Americans. In 1951, the Chiefs of Staff warned that the Russians might be provoked by Western rearmament into attacking in 1952. Under American pressure, Britain embarked on a costly rearmament programme in 1951 that undid the economic gains that had been made since 1948, and helped to strengthen the military commitment that has been such a heavy economic burden on post-war Britain. Defence spending has taken a higher percentage of gross national product than for other Western European powers.

The anti-Soviet political and strategic alignment was continued by subsequent governments, both Conservative (1951–64, 70–4, 79–97) and Labour (1964–70, 74–9, 97–). From 1960 American nuclear submarines equipped with Polaris missiles began to operate from the Holy Loch in Scotland and in 1962 Macmillan persuaded President Kennedy to provide Britain with the submarine-launched Poláris missile system, which offered Britain a global naval capability. That year, *Dr. No*, the first of the James Bond adventure films, had the hero of the British secret service saving American missile tests. In the 1980s, despite the protests of the Campaign for Nuclear Disarmament, American cruise missiles were deployed in Britain, and American bombers attacked Libya from British bases. In 2003, Britain joined the USA in invading Iraq.

Empire was replaced by NATO, Commonwealth and Europe. The dominion status given to the 'white' colonies especially Australia, Canada and New Zealand, was a preliminary to the establishment of the British Commonwealth as an association of equal and autonomous partners (1931). In 1949, the prefix British was discarded and it was decided that republics might remain members, a measure that allowed India to stay in. The Commonwealth was seen for a time as a source of British influence, or as the basis for an international community spanning the divides between first and third worlds, white and black, and its unity was fostered by a Secretariat, established in 1965, and by Heads of Government meetings. Relations with South Africa, immigration policies and the consequences of British concentration on Europe all, however, led to differences between Britain and Commonwealth partners, but the absence of common interests and views was of greater significance.

Economic, military and political links with former imperial possessions became less important. In the late twentieth century, New Zealand and, even more, Australia looked to Japan as an economic partner, while Canada became part of a free trade zone with the United States and Mexico. America replaced Britain as Canada's biggest export market after the Second World War, and as the biggest source of foreign investment there in the 1920s. The British share of this investment fell from 85 per cent in 1900 to 15 per cent in 1960, while the American rose from 14 to 75. The percentage of the Australian and Canadian populations that can claim British descent fell appreciably after 1945. Britain had little role to play as the Pacific became an American lake. In 1951, Australia and New Zealand entered into a defence pact with the United States without consulting Britain.

The United States served for Britain as a surrogate for empire in some respects, providing crucial military, political, economic and cultural links, and offering an important model. Part of the attraction was ideological. The American stress on the free market appealed to more groups in British society, not least to commercial interests, than the more statist and bureaucratic Continental European societies. From the 1970s, Anglo-American links have slackened, not least because anglophilia became less important in America and Britain had less to offer in terms of any special relationship. On the other hand, especially through the role of American programmes on British television, American or American-derived products in British consumer society, the American presence in the British economy and the more diffuse, but still very important, mystique of America as a land of wealth and excitement, America remains very important to Britain, especially to British culture, in the widest sense of the word. Not least for linguistic and, to a certain extent, commercial reasons, post-war American cultural 'hegemony' has been stronger in Britain than elsewhere in Europe, and has thus accentuated differences. The Atlanticism of the 1960s led to the creation of Schools of English and American Studies in new universities such as East Anglia and Sussex, separate to those of European Studies. Few Victorians would have thought it sensible to study their literature and history within this sort of a context. British film audiences have for long been under the sway of Hollywood, and American influence on television has been considerable. When 'J.R.', the leading character in the television series *Dallas*, was shot, it was reported on the BBC news, the fictional world displacing its less exciting real counterpart.

The postwar movement towards western European unity reflected the particular interests of the participant states. Britain did not share the concern of Italy and Germany to anchor their new democracies, nor the willingness of France to surrender a portion of its sovereignty in order to restrict German independence, and was not one of the founding members of the EEC, the European Economic Community, the predecessor of the European Union. The different nature of British commerce and investment was also important. Joining the EEC would be far more disruptive for Britain than it was for the other states, because their trade was overwhelmingly Euro-centric, while less than half of Britain's trade was. Thus, joining entailed a major economic dislocation; which for a country whose foreign trade was so vital to it was bound to make its adjustment to membership more difficult.

It soon became clear, however, that the EEC was going to be a success, and the costs of staying out seemed greater than those of joining. As a result, successive governments, both Conservative and Labour, applied to join in 1961 and 1967, only to be rejected by the veto of the French leader, Charles De Gaulle, who argued that Britain's claim to a European identity was compromised by her American links. De Gaulle's departure and a fresh application in 1970, by the Conservative government under Edward Heath (1970–4), led to the successful negotiation of British entry. Britain joined in January 1973, and in the sole national referendum ever hitherto held 67.2 per cent voted to remain in the EEC (1975), though voters' interest in and knowledge of the issues was limited and they were more influenced by the support for membership displayed by most politicians. The only areas showing a majority against staying in were in Scotland: the Shetlands and the Western Isles.

Concern about the European dimension, however, grew as the limited objectives of most of the politicians who constructed the EEC developed in more ambitious directions, with the call to create stronger institutions, and to transfer a considerable measure of authority, and thus sovereignty, from the nation states. Changing nomenclature registered the perception of new objectives. The European Community developed from being an economic organization, the EEC became the EC and, from 1993, the European Union (EU).

The 'duality of ocean and continent' in British foreign policy, discerned by Burrows and by a later Oxford Professor of Modern History, R.B. Wernham, depended on the 'defence of insularity' and 'the shield of sea power', but, as these were torn away by first air-power and then nuclear weapons, it was necessary to rethink totally Britain's strategic situation and policy. This was a crucial component in Anglo-American relations during the decades of defence from the 1940s to the late 1980s. This defence was not, however, simply bilateral, but part of a strategy for the whole of Western Europe. The largest sector allocation in the Defence White Paper of May 1989, 39 per cent, was to the British forces in what was then West Germany. The close of the Cold War reduced international tensions in Europe, and writers of spy stories had to search elsewhere than Moscow for villains, but international uncertainty remains acute, and at present the EU is unable to meet Britain's international and strategic requirements.

The extent to which England was 'truly' part of Europe vexed commentators after the Second World War. In some respects, England and the societies of Western Europe became more similar, although this is also true of societies such as Australia and Canada. This was a consequence of broadly similar social trends including secularization, the emancipation of women and the move from the land. Sexual permissiveness, rising divorce rates, growing geographical mobility, the decline of traditional social distinctions and the rise of youth culture were all shared characteristics. Deference, aristocracies, and social stratification all declined, though differences in wealth, both capital and income, within English society remained vast. The gradual virtual disestablishment of the Anglican Church, a process that really began with the Catholic Emancipation Act of 1829, gathered pace, a parallel to the process of disestablishment on much of the Continent. In England, as more generally throughout the British Isles and on the Continent, social paternalism, patriarchal authority, respect for age and the nuclear family, and the stigma of illegitimacy, all declined in importance, while rights to divorce, abortion and contraception were established across most of Western Europe (reducing the numbers available for adoption), and homosexual acts in private between consenting adults were decriminalized in England and Wales by the Sexual Offences Act of 1967. Cohabitation and one-parent families became more common, while the proportion of lifetime celibates declined. Working hours fell; populations 'aged', decreasing the economically active percentage and causing heavier pressures on the social welfare and health systems.

The speed of social changes can be gauged by considering earlier assumptions and assessing how dated they now appear. Detective stories offer one approach, as they tend to require realistic observation of behaviour and mores. In Patricia Wentworth's *The Listening Eye* (1957), Ethel Burkett writes to her aunt Maud Silver about her sister:

> who had taken the unjustifiable step of leaving an excellent husband whom she complained of finding dull. 'As if anyone in their senses expects their husband to be exciting!' wrote Mrs Burkett. 'And she doesn't say where she is, or what she is doing, so all we can hope and trust is that she is *alone*, and that she hasn't done anything which Andrew would find impossible to forgive. Because what is she going to live on!'

As across much of Europe, birth rates fell. Average rates of population growth in England as a whole were far lower in the inter-war period, when they fell to below replacement levels, than they had been in the nineteenth century, and, as a result, the number of children in an average family fell from three in 1910 to two in 1940. Despite a post-war birth-peak in 1947 and another in 1966, population growth-rates continued to decline in the 1950s and 1960s, to almost a halt in the 1970s and early 1980s, before a slight upturn from the mid-1980s. The population of surburban, commuter and Southern England increased more rapidly than that of the North and London.

Immigration, especially from former colonies, altered the ethnic composition of many Continental societies. In England much of the immigration was from Europe, Irish after the potato famine of 1847–8 and again strongly in the 1940s; Russian and Polish Jews from the 1880s until the Alien Act of 1905; Poles and Ukrainians in the 1940s. Thereafter, large-scale immigration was from the 'New Commonwealth', especially the West Indies and the Indian sub-continent. A labour-shortage in unattractive spheres of employment, such as foundry work and nursing, led to the active sponsorship of immigration. However, concern about its scale and growing racial tension led to immigration acts, beginning with the Commonwealth Immigrants Act of 1962, that progressively reduced Commonwealth immigration. Successive waves of immigrants faced poor housing and took on the less attractive jobs, the 'sweated' trades, such as tailoring, and casual labour in the docks and the building trade. Immigration also contributed greatly to the social and cultural variety of the country.

While some immigrants sought assimilation, others have striven to retain a distinctive identity, in certain cases linked to a lack of sympathy for generally accepted values. Over some issues, such as the mixed education of Asian Islamic women, this created administrative and legal problems. England has both 'multi-culturalism' and a degree of racial tension, and, though racial discrimination is illegal under the Race Relations Act, racial violence has played a role in the harrassment of non-whites, especially in attacks on housing estates. Black hostility to the police played a major role in the 1981 riots in south London and Liverpool and in subsequent violence. While the effects of immigration became more of an issue in England, emigration also rose. In the 2000s immigration became a more urgent issue, as the number of immigrants rose, in part due to a major increase from Eastern Europe, especially Poland, while the willingness of part of the Islamic immigrant population to suppport terrorism, which in 2005 extended to suicide bombings in London, challenged assumptions about integration.

As increased numbers travelled for pleasure, a consequence of greater disposable wealth among the bulk of the population, the development of the package holiday, the use of jet aircraft and the spread of car ownership, so far more inhabitants of England than ever before visited the Continent and far more than ever before made a regular habit of doing so. In 1991, there were 2.45 million British visitors to the USA, but far more to the Continent. If many visited 'little Britains' in nondescript Mediterranean resorts such as Benidorm, others did not. The metropolitan middle-class household that would have had servants seventy years ago may now have a second home in France, and *The Times* can carry regular articles on where best to purchase such properties. The opportunity of learning at least one foreign language is offered to all schoolchildren, and a certain number benefit.

Economically and politically, England has become closer to the Continent. The societies of Western Europe, including England, felt threatened first by Soviet power and then by the problems in Eastern Europe that followed the collapse of Communism; their economies were challenged by the staggering development of the 'dragon' countries of East Asia. Economically, England is more closely linked to Continental markets and suppliers than it was in 1973, while its attraction for 'inward investment', especially from Japan, America and the other countries of the EU, has largely arisen as a consequence of its access to the EU. Such investment was important. In the North of England, for example, manufacturing employment in foreign-owned companies rose between 1979 and 1989 from 11.8 per cent to 17.1 per cent. The adoption of the Single European Act in 1986 committed Britain to remove all barriers to the creation of the Single European Market (SEM), and also altered the framework of British economic activity. The EU and the domestic market were legally joined and it was necessary to comply with the SEM in order to operate in the EU and therefore in Britain. Politically, most British politicians proclaimed their commitment to Europe and the EU even when criticizing the practices or the objectives of the latter.

And yet there are also important strains in the relationship. Affinity is not the only reason for closeness or union. Complementarity is also involved. That was certainly believed to be the case with the empire in the later nineteenth century. The bases of imperial union were supposed to be twofold. There was a stress on common origins, customs, race and constitutions, but, secondly, an emphasis on the degree to which each complemented the others, especially economically.

Thus the dominions and crown colonies could exchange primary products for manufactured goods with industrial Britain, their common interests resting on the differences between the parts. This was also the relationship with transoceanic trading partners that were not part of the empire, most obviously South America. The EU was less amenable, because of the similarities between Britain and its neighbours, which made for a union of competitors rather than of partners.

There are also important political problems affecting the relationship. Scepticism about the notion of a European 'super state' and 'Euro-federalism' and resistance to the idea of 'pooled' or shared sovereignty was, and is, widespread, and some of the support for the European ideal in the 1980s was tactical and opportunistic, designed to attack Thatcher (Prime Minister 1979–90) who, though she signed the Single European Act, was not the most ardent admirer of European unity. Two very different indicators are the scarcity of the European flag in Britain, and the markedly patriotic response of the British public to the Falklands Crisis of 1982, when British forces drove out invading Argentine troops. Political identity is national, not international, but that raises the question of which nation, an issue pushed to the fore in the 1990s by successful pressure for Scottish and Welsh devolution. Like the Gulf War of 1990–1, in which Britain was part of a United Nations coalition, the Falklands war was a 'contained' conflict, comparable in some ways to nineteenth-century colonial wars, and also fairly popular. This can be seen as a sign of an assertive nationalism, although, if so, it was British rather than specifically English. In contrast, the invasion of Iraq in 2003 proved highly divisive.

Aside from the issue of political identity, there is also the question of social dimension. Over a long time span, there has been an ambivalence towards the democratization of society. This has different sources and takes different forms. Few were as sweeping as Halifax, an old Etonian who, aside from serving as Foreign Secretary (1938–40), was also Viceroy of India and Chancellor of Oxford University. He wrote to his father, 'what a bore democracy is to those who have to work it . . . I think it is a great pity that Simon de Montfort . . . ever invented our parliamentary system'. H.A. Gwynne, editor of the *Morning Post* (1910–37) and President of the Institute of Journalists (1929–30), hated democracy and regarded the First Reform Act of 1832 as the greatest error in recent British history: 'when we handed over the pistol to our masters in 1832 we let ourselves in for all the evils that pursued us'. Lady Bathurst, the paper's owner from 1908 to 1924, stated in 1918 that 'Democracy is idiotic'.

Such views have not been centre-stage, indeed far from it, but there has been a resistance to democratization. Hostility to democratic accountability was demonstrated in the unwillingness of often self-defining elites to accept popular beliefs and pastimes as worthy of value and attention, and their conviction that they were best placed to manage society and define social values. This was accentuated after 1945 by the spread of a 'public' sector that has frequently been anything other than responsive to the public. Instead, bodies such as the NHS and the education system were heavily influenced by 'producer lobbies'. Social and cultural condescension were linked to contempt for popular views on such matters as capital punishment or immigration. The Blair government was particularly prone to act as a 'nanny state', offering frequent strictures on the conduct of the population. Most institutions resisted unwelcome pressures, while political parties tempered their desire for popular support with their wish to maintain their ideological inheritance.

And yet, at the same time, there were powerful forces democratizing society. The most important was the emancipation of women. Their legal and social position was limited at the beginning of the twentieth century, not least because most adult women did not have an independent income. Frequent pregnancies were an important factor. In general, women lacked good jobs, and the employment rate among women with children was low, by modern standards. Working-class women frequently had appalling health. The change in the twentieth century was legal, economic and social.

Prior to the First World War, the suffragette movement won attention rather than support, as the Pankhursts urged their followers to acts of violence, but the war saw a substantial increase in the female work force as society was mobilized for total war. Men were conscripted, while nearly five million women were in employment at the start of 1918, although their wages remained much lower than men's. That year, the vote was given to all men over twenty-one and to most women over thirty; a decade later the voting age for women was dropped to twenty-one. The expansion of the First World War was partly reversed thereafter as men returned from the forces, but that of the second conflict was not, and the economic shift from manufacturing to service industries helped to create more opportunities for women workers. The Equal Pay Act (1970) was made more important by the major expansion of the female work force from the 1940s. Whereas previously most women had given up work when they married, older married women entered the labour force as clerical workers in large numbers from the 1940s. Clerical occupations are today the largest single occupational category for women.

There was opposition. The National Association of Schoolmasters was founded in 1922 from a splinter group of male teachers opposed to the National Union of Teachers' support for equal pay. Its leaflets included such titles as 'Making our boys effeminate' (1927). The National Union of Foundry Workers represented only men during its history (1920–46), despite there being about 50,000 foundrywomen in the 1940s. Yet, such opposition was overcome. Changes in the position of women cannot, however, be separated from other social questions. Class affected the recruitment for different tasks of women in both world wars. The mixture of classes in munitions work during the first war, though stressed in propaganda, was limited. Similarly, in the second war there was little mingling in the factories; social distinctions were maintained. 'Positive discrimination' in favour of hiring and promoting women in recent years has worked most to the benefit of middle-class women, and the practice of endogamy (marriage within the clan) may therefore ensure that social differences are thus fortified. Moreover, the combination of feminism and the decline of manual work led in the 1990s and 2000s to what was seen as a 'crisis of masculinity', seen for example in the marginality of men in many families, not least with the growing importance of single-mothers.

As with other movements lacking a centralizing structure, the 'women's liberation' movement of the 1960s and '70s was a diverse one. It included pressure for changes in lifestyles, and social arrangements that put women's needs and expectations in a more central position. The Abortion Act of 1967 was followed by a situation close to abortion on demand. Jobs and lifestyle became more important as aspirations for women, complementing, rather than replacing, home and family. The range of female activities expanded: the Women's Rugby Football Union was formed in 1983; the first English person in space was Helen Sharman. While numbers of full-time male undergraduates at universities increased by 20 per cent between 1970 and 1989, women's numbers increased by 30 per cent. By 1990 14 per cent of women were educated to over the age of eighteen compared with only 1 per cent in 1959. As with other developments of that period that led to pressure for change, the impact of the women's liberation movement diminished in the 1980s, which was ironically that of the first woman Prime Minister, Thatcher. Her rise showed that there was no ceiling of opportunity above which women could not rise; her determination and success, that a woman was easily capable of the job. Never rejected by the electorate, Thatcher was, in 1990, at the time she was toppled by disaffection among her MPs, who feared defeat in light of the government's unpopularity, the longest serving Prime Minister of the century, and the Prime Minister with the longest consecutive period in office since Lord Liverpool (1815–27). She had won three consecutive general elections – in 1979, 1983 and 1987.

Capitalism was another force shaping the democratization of society, for, at the same time as the differing wealth and income of individuals ensures that their purchasing power varies, each is a consumer able to make his or her own purchasing decisions. Market economics promoted democratization. Tax-payers were encouraged in the 1980s to see public expenditure as questionable and open to challenge. Taxes and public expenditure was 'our' money spent by the state. Under John Major, Prime Minister 1990–7, the Citizens' Charter (and all its variants: Patients, Schools, Further Education, etc.), promoted a culture of complaint and redress, admittedly most heavily used by the middle classes. Even the endless satisfaction survey/market research/focus groups of the 1990s promoted a sense of democratized (public) services.

The element of choice and the need to shape and cater to it combined to ensure a whole range of social shifts, among which the most striking was the emergence from the 1950s of the youth consumer and the development of cultural and consumer fashions that reflect the dynamism and volatility of this section of the market. It is easy to focus on 'pop culture', Rock to drug culture, via the Beatles and the Sex Pistols, Psychedelia and Punk, but more significance can be attached to the wish and ability of youth first to create an adolescent identity: not to be younger copies of their elders, and secondly, and more specifically, to reject the opinions of their parents; pop culture was only one manifestation of this. The willingness to try different foods, to holiday in different places, to move away from parental religious preferences, to go on to higher education or to purchase property are as interesting and possibly more important. The rejection by youth of established values was given theatrical force in 1956 with John Osborne's play *Look Back in Anger*; Jimmy Porter, the protagonist, expressed a sense of frustration that was to help produce change. Youth cultures became of greater importance.

The interrelationship between the aspirations of youth and socio-economic changes played a role in the major expansion of the middle class that was such a marked feature of the post-war world. In 1900, 75 per cent of the labour force were manual workers, members of the working class. By 1974 the percentage had fallen to 47, by 1991 to 36, although, alongside upward social mobility, there were many who still preferred to see themselves as working-class including, most improbably, Blair's Deputy Prime Minister, John Prescott. The manufacturing base declined; the service sector grew. White collar replaced blue collar, and average incomes for those in work rose appreciably, while tax rates fell; although many new jobs were part time, and an aspect of a casualization of much of the labour force. The increase in disposable income was skewed in favour of the middle classes, some of whom, also had and have a high propensity to be involved with the countryside, both by living there, and thus sponsoring counter-urbanization, and by influencing the way it is managed.

The long-term impact of the social revolution of recent decades, crucial aspects of which are falling union membership (the TUC had more than 12 million members in 1979, fewer than 8 million in 1992) and rising home ownership (three-quarters of trade unionists by the late 1980s), is still unclear; but the basic lineaments of society for the foreseeable future are of a capitalist, consumerist, individualist, mobile, predominantly secular and urban, property-owning democracy, with a substantial underclass. 'Who governs Britain?' was the slogan of the Heath government that, although it won more votes than Labour, was nevertheless defeated in February 1974. The defeat of the Miners' strike of 1984–5 answered the question and the Labour government elected in 1997 kept the trade unions at arm's length.

The substantial increase in individual and corporate debt in the 1980s as a consequence of the liberalization of the financial system and government encouragement of the widespread desire to own property, an increase that saw individual debt rise to unprecedented rates in the 2000s, combined with structural economic problems, however, ensured that many who are not in the underclass are in a vulnerable situation. A more general problem was posed by rising crime figures, the related perception of a more lawless and less safe society, and the difficulties of policing contemporary society. Widespread refusal to pay the unpopular poll tax, introduced by Thatcher, indicated a willingness to reject laws deemed unfair. The unpopularity of the tax, combined with a worsening economic situation, helped to lead to the crisis in confidence in her leadership in the parliamentary Conservative Party that led to her fall in 1990.

Despite the dependency culture actively fostered by Labour, there is little public confidence in central planning. Furthermore, there has been limited support for state collectivism, even in the Labour government elected in 1997. Under Tony Blair, it rejected 'old' or traditional Labour attitudes and policies, such as state ownership of much of the economy. Among other aspects of public values, more people prefer to shop than to go to church on Sundays, and fewer of the population express their religious faith through the Church of England than ever before. The rise of mass media and of consumer spending has been accompanied by a decline in democratic participation, with falling membership of political parties and trade unions and falling voting figures. Social differences remain, the working class eating less well, having poorer housing, fewer children and less access to higher education than the middle class. Thanks to the greater relative improvement of the middle-class conditions and the slower rise of those of the working class, class mortality differences have widened from the late 1950s.

Aside from those categorized as working-class, an 'underclass' defined by poverty, unemployment or low pay suffered limited opportunities. At the close of the 1990s one in five households had no current account and were reliant on moneylenders and pawnbrokers. This group included about half the council tenants and half the single parents in the country. In 1990, the death-rate for social class V males was 26 per cent higher than for social class I. For the latter, in place of a mid-century stress on a (then) sexy form of consumption – alcohol, cigarettes and gambling, all made glamorous in films – came healthy eating and an emphasis on firm stomachs, gyms and personal trainers. This was partly due to a (middle-class-dominated) shift from enjoying things that were supposed to be bad for one towards the vanities of trying to look good. Smoking (and not going to the gym) was very much part of a dwindling working-class culture.

Although there are clear variations between and within regions in many fields, including political preference, crime patterns, nuptiality, fertility and house ownership, these are less marked than in the past. National broadcasting, state education and employment, nationwide companies, unions, products and pastimes all brought a measure of convergence that can be seen in the decline of dialect and distinctive regional practices, as in cooking. Yet the granting of devolution to Scotland and Wales led in the late 1990s to questions about the future of England. Furthermore, Britain is a member of the European Union, but the future trajectory of that body and Britain's relations with it are both unclear.

The threat of Russian power has markedly diminished, and, although many other regions of the world are unstable and pose challenges to English interests, Western Europe appears reasonably safe for liberal democracy. The future of the environment is a growing concern, global warming and ozone depletion both being major problems; but the English can look back on over five decades without a major war. The experience of serving or losing loved ones in the two world wars, that greatly affected major politicians, such as Attlee, Bonar Law, Eden and Chamberlain, as well as millions of their contemporaries, is one that has not been repeated. History is so often a story of the move from one crisis to another, and that of modern England is no exception, but crisis can also be seen as an integral part of the functioning and development of any sophisticated society. Despite its serious problems, English society still has many attractive features.

History is like travel. To go back in the past and then to return, is to have seen different countries, other ways of doing things, various values. The traveller might not have the time or resources to appreciate fully what he or she is seeing, but is nevertheless made aware of variety and change. To travel today is to be made aware of some of the strengths and weaknesses of England and the English and also serves to confirm a sense of identity with place and people. A distinguished recent collective study of the history of Britain, *The Oxford Illustrated History of*

Britain edited by Kenneth Morgan (1984), concluded by stressing continuity. Using the structural image of geological constancy, it emphasized a constant expression of a deep sense of history, an organic, closely knit society, capable of self-renewal, as earlier the rooted strength of its institutions and its culture had been mentioned.

Writing at the start of the twenty-first century, it is possible instead to stress the role of chance. Much of the relative stability of this century was due to victory in both world wars. Most Continental countries were defeated and occupied with the accompanying strains. Many right-wing political groupings were contaminated, or at least stained, by collaboration; their left-wing counterparts affected by the rise of Communism. In England, in contrast, there was no foreign invasion, no seizure of power by undemocratic forces from left or right. Similarly, it was far from inevitable that England would survive French invasion attempts in the eighteenth century and the Napoleonic period. There have also been domestic crises whose peaceful resolution was far from inevitable; as well as civil conflicts whose outcome was far from certain to contemporaries. The result of the English Civil War and the '45 are obvious examples.

While stressing chance and contingency, it is also necessary to draw attention to those who were unsuccessful. English society can be presented as both organic and divided. The Glorious Revolution, for example, plays a major role in the English public myth, but many were not comprehended within the Whig consensus and both the Revolution settlement of 1688–9 and the Hanoverian regime were only established by force. For all their talk about being the natural party of government, only twice in the twentieth century (the Tories in

1900 and 1931) has either the Labour or the Conservative Party and its allies gained more than 50 per cent of the popular vote. Throughout, it is necessary to recall the role of different interests and opinions. Deterministic approaches to the past are suspect, and it is necessary to qualify any emphasis on patterns by stressing the role of chance and contingency. This has been made abundantly clear by the events of recent years, not least the consequences for the Blair government of the 2003 invasion of Iraq, and the extent to which Islamic assertiveness has challenged benign assumptions of the nature of England's changing society.

THIRTEEN
IDENTITIES

The issue of English identity gathered pace after the election of a Labour government in 1997. Earlier Labour governments had either been centralist in attitude or, if they had supported devolution, either had not made it a central strand of policy or had lacked the parliamentary strength to introduce it. Indeed, the interest which the Labour governments of 1974–9 displayed in devolution can be explained by their reliance upon the votes of Scottish Nationalist Party and Plaid Cymru MPs in the House of Commons. In contrast, in order, as it saw it, to modernize the United Kingdom, Tony Blair's government was determined to push through a policy of fundamental constitutional change, and, in particular, to alter the relationship between the parts of the British Isles. Initially this focused on Scotland and Wales. Referenda in 1997 won approval for devolved assemblies which were elected in 1999. The Welsh Assembly lacked the tax-varying powers of the Scottish Parliament, but the creation of both bodies was a major step. In 1999, powers were also devolved to the Northern Ireland Assembly and to a power-sharing executive of Nationalists and Unionists. The pace of change in England was slower, in part because, unlike in Scotland and Wales, there was no nationalist pressure to assuage or counter.

Instead, after Scotland and Wales, the constitutional focus moved onto the House of Lords. The bulk of the hereditary peerage lost their voting rights in 1999. This abolition took place without any agreement on what a reformed House of Lords would look like. The prospect of a nominated rather than a directly elected upper chamber has led to accusations of gross prime-ministerial patronage, and the 'cash for honours' scandal discredited the Blair government, making it appear highly corrupt.

From its election, the new Labour government also advocated the creation of regional assemblies within England. These were seen as a counterpart of the Scottish and Welsh assemblies. Furthermore, as in the case of Scotland and Wales, they were presented as legislative and executive bodies designed to match and control the developing pace of administrative devolution. In 1999, a new system began operation. Eight Regional Development Agencies began work. They were instructed to prepare an economic strategy for each region. The agencies were less exclusively under central government control. They were under a statutory duty to consult Regional Chambers, non-elected bodies, of whom 70 per cent were representatives from all the local authorities in the region, if such bodies met government standards for their composition. This process was pressed further in April 1999 when, following the Scottish model, the North-East Constitutional Convention, charged with drawing up a blueprint for a directly elected regional assembly, first met.

These moves suggested that directly elected regional assemblies would develop, although such an assembly was to be rejected when Labour tried it in North-East England. The alternative, a body for England as a whole, met no favour from Labour. Instead, in July 1999, it was the Conservative leader, William Hague, who suggested that when English matters came up for debate in the House of Commons, they should only be debated by English MPs. He did not press on to advocate English autonomy, let alone sovereignty, but his was an image of England very different to that of regional assemblies. It reflected the 'West Lothian question', by which Scottish MPs could legislate in Westminster for England while knowing that this legislation would not be applied in Scotland.

Both approaches – regionalism and action at the level of England – reflect aspects of England's history. It was one of the first European states to acquire a measure of unity and centralized control. This was always qualified and challenged, but, yet, the degree of cohesion achieved by the Old English state was impressive. When in 1962, Hugh Gaitskell, the leader of the Labour Party, warned, in a television interview, that entry into the EEC 'means the end of Britain as an independent nation; we become no more than Texas or California in the United States of Europe. It means the end of a thousand years of history', he should have been talking about England, not Britain, but his last comment would have been equally appropriate had he been able to glance ahead to his party's regional plans of a quarter-century later.

The cohesion of the English state was apparent again in the Middle Ages, after the abrupt discontinuity created by the Norman Conquest, in large part because the Normans and Angevins built on the Anglo-Saxon inheritance. Furthermore, national consciousness, nationalism, and a unitary state can all be seen in place in the fifteenth century. All three became stronger in the sixteenth century. A self-conscious cultural nationalism became far more apparent. Thereafter, however, statehood and culture had to adapt first to personal union and then parliamentary union with Scotland. Britishness was the major theme, although in the nineteenth century it was challenged by developments in Ireland, which represented the first sustained assault on the territorial integrity of the

United Kingdom. During the twentieth century, notions of Britishness were reinforced by the patriotic experiences of the two World Wars and the national bonding which took place during them.

Thus, at one level, independence for Eire, and devolution for Scotland, Wales, and Northern Ireland, provides the opportunity to recover an English identity. This might indeed be most in the interests of the English, by which term is understood the inhabitants of England, not some ethnic group. An English identity might lessen the divisions that would stem from regional governments and assemblies, both the difficulties that might stem from the creation of such bodies and their subsequent rivalries over policy and funding. Furthermore, it would provide a representation that could compete with those of Scotland and Wales in order to give due weight to English interests within both Britain and the European Union.

Regional assemblies reflect a very different emphasis. This links local politics to a sense that the very wide variations within England reflect regional identities. These have clearly been, and are, of importance. For example, the tension between the attitudes and interests that were most strongly represented in London and the South-East and those that focused in 'the North' was important to the dynamics of twentieth-century England. It challenged and, at times, undercut attempts to suggest that there was a consensus. The tension also provided much of the emotional dynamo behind class politics: a different sense of 'place', as well as of class attitude, was at issue.

More than image and perception were involved. There *are* important differences between parts of England. And indeed there may well be a resurgence of regional identity as well as Englishness as the counterpart to an assertive Welshness and Scottishness. Football loyalties are a precursor of this, as Merseyside shows. People do not identify with government-defined regions or development agencies, any more than they did with areas and bodies created in the early 1970s by local government reform, such as Humberside and Avon. However, they do identify with old counties, and the North/South divide still represents a difference and a division.

National and regional identities are not necessarily incompatible. It is possible to have overlapping senses of collective self-awareness. Yet, this process can be very difficult, and it is frequently the case that self-awareness at one level, most commonly the local or regional, is constructed or driven in large part from opposition to other levels of identity, as is certainly the case with Scottish nationalism. This is likely to be more pronounced when a new political system is put in place and there is dissension over the distribution of rights and responsibilities. Thus, in 1999, the creation of Scottish and Welsh assemblies helped to encourage calls for English identity and interests, which the Conservative Party has played some part in encouraging.

Noting the strength of both English and regional strains in collective consciousness is appropriate but only part of the conclusion. Two other points arise. First, the strength of the former is indicated by the limited role of regional identity in the most populous and economically dynamic part of England, the South-East. This is linked to the role of national economic and commercial policies, trends and products, as well as national education, leisure, and broadcasting policies, practices and institutions. All are particularly effective in the

South-East. Furthermore, it is possible that regionalism would not necessarily assist what is seen as modernization. Instead, it is possible that regional assemblies might become bodies expressive of regionalist conservatism, as local vested interests came to dominate or influence them.

Secondly, the place of particular moments in English history yet again emerges clearly. The attitudes of politicians and the electorate matter. It is too easy to blame impersonal forces or the structures of power. They play a role, but, if England is to have an identity, the next few years may well be crucial.

This issue is not simply a matter of politics and government, although, as the role of Labour and the West Lothian question indicate, these influences cannot be ignored. New Labour was intent upon devolution as a way of strengthening the Union, and upon modernizing notions of Britishness. Yet the impact of such schemes for 'repackaging' identity on the bulk of the population can be queried.

There are also wider questions of national identity to consider here. These are reflected and created not only in governmental structures but also in the wider character and depiction of the country. As already suggested, this process of identification has had a strong ruralist flavour. This can be seen for example on the back of the £10 note introduced in 1993. This features Dickens and, as an illustration of his work, the village cricket match from *The Pickwick Papers*, not one of the scenes of urban development or life that were more frequent in his novels.

The rural ideal was taken up by such leading inter-war politicians as Stanley Baldwin whose speeches were littered with respectful eulogies to the English countryside and the sons of the soil. He used his native Worcestershire to conjure up wonderfully evocative images of the rural England he loved so much. The rural ideal was also taken up by many (although by no means all) twentieth-century reformers. Thus, for example, the development of suburbia drew on the ideas of social improvement advanced by the garden city movement. The strength and endurance of the relationship between the ruralist tradition and Englishness derives from the fact that it is not just conservative but has been able to accommodate and place the apparently irreconcilable ideals of the Romantic right (country house, country church, squire, parson, and deferential society) and the Romantic left (folk society, the village, rural crafts and honest peasantry): that there are in short several ruralist traditions which co-exist. A comparable sense of place is lacking for the urbanist alternative, not least because of the remorseless process of new building and destruction that has affected so much of the urban environment.

Yet, ruralism clearly cannot describe the experience of the Western society that urbanized first, nor the assumptions and beliefs associated with this urbanization. Furthermore, not only has rural England become relatively less important, as was indeed the case from the eighteenth century. In addition, from the 1870s, it experienced acute difficulties, and that remains the case today. Rural England is very much under pressure. This pressure comes from within and from outside. Intensive agricultural land-use is generally unfavourable to the traditional conception of the countryside and, indeed, to most kinds of wildlife. Field enlargement and a general obsession with agricultural tidiness within a production-orientated economic regime have substantially reduced the habitat of many types of wildlife, helping produce the 'silent spring'. This process has been accentuated by the removal of hedgerows which have lost their functional but not aesthetic value. The demise of the traditional patterns of small farms with a diversity of crops has been a product of economic pressures and a standardization of farming practice. Much of rural England (and rural Britain) is assailed by poverty and uncertainty.

Pressures from non-agricultural 'development' are also acute. The love of the countryside threatens to destroy it. A powerful piece by Simon Jenkins in *The Times* of 23 July 1999, explaining why the English liked visiting rural France, suggested that South-West France offered 'the English an experience, not so much of France but of England, one which is fast disappearing. It is an England which many believe still lingers in the hills of Somerset and Devon, in the Welsh Marches or the Wolds of Lincolnshire, of cosy villages undefiled by modern estates, of idle roads bereft of hypermarkets, of horizons uncluttered with pylons or turbines, of woods, hedgerows and stone walls. It is a vision of a picturesque landscape, timeless, semi-ruined. It has all but gone.'

This is a misleading account of great swathes of France, many of which are increasingly derelict; but the pace of 'development' of rural England, especially the insistence on the building of very large numbers of new homes, is indeed undermining not only the rural environment, but also a ruralist concept of England and English life, although at the same time the desire to live 'in the countryside' is a testimony to the strength of this concept. There is, however, an urban alternative to this tradition, although it is not clear how effective it is, one that looks back to pragmatic, liberal, puritan and utilitarian accounts of identity and history, and was developed on the left. In the twentieth century, H.G. Wells was a central figure in this alternative. His novel *Tono-Bungay* (1909) provides a critique of the rural tradition in English/ British culture in terms which anticipate many of the discussions of the past two decades. In the novel, he attributes the chaotic sprawl of London to the fact that the values of the ruling elite are still essentially feudal and non-urban. He also finds the fake archaism of Tower Bridge to be indicative of a cultural failure to celebrate industrial function. Wells's analysis was similar to that of some later historians, such as Martin Wiener in his *English Culture and the Decline of the Industrial Spirit 1850–1980* (1981), who tried to explain the cause of Britain's economic problems in terms of conservative values.

In *Anticipations* (1901), Wells wrote positively about the role of satellite towns, of the suburbs, of transport networks making possible the expansion of cities into large metropolitan spaces. His *A Modern Utopia* (1905) was dynamic and scientific-industrial, not static and rural. In his feminist novel *Ann Veronica* (1909), Wells explores a key element of English urban society, the suburbs. In a film-script he wrote for *Things To Come*, Wells imagined a futuristic city on the lines sketched out by Le Corbusier. Wells's commitment to urban and industrial planning influenced the Labour Party. More generally, the belief in planning that was very strong in Britain from the 1940s until the late 1970s was different in spirit and intention from ruralist notions of national identity and interest.

There were other powerful exponents of positive urban images. If D.H. Lawrence established a powerfully Romantic and anti-industrial voice in English Modernism, the Vorticists, in contrast, celebrated industrial and urban life in 1910–16.

They were important to the overly neglected pro-urban, pro-industrial strain in Anglo-American Modernism. The documentary tradition of the 1920s and 1930s, especially Grierson's work, represented another pro-urban and pro-industrial strand. Alongside the pastoral tradition in English culture in the 1930s and 1940s, writers, film-makers and intellectuals in the 1930s were open to urban life. In the 1980s and 1990s, international cities and city life became fashionable again, but that was not the same as becoming popular.

More generally, the literary, pictorial, photographic, film and televisual representation of cities in English culture in the twentieth century suggests that this culture has not been pastoral in its identity. Furthermore, the largest city (or cities) in any region remain very important to cultural horizons. Manchester in the 1990s was spoken of in the same breath as Milan (although not by many Milanese). Manchester was not alone in developing cultural and other aspirations, but London's long-held reputation as England's premier city remained strong.

Yet, the rural conception of England has been the one which has arguably dominated artistic and popular images. Non-pastoral or urban constructions of English identity have never really eclipsed them. The key image for many remains that of England as a 'green and pleasant land', although the extent to which this resonates for example among Bangladeshis in Tower Hamlets is problematic.

There were major shifts in the understanding of Englishness from the second half of the twentieth century. The increasingly multicultural nature of society and the impact of globalization, specifically of American cultural hegemony, had a major impact. Within the United Kingdom, the tendency to blur England and Britain was heavily qualified, or, looked at differently, there was a greater understanding of different types of Britishness: British/Englishness, British/Scottishness, etc. were increasingly seen as very different. There was also greater sensitivity to regional, vocational, and class differences. Englishness was increasingly seen in the 1990s as something more like a set of interlocking identities, rather than an overarching phenomenon, even if certain tropes, such as ruralism, remain powerful. The empire was no longer really an issue.

Attempts in the late 1990s to suggest modish urban life, or, more generally, a supposed set of modish national values, as a replacement to earlier and other cultural traditions appear less likely to elicit popular support than an emphasis on the national dimension of the interlocked cultures of sport, television and celebrities. This may be the counterpart of the social trends of democratization and the cult of youth, but it is far from clear that it is attractive, uplifting, or capable of encouraging a sense of self-sacrifice for the good of a wider community. Possibly such values seem dated, in a hedonistic and individualistic world, yet it is far from clear that challenges that require some effective collective response have been overcome.

In part, this problem of identity is related to a collapse of cultural continuity. There was essentially such a continuity while England urbanized in the nineteenth century. This Victorian world persisted, despite the two world wars and the Modernism of the early decades of the twentieth century, but it blew apart in the social revolution of the 1960s. The consequences of this collapse are still being felt and come to terms with, and this affects the difficulty of searching for any widely held new (or old) basis for national identity. Thus, the destruction or weakening, in the 1980s, 1990s and 2000s, of traditional and, until then, still vital benchmarks of national identity – the Common Law, Parliamentary sovereignty, national independence, the monarchy, the Church of England, a culture of tolerance – was not followed by the creation of any viable alternatives.

It is not surprising that the natural environment continues to loom so large in culture – it has done so for centuries. What is more surprising is that ruralism is such a porous container for all manner of ideas about national identity. Possibly the place of the countryside in the twentieth and twenty-first centuries is both a reaction to the nineteenth-century identities as the world's leading industrial nation and greatest empire, and, in part also, the tale of how we have moved away from such identities to new ones. It is, however, impossible to generalize about the politics or geography of these new fragmented forms of Englishness. The countryside may simply be large and abstract enough to take all these different approaches. Yet ruralism is not universally powerful as a trope of Englishness and, to those for whom it is applicable, it is never the only reflection of Englishness. Because it can be anthropomorphized, the countryside carries such tropes as mildness, individualism and tradition, but it doesn't, for example, capture other characteristics that are seen as important, for example privacy, whimsy and irony.

'Englishness' in literature is no mere counterpart to ruralism, and English literature of course looks to many different impulses. 'Englishness' in literature is, for example, generally seen in terms of heightened imaginativeness (as in

Dickens), whimsy, solidity of description (as opposed to metaphysical ponderings), and respect for the underdog or individual. Indeed, these literary perceptions relate to a wider sense of Englishness as involving love of fair-play, friendliness and helpfulness to others, concern for the less fortunate, and both individualism and the amateur tradition, at once endearing and irritating. However, attempts consciously to embody 'Englishness' usually do not work, because it is too big and nebulous to be pinned down. As far as music is concerned, Elgar, Vaughan Williams and Walton were very different twentieth-century composers, yet each was regarded as quintessentially 'English'. They almost created their own 'Englishness' (as we call it) by taking certain elements of tradition, bonding them with foreign or modern influences, and producing something entirely fresh yet seemingly eternal, the invention of tradition in action.

To claim that traditions can be and are moulded, even created, is not the same as suggesting that they are without value. Nor is it the case that this process of moulding and creation necessarily justifies the replacement of existing practices and ideas that give people a sense of continuity, identity and values. At the start of the new millennium the continual process of change and its interaction with the particular strategies of politics has brought in a degree of remoulding of identities that has been unprecedented since the Reformation. Not only the sovereignty and the cohesion of the United Kingdom, but also the character and unity of England are being recast, or is it destroyed, in the name of modernity. It is difficult to feel optimistic about the outcome.

Selected Further Reading

Before turning to a brief listing of a few of the many relevant scholarly works, it is worth emphasizing the value of primary sources. These include correspondence, diaries, newspapers and travel accounts. The last are especially useful. Famous accounts include Daniel Defoe's *Tour of the Whole Island of Great Britain* (London 1724–7) and J.B. Priestley's *English Journey* (London, 1933). Recently published travel accounts include Z. Dovey, *An Elizabethan Progress. The Queen's Journey into East Anglia, 1578* (Stroud, 1999), and John Chandler, *Travels through Stuart Britain. The Adventures of John Taylor, the Water Poet* (Stroud, 1999). Old maps and historical atlases are also very useful. Coverage is patchy. There is nothing for the Midlands or North to match Roger Kain and William Ravenhill (eds), *The Historical Atlas of the South West* (Exeter, 1999). Important county studies include Susan Neave and Stephen Ellis, *An Historical Atlas of East Yorkshire* (Hull, 1996), David Dymond and Edward Martin (eds), *An Historical Atlas of Suffolk* (3rd edn, Ipswich, 1999), Kim Leslie and Brian Short (eds) *An Historical Atlas of Sussex* (Chichester, 1999), and Joan Dils (ed.), *An Historical Atlas of Berkshire* (Reading, 1999), although the last does not cover the pre-Anglo-Saxon period. Other counties recently covered include Durham (1992), Norfolk (1993), and Lincolnshire (1993).

This author has written at greater length in *The National Trust Historical Atlas of Britain. II The End of the Middle Ages to the Georgian Era* (Stroud, 2000), *III The Industrial Revolution to the New Millennium* (Stroud, 2000), *Britain since the Seventies* (London, 2004) and *The British Seaborne Empire* (New Haven, 2004). Norman Davies, *The Isles: A History* (Basingstoke, 1999) is stimulating. On the environment, see recently, John Hassan, *A History of Water in Modern England and Wales* (Manchester, 1998).

Concentrating on recent work, B. Jones and D. Mattingly, *An Atlas of Roman Britain* (Oxford, 1990) provides an excellent introduction to its period, and there is a very good short account of the Anglo-Saxon period in Ann Williams' *Kingship and Government in Pre-Conquest England, c. 500–1066* (Basingstoke, 1999). Barbara Yorke's *The Conversion of Britain. Religion, Politics and Society in Britain c. 600–800* (Harlow, 2006) offers much. See also recently, but, given the nature of the evidence, far more hypothetically, N.J. Higham, *An English Empire: Bede and the early Anglo-Saxon Kings* (Manchester, 1995). On Alfred, R. Abels, *Alfred the Great: War, Kingship and Culture in Anglo-Saxon England* (Harlow, 1998). For the Norman Conquest, Brian Golding, *Conquest and Colonisation. The Normans in Britain 1066–1110* (Basingstoke, 1994), and Ann Williams, *The English and the Norman Conquest* (Woodbridge, 1995). For the Middle Ages, M.T. Clanchy, *England and its Rulers 1066–1272* (2nd edn, London, 1998), W.H. Ormrod, *Political Life in Medieval England 1300–1450* (Basingstoke, 1995), Ormrod and A. Musson, *The Evolution of English Justice* (Basingstoke, 1998), Anne Curry, *The Hundred Years War* (Basingstoke, 1993), and A.J. Pollard, *The Wars of the Roses* (Basingstoke, 1998). On the law see recently, John Hudson (ed.), *The History of English Law: Centenary Essays on 'Pollock and Maitland'* (Oxford, 1996). For medieval social history, Alan Harding, *England in the*

Thirteenth Century (Cambridge, 1993), Richard Britnell, *The Commercialisation of English Society, 1000–1500* (Manchester, 1996), Helen Jewell, *Women in Medieval England* (Manchester, 1996), S.H. Rigby, *Chaucer in Context* (Manchester, 1996) and Heather Swanson, *Medieval British Towns* (Basingstoke, 1999). The English Monarchs series provides scholarly and accessible biographies. They are currently being republished by Yale University Press. Volumes include, David Douglas, *William the Conqueror* (2nd edn, New Haven, 1999), John Gillingham, *Richard I* (2nd edn, New Haven, 1999), and Charles Ross, *Richard III* (2nd edn, New Haven, 1999). A conventional chronological division is ably overcome in Britnell, *The Closing of the Middle Ages? England, 1471–1529* (Oxford, 1997).

For the Tudors, S.B. Chrimes, *Henry VII* (2nd edn, New Haven, 1999), Steven Gunn, *Early Tudor Government 1485–1558* (Basingstoke, 1995), David Loades, *The Mid-Tudor Crisis 1545–1565* (Basingstoke, 1992) and Penry Williams *The Later Tudors. England 1547–1603* (Oxford, 1995). For the Reformation, Richard Rex, *Henry VIII and the English Reformation* (Basingstoke, 1993), Diarmaid Macculloch, *The Later Reformation in England 1547–1603* (2nd edn, Basingstoke, 2000), and Christopher Marsh, *Popular Religion in Sixteenth-Century England* (Basingstoke, 1998). For the hostile response, Michael Bush, *The Pilgrimage of Grace* (Manchester, 1996). Sybil Jack, *Towns in Tudor and Stuart Britain* (Basingstoke, 1996) is a good guide to the most dynamic section of society. A more luxurious life is shown in J.T. Cliffe, *The World of the Country House in Seventeenth-Century England* (New Haven, 1999). For the seventeenth century, Mark Kishlansky, *A Monarchy Transformed. Britain, 1603–1714* (London, 1996), Roger Lockyer, *James VI and I*

(London, 1998), Michael Young, *Charles I* (Basingstoke, 1997), Ann Hughes, *The Causes of the English Civil War* (2nd edn, Basingstoke, 1998), John Morrill, *Revolt in the Provinces: The People of England and the Tragedies of War 1630–1648* (2nd edn, Harlow, 1999), Ronald Hutton, *The British Republic 1649–1660* (2nd edn., Basingstoke, 2000), Paul Seaward, *The Restoration 1660–1688* (Basingstoke, 1991), Eveline Cruickshanks, *The Glorious Revolution* (Basingstoke, 1999) and John Spurr *The Post-Reformation. Religion, Politics and Society in Britain, 1603–1714* (Harlow, 2006). For culture, Helen Jewell, *Education in Early Modern England* (Basingstoke, 1999) and Malcolm Smuts, *Culture and Power in England, c. 1585–1685* (Basingstoke, 1999).

For the eighteenth century, recent accounts include Frank O'Gorman, *The Long Eighteenth Century* (London, 1997), Wilfrid Prest, *Albion Ascendant. English History 1660–1815* (Oxford, 1998) and Jeremy Black, *George III* (New Haven, 2006). A very different approach is adopted by Tim Hitchcock, *English Sexualities, 1700–1800* (Basingstoke, 1997). National identities are tackled in Linda Colley, *Britons. Forging the Nation 1707–1837* (New Haven, 1992) and Gerald Newman, *The Rise of English Nationalism. A Cultural History, 1740–1830* (2nd edn, Basingstoke, 1998). For demographics see, most recently, E.A. Wrigley and others, *English Population History from Family Reconstitution 1580–1837* (Cambridge, 1997).

For the nineteenth century, Simon Dentith, *Society and Cultural Forms in Nineteenth-Century England* (Basingstoke, 1999), H.S. Jones, *Victorian Political Thought* (Basingstoke, 1999) and Alan Kidd, *Society and the Poor in Nineteenth-Century England* (Basingstoke, 1999). For biographical approaches, E.A. Smith, *George IV* (New Haven, 1999) and T.A. Jenkins, *Sir Robert Peel* (Basingstoke, 1998). Rivals can be approached through Jenkins, *Disraeli and Victorian Conservatism* (Basingstoke, 1996) and E. Biagini, *Gladstone* (Basingstoke, 2000). More generally see, A. Hawkins, *British Party Politics 1852–1886* (Basingstoke, 1998). A very different account is offered in Rohan McWilliam's *Popular Politics in Nineteenth-Century England* (London, 1998), and John Tosh's *A Man's Place. Masculinity and the Middle-Class Home in Victorian England* (New Haven, 1999). For another view of the same subject Deborah Cohen, *Household Gods, The British and their Possessions* (New Haven, 2006). There is much of interest in John Davis, *The Great Exhibition* (Stroud, 1999) and Steven Halliday, *The Great Stink of London. Sir Joseph Bazalgette and the Cleansing of the Victorian Metropolis* (Stroud, 1999). G.E. Mingay, *Land and Society in England 1750–1980* (London, 1994) is the best introduction to the topic.

Short biographies also offer an accessible approach to the twentieth century. It is worth reading Ian Packer, *Lloyd George* (Basingstoke, 1998) and Ian Wood, *Churchill* (Basingstoke, 1999). More wide-ranging accounts are provided by David Powell, *The Edwardian Crisis: Britain, 1901–1914* (Basingstoke, 1996), John Davis, *A History of Britain, 1885–1939* (Basingstoke, 1999) and David Childs, *Britain Since 1939* (Basingstoke, 1995). The two major protagonists are covered in John Charmley, *A History of Conservative Politics, 1900–1996* (Basingstoke, 1996) and Andrew Thorpe, *A History of the British Labour Party* (Basingstoke, 1997). Faddishness is avoided in Brian Harrison's *The Transformation of British Politics, 1860–1995* (Oxford, 1996). Useful collections of documents include Stuart Ball, *The Conservative Party since 1945* (Manchester, 1998), Alan Booth, *British Economic Development since 1945* (Manchester, 1996), Stephen Brooke, *Reform and Reconstruction. Britain after the War, 1945–51* (Manchester, 1995), and Steven Fielding, *The Labour Party. 'Socialism' and society since 1951* (Manchester, 1997), and for social, political and cultural criticism, Patrick Deane (ed.), *History in Our Hands. A Critical Anthology of Writings on Literature, Culture and Politics from the 1930s* (1999). Very different flavours of the period can be captured through Lesley Hall, *Sex, Gender and Social Change in Britain since 1880* (Basingstoke, 2000) and Callum Brown *Religion and Society in Twentieth-Century Britain* (Harlow, 2006). For twentieth-century development, Standish Meacham, *Regaining Paradise. Englishness and the Early Garden City Movement* (New Haven, 1999) and Andrew Saint (ed.), *London Suburbs* (London, 1999). For the crafts movement, Tanya Harrod, *The Crafts in Britain in the Twentieth Century* (New Haven, 1999).

On national identity, G.R. Elton, *The English* (Oxford, 1992); R. Samuel (ed.), *Patriotism: The Making and Unmaking of British National Identity* (London, 1989); Alexander Grant and Keith J. Stringer (eds), *Uniting the Kingdom: The Making of British History* (London, 1995); Keith Robbins, *Great Britain: Identities, Institutions and the Idea of Britishness* (Harlow, 1998); Jeremy Paxman, *The English* (London, 1998); David Cressy, *Bonfires and Bells: National Memory and the Protestant Calendar in Elizabethan and Stuart England* (London, 1989); R. Helgerson, *Forms of Nationhood: The Elizabethan Writings of England* (Chicago, 1992); Laurence Brockliss and David Eastwood (eds), *A Union of Multiple Identities. The British Isles, 1750–1850* (Manchester, 1997), Margot Finn, *After Chartism:*

Class and Nation in English Radical Politics, 1848–1874 (Cambridge, 1993); R. Colls and P. Dodd (eds), *Englishness: Politics and Culture 1880–1920* (London, 1986). Roy Porter (ed.), *Myths of the English* (Cambridge, 1992); Jeffrey Richards's *Films and British National Identity. From Dickens to 'Dad's Army'* (Manchester, 1997); David Matless, *Landscape and Englishness* (1998); Stefan Collini, *English Pasts. Essays in History and Culture* (Oxford, 1999) and Peter Mandler, *The English National Character. The History of an Idea from Edmund Burke to Tony Blair* (New Haven, 2006). On the construction of the English past, J.W. Burrow, *A Liberal Descent: Victorian Historians and the English Past* (Cambridge, 1981). For regionalism, David Smith, *North and South: Britain's Economic, Social and Political Divide* (Harmondsworth, 1989), Edward Royle (ed.), *Issues of Regional Identity* (Manchester, 1998) and John Mohan, *A United Kingdom? Economic, Social and Political Geographies* (1999).

INDEX